# CAPSTONE

Exemplary Lessons for **High School Economics**

# CAPSTONE

Exemplary Lessons for **High School Economics**

# Teacher's Guide

**National Council on Economic Education**

*This publication was made possible through funding from the
Calvin K. Kazanjian Economics Foundation.*

# AUTHORS

**Jane S. Lopus**
*Professor of Economics and Director, Center for Economic Education*
California State University, Hayward
Hayward, California

**John S. Morton**
*Vice President for Program Development*
National Council on Economic Education
Scottsdale, Arizona

**Robert Reinke**
*Professor of Economics and Executive Director, South Dakota Council on Economic Education*
University of South Dakota
Vermillion, South Dakota

**Mark C. Schug**
*Professor of Curriculum and Instruction and Director, Center for Economic Education*
University of Wisconsin-Milwaukee
Milwaukee, Wisconsin

**Donald R. Wentworth**
*Professor of Economics and Director, Center for Economic Education*
Pacific Lutheran University
Tacoma, Washington

Cover photos by: © Zoran Milich / Masterfile, © Ron Fehling / Masterfile, © David Muir / Masterfile, © Carl Valiquet / Masterfile and © Daryl Benson / Masterfile

Copyright © 2003, National Council on Economic Education, 1140 Avenue of the Americas, New York, New York 10036. All rights reserved. Some materials in this publication were previously published in *Capstone: The Nation's High School Economics Course*, copyright © 1989 by the National Council on Economic Education. The visuals and student activities may be duplicated for classroom use, the number not to exceed the number of students in each class. Notice of copyright must appear on all pages. With the exception of the visuals and student activities, no part of this book may be reproduced in any form by any means without written permission from the publisher. Printed in the United States of America.

ISBN: 1-56183-515-3

Teacher's Guide

# TABLE OF CONTENTS

Foreword ........................................ vi

Acknowledgments ........................... vii

Introduction .................................... ix

A User's Guide to Capstone ............... xi

## Unit 1  The Economic Way of Thinking

1. Economic Reasoning:
   Why Are We a Nation of Couch Potatoes? ....... 3
2. Scarcity and Abundance ...................... 11
3. Economic Magic:
   Creating Something from Nothing ............. 15
4. To Choose or Not to Choose?
   That Is Not the Question ..................... 19
5. Rules Influence Economic Behavior ........... 23

## Unit 2  The Invisible Hand at Work

6. Why Did Communism Collapse? ................ 33
7. A Silver Market .............................. 41
8. A Picture Is Worth a Thousand Words: Demand . 49
9. A Picture Is Worth a Thousand Words: Supply .. 57
10. Equilibrium Prices and Equilibrium Quantities .. 63
11. Do Prices Matter to Consumers? .............. 69
12. How Do Prices Influence My Behavior?
    Price Elasticity ............................. 73
13. How Markets Allocate Resources .............. 79
14. Secondary Effects: Price Ceilings and Floors ... 85

## Unit 3  How You Can Prosper in a Market Economy

15. Why Do Some People Earn More than Others? .. 91
16. Making Choices about Saving and Investing .... 97
17. Creating and Using a Budget ................. 103
18. Credit Management .......................... 113
19. Earning an Income ........................... 119

## Unit 4  The Business of Doing Business

20. Why Helping Yourself Helps Others ........... 129
21. Productivity, Diminishing Marginal Returns,
    and the Demand for Labor .................... 139
22. How Competitive Is the Industry? ............ 145
23. Make a Profit: Do the Math .................. 147

## Unit 5  The Visible Hand: The Role of Government in a Market Economy

24. Government and the Environment ............ 153
25. The Economics of the U.S. Constitution ....... 161
26. Public versus Private Goods .................. 167
27. The Economics of Special Interest Groups ..... 171
28. The Economics of Voting ..................... 179
29. Can Taxes Be Incentives? ..................... 187
30. Poverty and Income Inequality ............... 195

## Unit 6  The Macroeconomy

31. Measuring Unemployment:
    A Labor Market Mystery ...................... 205
32. The Effects of Inflation ...................... 211
33. Gross Domestic Product (GDP)
    and How to Measure It ....................... 215
34. Money and Monetary Policy .................. 221
35. Fiscal Policy: A Two-Act Play ................. 229
36. Should We Worry about the National Debt? .... 233
37. Can Government Manage
    the National Economy? ...................... 239
38. Aggregate Demand and Aggregate Supply ..... 245

## Unit 7  Markets without Borders: The Global Economy

39. Why Go Global? .............................. 259
40. Why Do People Trade across National Borders? . 265
41. Why People Trade: Comparative Advantage ... 271
42. Foreign Currencies and Foreign Exchange ..... 275
43. Why Are Some Nations Wealthy? ............. 281
44. World Environmental Issues:
    Is the Market at Fault? ....................... 289
45. International Trade:  How Do We
    Measure Trades across Political Borders? ...... 293

Glossary ...................................... 297

# FOREWORD

The National Council on Economic Education is proud to present *Capstone: Exemplary Lessons for High School Economics*. *Capstone* provides teachers with an important new tool for improving the economic understanding of high school students. Attaining that goal at the high school level is essential. Many young people, even those who pursue post-secondary education, will not have an opportunity after their high school years to study economics. It is important that we get this right.

*Capstone* presents an exciting approach to economics, formulated specifically for high school classroom use. It stresses economic reasoning, guided by a set of principles derived from basic assumptions about human behavior. It invites students to apply these principles in analyzing an array of economic mysteries, some of them markedly novel in their content. The emphasis on principled reasoning and intriguing points of application enables students to experience the study of economics as a source of insight into a surprisingly wide range of problems and issues.

In emphasizing economic reasoning, *Capstone* attends to key curricular objectives for high school economics courses. By reference to such basics as the laws of supply and demand and the role of prices and profits in market systems, it enables students to learn how market systems work. Through lessons on earning an income, money management, saving, and investing, it helps students to envision their future as participants in a market economy. Through lessons on fiscal policy, monetary policy, economic growth, inflation, labor markets, and environmental protection, it engages students in assessing the government's role in the macro economy. And by addressing markets without borders, it introduces students to the international economy and issues related to global trade.

We know from research that before students can gain insight and skills from the discipline of economics, someone — most often a talented teacher — must teach it to them in an appropriate manner. *Capstone* will provide talented teachers with a great new instructional tool, enhancing their capacity to help students understand our market system and participate in it.

I would like to thank the Calvin K. Kazanjian Economics Foundation, Inc., for funding *Capstone* and for supporting economic education for many years. I also would like to thank Mark C. Schug, *Capstone* project director, for his leadership and hard work in managing this project and for his continued commitment to economic education.

Robert F. Duvall, Ph.D.
President & Chief Executive Officer
National Council on Economic Education

# ACKNOWLEDGMENTS

The National Council on Economic Education expresses its deepest gratitude to the many individuals who were involved with this project.

**PROJECT DIRECTOR:**

**Mark C. Schug**
*University of Wisconsin-Milwaukee*
Milwaukee, Wisconsin

**EDITOR:**

**Richard D. Western**
Milwaukee, Wisconsin

**REVIEWERS:**

**Donald Fell**
*President, Florida Council on Economic Education*
Tampa, Florida

**Donna Miller**
Milwaukee, Wisconsin

**Timothy T. Taylor**
*Managing Editor, The Journal of Economic Perspectives*
Macalester College
Saint Paul, Minnesota

**FIELD TEST TEACHERS:**

**Jacque Bowman**
*San Ramon Valley Unified School District*
San Ramon, California

**Thomas J. Fugate**
*Mequon-Thiensville School District*
Mequon, Wisconsin

**Carol Hyatt**
*Denton Independent School District*
Denton, Texas

**Rich Larsen**
*Fremont Unified School District*
Fremont, California

**Lennis Larson**
*Spearfish High School*
Spearfish, South Dakota

**Matt McWenie**
*Phoenix Union High School District*
Phoenix, Arizona

**Cheryl K. Rudd**
*Colville School District*
Colville, Washington

**Alice Temnick**
*Cave Creek Unified School District*
Cave Creek, Arizona

**Debbie Tettleton**
*Grand Prairie Independent School District*
Grand Prairie, Texas

**George Thornton**
*Oroville School District*
Oroville, Washington

**Anna Vanlandingham**
*Seminole County Public Schools*
Sanford, Florida

**Erica Vonk**
*Sioux Falls School District*
Sioux Falls, South Dakota

# TEACHER'S GUIDE

# INTRODUCTION

## THE CHALLENGE AND OPPORTUNITY OF TEACHING HIGH SCHOOL ECONOMICS

Teaching economics to high school students offers an enormous challenge and an even larger opportunity.

The challenge is that the subject matter and approach of economics are unfamiliar, and may even seem alien, to many high school students. To be sure, many students have some direct experience with the economy — in buying clothes or movie tickets, holding a job and filing for a tax refund, receiving interest payments from a bank account, or paying interest on a credit card balance or a small loan. These interactions with the economy can offer a toehold for a high school economics teacher.

But for most high school students, economics involves a manner of thinking that lies outside their personal experience. The students' idea of scarcity sometimes involves little more than asking their parents for spending money. Their idea of the trade-offs associated with a budget tend to focus on small marginal purchases of entertainment and clothing, not on essentials like food, housing, transportation, and medical care. They often expect to be working at a job for only a few months or a year, so the notion of building skills for a career path is apt not to be on their personal agendas. Similarly, their idea of saving or borrowing money often involves a time horizon of six months or a year, which is not very useful for learning about the power of compound interest.

Moreover, high school students tend to see the economy as an impersonal force of nature acting upon them — like the weather — not as a social system in which people make choices in a world of scarcity and trade-offs. For many high school students, the decisions business leaders make about pricing or hiring can appear to be highly arbitrary, as if the gods on Olympus were playing games of chance to determine the fates of humans back down on Earth. Decisions of the Federal Reserve about monetary policy or deliberations of Congress about the federal budget are also apt to seem curious and inscrutable, like the social or culinary practices of a remote and unvisited country.

Learning economics is difficult because it requires a combination of structure and flexibility. High school students are often comfortable with either a free-form assignment, like writing about their personal reactions to a novel, or with a highly constrained problem, like regurgitating a list of U.S. presidents or the capitals of all 50 states. But economics imposes a structure of analytical frameworks, presented in a language that sounds remarkably like standard English while actually it is dotted with terms that have quite specific definitions. It then asks students to use these tools flexibly — a delicate balance. A supply and demand problem in an economics class, for example, is similar in structure to the story problems that students so often dread in math classes. Structure can enable students to extend the reach of their insights — but only after they have mastered the structure in question.

The opportunity offered by teaching economics at the high school level is nothing less than the chance to foster economic literacy for the country. Nearly half of U.S. high school students now enroll in an economics course. That proportion rose substantially in the 1990s as a number of states began to require an economics course in high school. However, only about two-thirds of U.S. high school students continue their education in colleges or universities, and only about 40 percent of those who do go on to college will take a college-level economics class. Thus, for many students, high school provides the last chance: if they do not study economics in high school, they will probably never get even a whiff of the subject.

The typical high school course in economics — setting aside the Advanced Placement classes, which represent only about two percent of all students who take a high school economics course — also differs in tone from the introductory college course. At the college level, introductory economics courses are substantially concerned with preparing students for additional courses in economics. The tone of the introductory course is often heavily conceptual, with lots of graphs and definitions and structured problems. Although high school economics courses do typically include a component of terminology, they focus primarily on expanding the horizons of young citizens.

The study of economics gives students a backstage tour of the world around them, revealing many things that had previously been hidden from view. With a working knowledge of economic terms and institutions, students can find meaning in newspaper headlines and TV news reports that had previously seemed to be empty words. Magazines like *Business Week, Fortune,* and *The Economist* may never be juicy reading, but their articles can become accessible. Claims of political figures with regard to economic policy — especially claims that offer free lunches for all constituents — can be evaluated.

For many students, early courses in economics open up a new way of seeing the world. Some of the lessons may feel harsh — those emphasizing, for example, the economist's insistence that a person or society can't have everything, but must choose. High school students often like to believe that their causes — say, environmental protection — amount to absolute crusades, not projects that must be nuanced by trade-offs. But the study of economics also helps students to gain a sense of order and interconnection among things in the world. It opens up the topic of responsible adulthood — in personal, career, and financial choices and in the practice of informed citizenship — in a way that is distinct from any other high school course.

All of us who have worked on this revision of *Capstone* hope that it will provide a reliable and even inspirational set of curriculum materials on which high school teachers can build as they seek to open their students' minds to the insights and empowerment that the study of economics offers.

*Timothy T. Taylor*

# Teacher's Guide

# A User's Guide to Capstone

In its organization and format, *Capstone* is similar to other publications of the National Council on Economic Education. Nonetheless, we thought it might be useful to anticipate questions about its features and to explain some of them briefly.

As a result of our field testing, we find that teachers are likely to ask whether they still will need to use a high school economics textbook if they use *Capstone*. Our answer is: "Yes." *Capstone* contains 45 lessons, and these lessons could provide a solid basis for a typical high school economics course. They introduce and reinforce many concepts and principles that all teachers of economics are likely to regard as fundamental. But *Capstone* is not a textbook, and it is not designed to survey concepts and principles comprehensively. Nor does it present an uninterrupted narrative linking key ideas across lessons. Instead, *Capstone* presents an approach to teaching economics — emphasizing economic reasoning — and a set of lessons designed to illustrate that approach concretely. It could stand alone, but we recommend that teachers use it together with a good high school economics textbook

*Capstone* consists of two main parts: a Teacher's Guide and a Student Activities book. The Teacher's Guide provides lesson objectives, concept lists, links to content standards from the *Voluntary National Content Standards in Economics* (NCEE, 1997), and instructional procedures. The procedures provide step-by-step directions for teachers, including lesson introductions, discussion questions, instructional activities, visuals (overhead transparency masters), and assessments. Answers to questions posed in the Student Activities book are also provided in the teaching procedures, usually set in italic type and enclosed in parentheses.

Nearly all student activities (exercises) appear in *Capstone*'s Student Activities book. Some exercises, however, involve simulations that call for cards or other materials to be prepared by the teacher. These materials are contained and noted in the Teacher's Guide. While most visuals appear only in the Teacher's Guide, some are also included in the Student Activities book so that students can work easily with them during class discussions.

There is a glossary in the Teacher's Guide and the Student Activities book. The glossary provides definitions for all concepts listed in the lessons, plus others that some teachers may wish to consider in developing their teaching plans.

*The Authors*

# Unit 1
# The Economic Way of Thinking

Lesson 1    Economic Reasoning: Why Are We a Nation of Couch Potatoes?
Lesson 2    Scarcity and Abundance
Lesson 3    Economic Magic: Creating Something from Nothing
Lesson 4    To Choose or Not to Choose? That Is Not the Question
Lesson 5    Rules Influence Economic Behavior

# Unit 1 | Teacher's Guide

## Unit 1 Lesson 1

## Economic Reasoning: Why Are We A Nation of Couch Potatoes?

### INTRODUCTION

**Economics** This lesson identifies the key principles that guide economic analysis. It introduces students to the basic economic problems of scarce resources, unlimited wants, the need to choose among alternatives, the consequences of cost, and the importance of incentives. While noting that nothing of value is free, the lesson explains how voluntary trade helps to provide more goods and services. While today is important, people are forward-looking in the decisions they make.

**Reasoning** Economic reasoning proceeds from basic assumptions about human activity. This lesson introduces students to these basic assumptions and uses them to model economic reasoning about an issue. It shows students how to apply the assumptions in the case of what seems to be a mystery: Why would people who admire a trim, slender appearance in others choose to eat too much and be inactive?

### CONCEPTS

- Choice
- Economic system
- Future consequences
- Incentives
- Opportunity cost
- Voluntary trade

### OBJECTIVES

*Students will:*

1. Identify basic principles of economic reasoning, including choices, costs, incentives, rules of the system, voluntary trade, and future consequences.

2. Apply principles of economic reasoning in an analysis of exercise and diet in the United States.

### CONTENT STANDARDS

- Productive resources are limited. Therefore, people cannot have all the goods and services they want; as a result, they must choose some things and give up others. (NCEE Content Standard 1)

- Effective decision making requires comparing the additional costs with the additional benefits. Most choices involve doing a little more or a little less of something; few choices are all-or-nothing decisions. (NCEE Content Standard 2)

- Different methods can be used to allocate goods and services. People, acting individually or collectively through government, must choose which methods to use to allocate different kinds of goods and services. (NCEE Content Standard 3)

- People respond predictably to positive and negative incentives. (NCEE Content Standard 4)

- Voluntary exchange occurs only when all participating parties expect to gain. This is true for trade among individuals or organizations within a nation, and among individuals or organizations in different nations. (NCEE Content Standard 5)

### LESSON DESCRIPTION

Students examine visuals to identify an economic mystery regarding exercise and diet. They use the **Guide to Economic Reasoning** to analyze the costs and benefits of decisions about diet and exercise. They discover that human behavior is influenced by choices, costs, incentives, rules, voluntary exchange, and future consequences, even in decisions about diet and exercise.

*Time Required: 45 minutes*

### MATERIALS

- A transparency of Visuals 1, 2, and 3
- Activity 1

### PROCEDURE

1. Welcome the class to the world of economic reasoning. Explain that economics is sometimes thought to be a dry, remote subject. This economics course will be different. It is designed to provide young people with a new way to look at issues and questions. It asks students to consider problems in a mature, real-world sort of way. It even invites students to have fun in doing economics.

2. Explain that the purpose of this lesson is to show how economic reasoning can be applied in the analysis of a wide range of human behavior. Specifically, this lesson uses economic reasoning to examine why it is that America is becoming a land of couch potatoes.

3. Explain that exercise and diet have recently become an important issue in the United States. Display Visual 1. Ask:

    - Which well known people do Americans tend to admire?

    *(The trim, slender people depicted in the media.)*

# ECONOMIC REASONING:
# WHY ARE WE A NATION OF COUCH POTATOES?

- How are Americans' exercise and diet habits changing?

    *(Americans appear to be exercising too little and eating too much.)*

- What is the mystery?

    *(Why do an increasing number of Americans, the same ones who admire the trim, slender people often featured in the media, exercise too little and eat too much?)*

4. Display Visual 2. Ask the students to speculate about whether each statement is true or false.

    - Few Americans know that exercising more and eating less can help many people become healthier. *(False)*

    - Exercise and a healthful diet are free. *(False)*

    - In jobs that involve physical work, exercise is like a fringe benefit. *(True)*

    - The price of food has been increasing. *(False)*

    - Passive modes of entertainment — like television and video games — are popular with many Americans. *(True)*

    - Common jobs in the past — in mining, farming, and manufacturing, for example — were much safer than today's jobs in technology, law, and finance. *(False)*

5. Refer the students to Activity 1 and ask them to read it. Then ask:

    A. What is the economic view of choice?

    *(People strive to choose the best combination of costs and benefits in making decisions.)*

    B. How do choices influence people in respect to exercise and diet?

    *(The level of exercise people maintain and the diet they favor reflect their personal choices.)*

    C. What is an opportunity cost?

    *(The opportunity cost is the second-best choice.)*

    D. How does opportunity cost influence people in their decisions about exercise and diet?

    *(The opportunity cost of exercising used to be much lower when many occupations involved more physical effort.)*

    E. What is an incentive?

    *(A reward.)*

    F. Why is money such an attractive incentive?

    *(Money can be exchanged for many other things that people desire.)*

    G. What incentives influence people in their decisions about exercise and diet?

    *(The incentives that influence decisions about exercise include forms of passive entertainment, like television and computer games. One incentive influencing decisions about diet is the reduced cost of food.)*

    H. Why are the rules of the economic system important?

    *(Economic behavior occurs in a climate of formal and informal rules. These rules often act as incentives and influence the choices people make.)*

    I. How do the rules of the economic system influence people in their decisions about exercise and diet?

    *(The American economy responds to changes in technology. Many of these changes have eased the physical demands of working. Consumer demand also has encouraged the development of work-saving products.)*

    J. What is voluntary trade?

    *(Voluntary trade is a cooperative activity in which people exchange something they value less for something they value more.)*

    K. How does voluntary trade influence people in their decisions about exercise and diet?

    *(Many people today are exchanging their labor for service jobs in which they are less likely to be injured and more likely to live longer.)*

    L. What does it mean to say that people's choices have future consequences?

    *(People strive to make decisions they hope will benefit them in the future.)*

    M. How do future consequences influence people in their decisions about exercise and diet?

    *(Many Americans have in effect decided to be less thin today in order to live longer and healthier lives by working in a service-based economy that demands little in the way of physical work. However, this choice comes with costs; losses in physical fitness may spur people to search out new ways to exercise.)*

# Unit 1 | Teacher's Guide

N. Solve the mystery.

*(The analysis in this lesson suggests that Americans are gaining extra weight not because they are lazy or because of a sudden increase in the desire to eat fatty foods. Instead, many Americans have accepted the new jobs created in a changing market system — jobs that involve less exercise than the jobs of an earlier era. In an economic sense, American employees have traded thinness and some of the health benefits that came with strenuous, dangerous work for other values and work-related benefits that enable them, in the aggregate, to live longer and healthier lives. Outside the workforce, some Americans have benefited from engagement with new forms of passive entertainment. The opportunity cost of physical activity has gone up, prompting people to make new choices regarding exercise.)*

## Closure

Review the key points of the lesson. Ask:

- What are the principles of the **Guide to Economic Reasoning**?
    1. People choose.
    2. People's choices involve costs.
    3. People respond to incentives in predictable ways.
    4. People create economic systems that influence individual choices and incentives.
    5. People gain when they trade voluntarily.
    6. People's choices have consequences that lie in the future.

- What are some of the costs associated with failure to exercise enough and being overweight?

    *(Many health risks are associated with obesity and the failure to exercise, including heart disease, diabetes, and cancer.)*

- What incentives might influence people to exercise less and eat more?

    *(People used to get exercise "on-the-job." Today's service economy has enabled people to choose occupations that involve less physical effort. These jobs are much less dangerous than were jobs in mining, farming, and manufacturing. Other incentives include the reduced cost of food and the increased attractiveness of passive entertainment.)*

- How might you solve the mystery?
  Display Visual 3 to reinforce the solution.

    *(Americans are gaining extra weight not because they are lazy or because of a sudden increase in the desire to eat fatty foods. Instead, the new jobs created in a changing market system have resulted in less exercise. Many Americans have traded thinness and some of the health benefits that came with strenuous, dangerous work for other values and work-related benefits that enable them, in the aggregate, to live longer and healthier lives. Outside the workforce, some Americans have benefited from new forms of passive entertainment. The opportunity cost of physical activity has gone up, prompting people to make new choices regarding exercise.)*

- What are some ways to change the incentives associated with exercise and diet?

    *(Suggestions might include increasing health education, finding ways to reward exercise on-the-job, imposing a "calorie" tax on certain foods, and so forth.)*

Source note: This lesson is based in part on Philipson, T.J., and Posner, R. A. (1999), The Long-Run Growth in Obesity as a Function of Technological Change. Working Paper 7423, National Bureau of Economic Research, www.Nber.org/papers/w7423.

## Multiple-Choice Questions

### (Correct answers shown in bold)

1. Recent evidence suggests that Americans are not exercising enough and are eating too much. Using economic reasoning, how would you explain this behavior?

    A. Americans are lazy.

    B. Americans cannot resist fatty foods.

    C. No one has ever told Americans about the advantages of exercise and a healthy diet.

    **D. The overall benefits associated with working in service jobs outweigh the costs of reduced physical activity.**

2. Claire decided to try out for the soccer team last season even though she had a serious knee injury. Her parents and friends have decided that she is crazy. Her friend Linda told Claire that she obviously did not care one bit about her future health. Using economic reasoning, how would you explain Claire's action?

    A. Claire had no respect for her health.

    B. Claire's parents and friends must not care for Claire.

    C. Claire is prone to make irrational decisions.

    **D. Claire thought that the benefits associated with playing soccer outweighed the costs.**

## ECONOMIC REASONING: WHY ARE WE A NATION OF COUCH POTATOES?

**ESSAY QUESTION**

Molly received a grade of D in economics because she did not complete enough of the homework assignments. She asked her teacher: "How could I complete all those assignments when I have so many things to do? I have a job after school. On Saturdays I am supposed to babysit while my mother goes to the grocery store. On Sundays, half the day is tied up at church. Who has time to do school work?" What would an economics teacher tell Molly?

*(Molly made a choice regarding her economics homework. She assumed that the benefits of not doing her homework were worth the costs. The opportunity cost of a good grade was the combination of all the other things she chose to do rather than doing homework. Molly traded off getting a good grade in economics in order to gain the benefits of employment and family obligations, which were of greater value to her.)*

# Unit 1 | Teacher's Guide

**Unit 1, Lesson 1**
Visual 1

## WHY ARE WE A NATION OF COUCH POTATOES?

- Surf the television channels, glance at any news stand, or open a clothing catalog, and it becomes clear: Americans admire people who look slender and physically fit.

- Yet, according to the Center for Disease Control and Prevention, only about 25 percent of Americans are getting enough exercise and about 35 percent of American adults are overweight.

- The percentage of children who are overweight has doubled since the early 1970s.

- *Why do an increasing number of Americans, the same people who admire the trim, slender look so often featured in the media, exercise too little and eat too much?*

**Unit 1, Lesson 1**
Visual 2

# True/False Clues

- Few Americans know that exercising more and eating less can help many people become healthier.

    True or False?

- Exercise and a healthful diet are free.

    True or False?

- In jobs that involve physical work, exercise is like a fringe benefit.

    True or False?

- The price of food has been increasing.

    True or False?

- Passive modes of entertainment — like television and video games — are popular with many Americans.

    True or False?

- Common jobs in the past — in mining, farming, and manufacturing, for example — were much safer than today's jobs in technology, law, and finance.

    True or False?

# Unit 1 | Teacher's Guide

**Unit 1, Lesson 1**
Visual 3

## SOLUTION TO THE COUCH POTATO MYSTERY

### THE MYSTERY

Why do an increasing number of Americans, the same ones who admire the trim, slender look so often featured in the media, exercise too little and eat too much?

### THE SOLUTION

- Americans are not gaining extra weight because they are lazy or because of a sudden increase in the desire to eat fatty foods.

- Instead, they are choosing new jobs created in a changing market system — new jobs that have resulted in less exercise.

- Americans have in effect traded thinness for other values and work-related benefits enabling them to live longer and healthier lives.

- Some Americans enjoy new forms of passive entertainment; for them, the opportunity cost of physical activity would include giving up time they now spend watching TV or playing video games.

# Unit 1 | Teacher's Guide

## Unit 1 Lesson 2

# Scarcity and Abundance

### INTRODUCTION

**Economics**  Economists insist that scarcity exists and forces people to make choices about the use of resources. But people in the United States and elsewhere see many signs of abundance around them in their day-to-day lives. They also see that certain important resources like water and food are wasted regularly. How important can the concept of scarcity be, given widespread evidence of abundance and waste?

Economists do not see a paradox here. Abundance and scarcity can exist together. People may treat scarce goods as abundant if they receive misleading signals about the scarcity problem. Scarcity exists when resources are limited and people's wants are unlimited. Usually people's wants for consumer goods, leisure time, and environmental quality exceed the time and resources needed to produce these goods and services. Economists describe this condition as one of scarcity because it forces people to choose how they will use the resources in question. For every good and service produced, a decision must be made not to produce a different good and service.

**Reasoning**  In economic reasoning, scarcity is a relative concept, not an absolute one. Many people think it means "not plentiful," but in economics something is scarce when it has more than one valuable use. For example, it is obvious to a thirsty person that water is scarce (not plentiful) in the desert. But water that seems plentiful in a large lake or river is scarce nonetheless because it has many mutually exclusive uses — including, for example, crop irrigation, the production of electricity, a venue for shipping lanes, fish habitat, and many forms of recreation. Water, like many resources, can be abundant and scarce at the same time.

### CONCEPTS

- Alternatives
- Choice
- Scarcity

### OBJECTIVES

*Students will:*

1. Identify two definitions of the term *scarcity*.
2. Select examples consistent with the two definitions.
3. Identify conditions that might cause people to treat scarce resources as if they were not scarce.

### CONTENT STANDARD

- Productive resources are limited. Therefore, people can not have all the goods and services they want; as a result, they must choose some things and give up others. (NCEE Content Standard 1)

### LESSON DESCRIPTION

The lesson provides students with two definitions of the term scarcity. They apply these definitions to several examples of human behavior. In the second part of the lesson they use the definitions to explain why people may treat scarce resources as if they were not scarce.

*Time Required: 60 minutes*

### MATERIALS

- A transparency of Visual 1
- Activities 1 and 2

### PROCEDURE

1. Explain that the purpose of this lesson is to clarify the concept of scarcity and to demonstrate how that concept can be used in analyzing human behavior.

2. Ask the students what they think the term scarcity means and to provide an example of scarcity.

    *(Usually students will suggest that scarcity means not enough of something, or a condition in which something is not plentiful. Examples might be one car and eight people who wish to ride, or five bagels and nine hungry people to eat them. Write the students' definitions and examples on the chalkboard and leave them there.)*

3. Display Visual 1 and explain the two definitions it provides. Ask the students how the definitions in Visual 1 differ from their definitions.

    *(Definition 1 involves a relative relationship in which scarcity depends on how much of something is available relative to how much is wanted. Usually students use an absolute relationship in their definitions: If a small amount of something is available, that something is scarce. Definition 2 emphasizes a second aspect of the concept: the importance of more than one valuable use. Goods are scarce if choosing one valuable use of them means giving up another valuable use.)*

4. Refer the students to Activity 1 and ask them to read it. Ask the students to work in pairs to decide which examples do and do not illustrate the concept of scarcity.

# SCARCITY AND ABUNDANCE

*Answers to Activity 1*

A. Old economics textbooks collected in a bookcase near the teacher's desk with a sign that says "Free books, take as many as you want." The books have been there for three years.

(*Not scarce. No alternative valuable use.*)

B. Old economics textbooks collected in a bookcase near the teacher's desk with a sign that says "Free books, take as many as you want." Another sign posted in the hallway says "$10 paid for any recycled textbook. Bring books to the Principal's office."

(*Scarce. The books may be read or they may be recycled. Two valuable uses.*)

C. One economics textbook, five students who wish to do well in the economics course, and an important test in class the next day.

(*Scarce. The one book could be used by five different people; it has valuable alternative uses.*)

D. One economics textbook, five students who are not taking economics, and an important test in the economics class the next day.

(*Not scarce. Same number relationship, but the information in the book is not valuable to the five students.*)

E. Petroleum in Japan, a country without its own oil fields and without oil reserves.

(*Scarce. Petroleum has many valuable uses in Japan.*)

F. Petroleum in Saudi Arabia, a country with many oil fields and oil reserves.

(*Scarce. Petroleum has many valuable uses in Saudi Arabia, and it can be sold to other people in other countries. Several valuable uses.*)

5. Describe situations (see two examples below) where scarce resources are treated as if they were not scarce because the people involved don't personally find the resources to be scarce. Behavior in these cases often leads to waste and poor use of the resource.

- Teachers assign unnecessary homework to their classes, not recognizing that the students have many assignments from many classes. The teachers do not bear the cost of the assignment overload (how to spend scarce study time?), so they may neglect to take scarcity into account when they assign students their homework.

- Land used as a site for new school buildings was once prime wildlife habitat. The people designing the school had no interest in wildlife, so to them there was no cost in using the land for construction of a school.

6. Refer the students to Activity 2 and ask them to read it. Ask the students again to work in pairs to decide which examples show people treating scarce resources as not scarce and which examples show people treating scarce resources as scarce.

*Answers to Activity 2*

A. Water fountains in Rome flow continuously with water carried by viaducts from the Italian mountains. People walking in Rome quench their thirst by drinking from these fountains. But most of the water flows into the street and down the drains to a river that passes through the city.

(*Scarce resource treated as not scarce. The water has other valuable uses, such as irrigation or sewer treatment.*)

B. At closing time, restaurants in the United States are required to throw away all uneaten food. To meet health standards for food preparation and the safety of consumers, the food cannot be stored for use the next day. Also, the law prohibits restaurant employees from giving the food to the poor or dispersing it to local food banks.

(*Scarce resource treated as not scarce. The food could feed hungry people; it could be stored for future consumption; or it could be used as compost to improve soil conditions in gardens.*)

C. Oxygen is taken from the air and stored in containers. When divers wish to stay underwater for long periods of time, they purchase container-stored oxygen and breathe from it during their underwater activities.

(*A difficult example. Oxygen in the air around us is not scarce. People routinely acquire it at no cost. There is more of it than individuals can use. But oxygen underwater is scarce, as are the resources needed to capture oxygen and store it in containers for underwater use. So container-stored oxygen is scarce.*)

D. Pebbles are taken from a beach to build a walkway in a homeowner's lawn. No one else wants the pebbles. The pebbles are not necessary for the lake's ecosystem or animal habitat.

(*Not scarce. The pebbles have no valuable alternative use. The resources necessary to move the pebbles [time and effort, for example] are scarce. They could be used for other valuable purposes.*)

E. A farmer has a water irrigation contract that requires the water user to use the entire allocation of water to water crops, whether or not all the water is needed for crop irrigation. If the farmer does not use all the water, he or she will receive a smaller allocation next year.

*(Scarce resource treated as not scarce. The farmer is prohibited from considering other valuable uses for the water.)*

## Closure

Ask the students to review the key ideas in this lesson by explaining why there is a lot of wasted food in the school cafeteria.

*(Food is scarce, according to both definitions. Students, however, cannot store it or resell it. Often they do not pay for it. For the students, therefore, food in the school cafeteria has only one valuable use — eat it or throw it away. This helps to explain why some of the food is treated as not scarce.)*

## Multiple-Choice Questions

### (Correct answers shown in bold)

1. Which of the following statements is *not* consistent with the concept of scarcity?

   A. People are scarce because they have many valuable uses in the world.

   **B. Trash is scarce because you rarely see much of it around unless you go to a landfill.**

   C. Knowledge is scarce because what we wish to know is so great relative to what we do know at this time.

   D. Electricity is scarce because it has many valuable uses.

2. Which of the following resources was considered scarce in 1000 AD?

   A. Petroleum

   B. Aluminum

   C. Computers

   **D. None of the above**

3. Which of the following people must deal with scarcity when they make decisions during the day?

   A. The richest person in the world

   B. A homeless person living in New York City

   C. A commuter living in the suburbs and working in the city

   **D. All of these people must deal with scarcity.**

## Essay Question

Do students face scarcity? Define scarcity and provide two examples showing how students are confronted with scarcity if a teacher assigns them homework.

*(Answer: Scarcity is a circumstance in which human wants exceed the capacity of available resources to provide for those wants. It is also a situation in which a resource has more than one valuable use. Students are resources. They may want to use their time for work, leisure, fun, relaxation, and gaining knowledge. A homework assignment requires students to make a decision: whether to give up other valuable uses of their time and energy to do homework or to ignore the homework, do other valuable things instead, and bear the consequences of not doing as well in the class.)*

SCARCITY AND ABUNDANCE

**Unit 1, Lesson 2**
Visual 1

## TWO DEFINITIONS OF SCARCITY

- A situation in which human wants are greater than the capacity of available resources to provide for those wants.

- A situation in which a resource has more than one valuable use.

# Unit 1 | Teacher's Guide

## Unit 1 Lesson 3

## Economic Magic: Creating Something from Nothing

### INTRODUCTION

**Economics** Economics is the study of how human beings choose to use scarce resources. In this lesson, students must decide, given a special set of circumstances, which resources are scarce and what the alternative uses for them might be. The circumstances seem to require the students to make something from nothing, since they are stuck on an island and have, apparently, no resources to use for survival. They soon discover, however, many items that may be used to produce goods and services. Then they must answer the three basic questions of economics: What to produce? How to produce it? For whom will it be produced? As the students answer these questions, they are effectively establishing an economic system.

**Reasoning** As individuals are confronted with scarcity, they must decide how to cope. They typically find that some resources are more valuable than others. Some rules, similarly, serve as incentives for cooperation more effectively than others do. Given the possibilities, people work purposefully to find the alternatives best suited to their production and distribution problems. Their choices may work well or poorly depending upon their judgment, knowledge, imagination, and ability to work with other people.

### CONCEPTS

- Distribution
- Economics
- Production
- Resources
- Scarcity

### OBJECTIVES

*Students will:*

1. Identify scarce resources.
2. Define the opportunity cost of a decision as the most valuable alternative forgone.
3. State the three fundamental questions that people in every economy must answer.
4. Recognize that people try purposefully to make the best choices they can, given the alternatives available.

### CONTENT STANDARDS

- Productive resources are limited. Therefore, people cannot have all the goods and services they want; as a result, they must choose some things and give up others. (NCEE Content Standard 1)
- Different methods can be used to allocate goods and services. People, acting individually or collectively through government, must choose which methods to use to allocate different kinds of goods and services. (NCEE Content Standard 3)

### LESSON DESCRIPTION

Students participate in a small-group survival activity designed to illustrate the basic economic decisions people in every economy must address. They must decide which resources are scarce and they must answer three basic questions: What to produce? How to produce it? For whom will it be produced?

*Time Required: 90 minutes*

### MATERIALS

- A transparency of Visual 1
- Activity 1

### PROCEDURE

1. Explain that in every economy, people must make decisions about production and distribution. They must decide which resources are scarce and how to use them. This lesson will help the students to understand these ideas and relationships.

2. Read the following account of a hypothetical situation to the class:

*Picture yourself on vacation in spectacular Southeast Alaska, kayaking with a group of friends. You can't believe you are there. You have never kayaked before in your life, but the school had a special deal enabling students to spend a few days sea kayaking and whale watching. It sounded great, so you went along.*

*It's the end of July. The weather is warm and the scenery is spectacular. You've had good times and easy paddling so far, but today you've noticed clouds gathering and a chill in the air. Still, you and your friends climb into the kayaks and get started, thinking that if it does rain you will be able to dry off later, after you travel the day's course and make camp.*

*Just as you expected, rain begins to fall, and it shows no sign of stopping soon. The clouds get darker, the rain pours down harder and harder, and THE WIND COMES UP! It becomes difficult to paddle in the waves. You might be in trouble. Then a huge wave hits the kayak*

# Economic Magic: Creating Something from Nothing

*and, very quickly, you capsize. But you and your friends remember your safety training. You grab hold of the kayaks and paddles and swim for shore. Thank goodness you were careful to travel near land at all times. Gasping for breath and shivering from exposure to the cold water, you eventually drag yourself up onto the shore.*

*Now you have a new problem. You and your friends are stranded on a small, deserted island, and you don't know how long you will have to be there. The nearest settlement is over 75 miles away. Your task: Survive!*

3. Refer the students to Activity 1 and ask them to decide which of the resources listed there are scarce (have more than one valuable use) and which are not scarce.

4. Display Visual 1. Encourage the students to use their imagination to solve their problem, but remind them also to consider the opportunity cost of each of their choices.

5. Divide the class into groups.

6. Refer the students to Activity 1 and ask them to review the island's environment and the equipment that remains from the kayaks.

7. Tell the students that each group has no longer than 10 minutes to figure out how it will survive. The students in each group should settle on their plan and describe the plan briefly at the end of Activity 1.

8. After 10 minutes, call time and have one person from each group report the group's survival plan to the entire class. Summarize each plan on the chalkboard.

9. Instruct the students to take notes on the back of their survival sheets during the questioning. Ask:

   - What general type of behavior seems to be the same among groups of people trying to keep themselves alive? What choices were they making?

     *(Creating a survival plan forced the members of each group to decide which items were scarce resources and to make choices about alternative ways to use those resources.)*

   - What opportunity costs did people encounter in making their decisions?

     *(Many items can be used in different ways, and the alternatives may be mutually exclusive. The students should have many examples.)*

   - Explain that people in all economies must decide what to produce, how to produce it, and for whom it will be produced. The students then should share examples of their decisions as they relate to these three questions. If the students cannot see how their decisions relate to these questions, probe further:

     1. What did you make to eat or for shelter?
     2. How did you make it?
     3. Who made it?
     4. What natural resources were used?
     5. What tools were used?
     6. Did everyone get a share of what was produced?
     7. Did the goods produced go only to those who helped to produce them?
     8. Did a leader decide who got what?
     9. Did those who did no work get any of the goods produced?

   If the students cannot answer these questions, instruct them to go back into their groups and figure out the rest of their survival plan.

   - Ask the students how they made their choices.

     1. Were your choices made randomly (by chance) or purposefully (considering alternatives)?

        *(They probably considered alternatives, choosing those deemed most useful for survival.)*

     2. What alternatives did you consider before you made choices about production and consumption?

        *(Most students will have looked at a variety of alternatives and implicitly considered the costs and benefits of each choice. This process indicates that the choices were purposeful.)*

   - How do anticipated costs and benefits explain the choices you made to survive?

     *(Groups probably sought to gain survival-related benefits at the lowest possible costs.)*

## Closure

Ask the students to summarize and explain the following key ideas:

- Scarce resource
- Opportunity cost
- Three basic economic questions
- Purposeful decision making

# Unit 1 | Teacher's Guide

## Multiple-Choice Questions
(correct answers shown in bold)

1. Shipwrecked survivors on a deserted island, even if they did not have a boat, might consider a wood paddle to be a scarce resource because:

   A. It reminds them of home.

   B. It can be burned for heat.

   **C. It can be used for several valuable purposes.**

   D. They would not consider it a scarce resource.

2. Which of the following statements is not an economic question people in every society must answer?

   A. What to produce?

   **B. Who decides what is fair?**

   C. How to produce it?

   D. For whom will it be produced?

3. Carla was showing her friend Debbie the new car she had just purchased. She told Debbie that the car cost her a two-month vacation in the Bahamas. Debbie got on Carla's case. "That is not the cost," she said; "you gave up $10,000." If they were talking about opportunity cost, who was correct?

   **A. Carla**

   B. Debbie

   C. Both were correct.

   D. Both were wrong.

## Essay Question

Several students were talking about taking time off after graduating from high school so that they could spend two years traveling around the world. One student remarked, "It's a great idea, but can you imagine how much it would cost? Even if you backpacked and camped out, it would still cost you $10,000!" An economics student replied that that sum of money would not amount to even half the cost. Explain what the economics student was talking about.

*(Opportunity cost is the key concept in this conversation. The obvious financial cost [perhaps $10,000] is important, but the lost opportunities are even greater. The next-best alternative is also a cost. If the next-best alternative for these students is to stay home and take a job for $25,000 a year, their total cost for the world tour would be $60,000. That total includes the $10,000 in monetary cost plus $50,000 in two years of lost wages.)*

# ECONOMIC MAGIC: CREATING SOMETHING FROM NOTHING

**Unit 1, Lesson 3**
Visual 1

## OPPORTUNITY COST

As you make choices about how to survive, consider the consequences of each choice. These consequences include anything you might give up in making a particular choice. Economists call this an analysis of opportunity cost, because using a resource in one way may foreclose the opportunity to use it differently.

### DEFINITION:

In any choice, the opportunity cost is the highest-valued alternative that must be forgone when another alternative is chosen.

### EXAMPLES:

1. If you use the kayak paddle for firewood, you cannot use it as a fishing pole.

2. If you use the drinking water collected from the rain for taking a shower, you cannot use it to satisfy your thirst.

# Unit 1 | Teacher's Guide

**Unit 1 Lesson 4**

## To Choose or Not to Choose? That Is Not the Question

### INTRODUCTION

**Economics**  This lesson emphasizes the concepts of scarcity and choice. People engage in economizing behavior; consciously or tacitly, they weigh the relative benefits and costs of each alternative and try to choose the one that will provide them the greatest net benefits. In some situations it may appear that people "have no choice." Even in tough situations, however, there are alternatives; when there seem to be none, it is usually because the alternatives in question come with costs so high that they are not given serious consideration. The economizing choice that follows in such a case scarcely seems to be a choice at all. This lesson helps students to identify alternatives and anticipate their associated costs and benefits; it also requires them to make choices among given alternatives.

**Economic Reasoning**  This lesson helps to establish the economic assumption that people choose. Students identify the alternatives that exist in "no choice" circumstances.

### CONCEPTS

- Alternatives
- Choices
- Economizing behavior
- Scarcity

### OBJECTIVES

*Students will:*

1. Identify alternatives in various choice situations.
2. Identify costs and benefits associated with various alternatives.
3. Make economizing choices, given competing alternatives.

### CONTENT STANDARDS

- Productive resources are limited. Therefore, people can not have all the goods and services they want; as a result, they must choose some things and give up others. (NCEE Content Standard 1)
- Effective decision making requires comparing the additional costs of alternatives with the additional benefits. Most choices involve doing a little more or a little less of something; few choices are all-or-nothing decisions. (NCEE Content Standard 2)

### LESSON DESCRIPTION

Students make a decision after identifying the alternatives and their anticipated costs and benefits.

*Time Required: 45 minutes*

### MATERIALS

- Activity 1

### PROCEDURE

1. Explain that the purpose of this lesson is to help the students develop their ability to solve economic problems. To do that, they need to learn some basic assumptions of economics. One assumption has to do with whether or not people have choices.

2. Point out to the class that people often think they have no choice. Read this example to the class:

    *Todd recently purchased his own car on credit. He works at a part-time job at an auto-wrecking firm to earn the money he needs to make payments on his new car. Lately, his work in school has declined. When his teacher asked him if he was studying for the tests, he replied, "Not really. I'd like to study more, but I have no choice. I've got to keep working to pay off my car loan."*

    Ask: Did Todd have alternatives in his situation? Encourage the students to suggest some alternatives Todd had in addition to reducing his study time.

3. Ask the students to describe situations where they may have felt they had no choice. For example: "I have to put gas in the car so I can get to work tonight."

4. Refer the students to Activity 1. Ask them to read the first case. Discuss the first example with the class. Ask:

    A. What was Ashley's problem?
    B. What alternatives did Ashley have?
    C. What were the costs of each alternative?
    D. What were the benefits?

5. Encourage the students to practice this way of thinking by completing the choice grids in Activity 1, listing the alternatives and the expected costs and benefits in each case.

# To Choose or Not to Choose?
# That Is Not the Question

*Possible answers to Activity 1, examples 2 and 3.*

*Example 2:*

| Alternatives: | Possible Cost | Possible Benefit |
|---|---|---|
| Keep the price the same. | Reduce profits, maybe lose money and go out of business. | Keep prices the same and customers happy. |
| Keep the price the same by discontinuing some of sandwiches' special features (e.g., use cheaper tomatoes). | Customers might not buy as many sandwiches — reduced sales. | Keep prices and profits about the same. |
| Discontinue selling sandwiches and introduce less expensive lunches. | Customers might not like the new product, maybe lose sales. | Keep profits about the same. |
| Raise prices of sandwiches. | Customers might buy less, maybe lose money. | Keep profits about the same. |

*Example 3:*

| Alternatives: | Possible Cost | Possible Benefit |
|---|---|---|
| Produce a different product. | Difficult to transform the plant and equipment. | Keep profits about the same. |
| Produce airbags and GPS or a foreign producer. | Difficult to get a contract. | Increased sales. |
| Close the plant and go bankrupt. | Lose money Employees out of work. | No more worries about competing with foreign producers. |
| Restrict imports. | Few obvious costs to this owner and workers but increased costs for others. | Increased sales and jobs for his workers. |

6. Discuss the students' responses to one or more of the cases in Activity 1. Stress the choices that may not be obvious.

## Closure

Conclude the lesson by reviewing the choice principle with a new example. Have the students provide an example from a recent experience in which they had to make a choice.

## Multiple-Choice Questions

(Correct answers shown in bold)

1. Everyone must wake up and start the day. Which of the following actions requires people to make a choice among alternatives?

    A. Take a shower.

    B. Say "Good Morning" to the family.

    C. Get dressed.

    D. Listen to the radio.

    **E. All of the actions require people to make choices and consider alternatives.**

2. Economists encourage people to think carefully about decisions because there are no "costless" decisions. Which of the following statements best explains this idea?

    **A. In choosing one alternative, you give up the other alternatives.**

    B. If you choose one alternative, you are forced to pay the money.

    C. There are no consequences for a poor decision.

    D. Economists tend to confuse money and consequences.

3. A professional hockey team offers Kyle $5 million a year to play hockey. Kyle tells his parents that he has "no choice" but to skip college and play hockey. Which of the following alternatives is Kyle not considering?

    A. Stay at home and loaf.

    B. Go to college.

    C. Choose a career outside hockey.

    **D. All of the above are alternatives to playing hockey.**

## Essay Question

A hay farmer is approached by an environmental group with a plan to save fish in the nearby river. The environmentalists will pay him for all the hay he planned to grow if the farmer agrees not to use water from the river to irrigate the hay crop. Does the farmer have a choice? Explain your answer, using the concepts of scarcity, choice, and alternatives.

*(The water is scarce. It has at least two valuable uses. It can be used to provide habitat for fish or to grow hay, but it cannot be used for both alternatives. The farmer now has a choice of how to gain income. He can gain income by growing and selling hay or by receiving payments from the environmental group for not irrigating the hay.)*

# Unit 1 | Teacher's Guide

## Unit 1 Lesson 5

## Rules Influence Economic Behavior

### INTRODUCTION

**Economics** In successful economies, many people work together on specialized tasks to produce and distribute goods and services. Rules (both formal and informal) foster these relationships. Rules help to create social systems in which strangers may work independently in an interdependent relationship. Specialization and interdependence are obviously important. Most people, after all, do not sew the clothes they wear, grow the food they eat, or build the homes they live in. Instead, one person's work and output are exchanged for another person's work and output. Rules can help make interaction of this sort regular and predictable.

**Reasoning** In this lesson students experience an unanticipated change of rules and take note of the changes in behavior that follow. Then, using assumptions about rules, choices, and incentives, they explain the observed changes in behavior.

### CONCEPTS

- Choices
- Incentives
- Interdependence

### OBJECTIVES

*Students will:*

1. Identify incentives that influence their test-taking behavior.
2. Explain how rule changes can affect incentives.
3. Explain how rules influence people's choices and the level of economic activity observed in different economies.

### CONTENT STANDARDS

- Effective decision making requires comparing the additional costs of alternatives with the additional benefits. Most choices involve doing a little more or a little less of something; few choices are all-or-nothing decisions. (NCEE Content Standard 2)
- People respond predictably to positive and negative incentives. (NCEE Content Standard 4)

### LESSON DESCRIPTION

The lesson begins with a demonstration of how rules and incentives influence students' behavior in the classroom. Then students apply the same analysis to behavior in the larger economy. (WARNING: Given the unusual grading procedure specified in Procedure 5, this lesson may be hazardous to the teacher's health.)

*Time Required: 45 minutes*

### MATERIALS

- A transparency of Visuals 1, 2, 3, and 4
- Activities 1, 2, 3, and 4

### PROCEDURE

1. Explain that this lesson will demonstrate how rules and changing incentives can influence people's economic behavior.

2. Display Visual 1. Review each of the principles in the **Guide to Economic Reasoning**.

3. Refer the students to Activities 1 and 2. Ask them to do the following:
   - Do their very best on the quiz.
   - Make no marks on the quiz.
   - Mark all answers on Activity 2, First Answer Sheet.
   - Finish in five minutes.

4. Call time after five minutes. Ask the students to exchange their answer sheets with a neighbor for correcting. Read the correct answers and have the students record scores (number correct) for the quizzes they correct in the space provided on the answer sheet.

   *(Quiz answers are: 1-A, 2-D, 3-C, 4-A, 5-B, 6-C, 7-B, 8-C, 9-B, 10-D. Read the original questions along with the correct answers. This will help reinforce the economic concepts being taught.)*

5. Display Visual 2. Tell the students that grades on the quiz will be assigned as follows:

   | Number Correct | Grade |
   |:---:|:---:|
   | 4 or more | F |
   | 3 | D |
   | 2 | C |
   | 1 | B |
   | 0 | A |

   Tell the graders to record grades on Activity 2, First Answer Sheet.

# Rules Influence Economic Behavior

6. How well did the students do? Survey class performance, asking correctors to provide data by raising their hands. Ask: How many of you corrected a First Answer Sheet that has a grade of A?, B?, C?, D? or F? Record the data for future reference, using Visual 3. Return the quizzes to the owners after the tally.

7. Discuss the students' reactions to the results. Ask:
   - How many of you usually try to earn as high a grade as possible? Why?
   
   *(Most students see earning high grades as having something in it for them — e.g., personal satisfaction, getting a good course grade, or getting parental, teacher, or peer approval.)*
   
   - Why did so many of you end up with low grades on the quiz?
   
   *(Students made an incorrect assumption about the grading rules.)*
   
   - What is an incentive?
   
   *(Refer the students to question 3 on the quiz if they need to review the definition of incentive.)*
   
   - What incentive influenced the choices you made in selecting answers to the quiz questions?
   
   *(The incentive for most students was to do well, demonstrate their accurate knowledge, and get a good grade.)*
   
   - If you had known before you took the quiz that the grading scale was inverted, how many quiz questions would you have tried to answer correctly? Why?
   
   *(Many students would have tried deliberately to answer questions incorrectly, since the lowest score would have earned the highest grade.)*

8. Tell the students that the grades from the quiz they just took will not count. Instead, they will be permitted to take the same quiz a second time in order to have a chance to improve their grades. Distribute Activity 3. Display Visual 4 and discuss the new grading scale:

   | Number Correct | Grade |
   | --- | --- |
   | 10 | A |
   | 9 | B |
   | 8 | C |
   | 7 | D |
   | 6 or less | F |

*NOTE:* All students earning a grade of A will be given a writing assignment which will be due at the end of the period. Other students may use the rest of the period for reading or working quietly on anything of their choice.

9. Ask the students to do the following:
   - Use the same quiz they took for Activity 1.
   - Make no marks on the quiz.
   - Mark all answers on Activity 3, Second Answer Sheet.
   - Finish in five minutes.

10. Call time after five minutes and tell the students to exchange their quizzes with a neighbor for correcting. Read the correct answers and have the students record scores (number correct) for the quizzes they corrected in the space provided on the answer sheets. Then tell the correctors to mark grades on the answer sheets according to the grading scale provided on Visual 4.

11. How well did the students do this time? Survey class performance, asking correctors to report grades by raising hands in response to your questions. Record the data for future reference, using Visual 3 again. Ask:
    - Why didn't everyone earn a grade of A, since all of you knew what the correct answers were before you took the quiz?
    
    *(The incentives changed. The grade of A was too costly relative to the benefits for many students.)*
    
    - How many students tried to miss at least one question on the quiz? Why?
    
    *(Students probably missed a question to avoid the extra assignment and to get time for free reading or study.)*
    
    - What incentive influenced the choices you made about selecting answers to the quiz questions this time?
    
    *(Most students probably wanted the highest grade possible without incurring any extra work.)*
    
    - What caused the incentive change?
    
    *(The teacher changed the rules.)*

12. Place the following diagram on the board:

    **Rules →Incentives →Choices**
    
    Ask: What is the relationship among choices, incentives and rules?
    
    *(Rules influence incentives, and incentives influence choices.)*

13. Explain that all countries establish rules for their economies, and these rules influence behavior. Some rules encourage people to use resources and exchange goods and services. Some rules discourage people from using resources and exchanging goods and services. Refer the students to Activity 4. Ask them to decide whether the rules described there would encourage or discourage economic activity. (Note: Some examples in Activity 4 involve important religious beliefs or cultural norms. This activity implies no moral judgment of those beliefs or norms; it focuses only on whether the rules in question would be likely to encourage or discourage economic activity.)

*Answers to Activity 4*

A. In Afghanistan, under Taliban rule, women could not go to school, hold jobs, or move around in public without an escort.

   Encourage _____

   Discourage __X__

   *(This policy prohibited 50 percent of the population from providing goods and services to other people [except family members]. In that respect it reduced the society's capacity to provide goods and services.)*

B. In Russia when it was part of the former Soviet Union, managers of nail factories were rewarded for producing large numbers of nails. No reward was given for making nails in several different sizes.

   Encourage __X__

   Discourage _____

   *(This policy encouraged economic behavior, but it was wasteful. The managers made many small nails which were not useful to people who wanted nails in other sizes.)*

C. In the United States, if the water in a river provides the habitat for an endangered species, the water cannot be used to irrigate crops, create electricity, or water livestock.

   Encourage _____

   Discourage __X__

   *(The cost of saving endangered species in this manner is the value of other economic activity, associated with other uses of water, prohibited by the rule.)*

D. In many parts of India, cows are considered sacred, and people are not allowed to use beef as a food.

   Encourage _____

   Discourage __X__

   *(This religious belief obviously discourages the use of cows as a food source. It has also encouraged people in India to concentrate on providing alternative food sources.)*

E. In Argentina, beef is considered an important food source, and Argentine cows are sold to people around the world.

   Encourage __X__

   Discourage _____

   *(The high value attached to eating beef encourages the use of cows as a food source. Large ranches produce cows in large numbers. Vegetarians observe that the emphasis on beef ranching discourages efforts to develop other, non-meat food sources in Argentina.)*

## CLOSURE

Conclude the lesson with a quick review. Ask:

- How do rules influence economic behavior? Provide an example.

- Would a new rule about economic behavior (for example: no one is allowed to eat meat) influence people if it was not enforced?

   *(If rules are not enforced, people tend to disregard them and act as if no rule existed.)*

## MULTIPLE-CHOICE QUESTIONS

(CORRECT ANSWERS SHOWN IN BOLD)

1. Which of the following rules would encourage high school seniors to study during their last semester in high school?

   **A. Seniors who do not equal their highest semester GPA during their last semester in high school will not graduate.**

   B. Seniors who have passed all their courses before the last semester in high school must average at least a D in all their courses to graduate.

   C. All seniors who are voted "friendly" by their classmates will graduate, no matter what grades they achieve in the last semester.

   D. All seniors will graduate except for five students voted "most uncooperative" by the teachers.

# Rules Influence Economic Behavior

2. Which of the following rules will encourage workers to work harder and produce more at their jobs?

    A. After working at a firm for six months, workers are guaranteed a job in that firm for the rest of their lives.

    **B. Workers receive 50 percent of all the money made on sales of items produced by the firm.**

    C. Workers receive the same pay no matter how much they work and produce.

    D. Workers receive raises based on how many times they volunteer to do community work.

3. In Africa, poachers kill many elephants. Local people who live near elephants often do not protect the elephants from poachers. Which of the following rules will most likely help reduce the poaching of elephants?

    A. Elephants cannot be owned or claimed by anyone. They are to be left unharmed, even if they move through villages, harm people, and trample crops.

    B. People should love elephants and respect nature's great beasts.

    **C. People living near elephant herds can treat elephants as their own beasts — using them for food or charging fees for tourists who want to view the animals.**

    D. Anyone who provides the evidence needed to arrest and convict a poacher will be paid a reward of $10.

## Essay Question

Public officials are concerned about traffic congestion on freeways during rush hour in large cities. They want to reduce the number of cars on the freeways from 7:00 to 9:00 a.m. and from 4:00 to 6:00 p.m. To achieve this, they introduce a rule that requires drivers to pay $30 per car to drive during rush hour. How do you think people will respond?

*(More people will drive before 7:00 a.m., after 9:00 a.m., before 4:00 p.m., and after 6:00 p.m. People who do drive during rush hour will be more inclined to ride in car pools so that they and their car-pool partners can share the cost. People may also strive to use other roads and stay off the freeway during rush hour.)*

# Unit 1 | Teacher's Guide

**Unit 1, Lesson 5**
Visual 1

## GUIDE TO ECONOMIC REASONING

1. People choose. People choose the alternative that seems best to them because it involves the least cost and the greatest benefit. People economize.

2. People's choices involve costs — monetary costs and opportunity costs. Opportunity cost is the second-best alternative people give up in making a choice.

3. People respond to incentives in predictable ways. Incentives are benefits or rewards that encourage people to act. When incentives change, people's choices change.

4. People create economic systems, and these systems influence incentives and people's choices. How people cooperate is governed by written and unwritten rules. As rules change, incentives change and choices change.

5. People gain when they trade voluntarily. People can produce more in less time by concentrating on what they do best. The surplus goods or services they produce can be traded for other valuable goods or services.

6. People's choices have consequences that lie in the future. The important costs and benefits in economic decisions are those that will appear in the future. Economics stresses the importance of making choices about the future. People cannot choose to change the past.

**Unit 1, Lesson 5**
Visual 2

# GRADES

| NUMBER CORRECT | GRADE |
|:---:|:---:|
| 4 or more | F |
| 3 | D |
| 2 | C |
| 1 | B |
| 0 | A |

# Unit 1 | Teacher's Guide

**Unit 1, Lesson 5**
Visual 3

## Class Tally of Quiz Grades

| Possible Grades | First Quiz<br /># of students who earned | Second Quiz<br /># of students who earned |
|:---:|:---:|:---:|
| A | _____ | _____ |
| B | _____ | _____ |
| C | _____ | _____ |
| D | _____ | _____ |
| F | _____ | _____ |

**Unit 1, Lesson 5**
Visual 4

# Grades Again

| NUMBER CORRECT | GRADE |
|:---:|:---:|
| 10 | A |
| 9 | B |
| 8 | C |
| 7 | D |
| 6 or less | F |

**NOTE:** All students earning a grade of A will be given a writing assignment which will be due at the end of the period. Other students may use the rest of the class period to read or work quietly on anything of their choice.

# CAPSTONE

## UNIT 2

# THE INVISIBLE HAND AT WORK

Lesson 6     Why Did Communism Collapse?

Lesson 7     A Silver Market

Lesson 8     A Picture Is Worth a Thousand Words: Demand

Lesson 9     A Picture Is Worth a Thousand Words: Supply

Lesson 10    Equilibrium Prices and Equilibrium Quantities

Lesson 11    Do Prices Matter to Consumers?

Lesson 12    How Do Prices Influence My Behavior? Price Elasticity

Lesson 13    How Markets Allocate Resources

Lesson 14    Secondary Effects: Price Ceilings and Floors

# Unit 2 | Teacher's Guide

## Unit 2 Lesson 6

# Why Did Communism Collapse?

### INTRODUCTION

**Economics** People in every society make choices regarding what goods and services to produce, how to produce them, and how to allocate them. The command economies of the twentieth century, in nations such as the former Soviet Union and the People's Republic of China, relied primarily on government to make these choices. In contrast, the market economies of the West, including such nations as the United States, Canada, and Great Britain, relied primarily on market forces — private ownership, the profit motive, and market prices — in making these choices. The contrast shows that market systems are by and large more successful and more sustainable than command systems.

**Reasoning** What happens when people in positions of authority ignore or flout basic economic principles? Some answers can be inferred from the recent history of experimentation with command economies in the former Soviet Union and its satellite states in Eastern and Central Europe. Drawing upon principles from the **Guide to Economic Reasoning** — especially the importance of incentives — this lesson challenges students to explain why communism collapsed.

### CONCEPTS

- Choice
- Command economy
- Economic systems
- Market economy
- Incentives

### OBJECTIVES

*Students will:*

1. Analyze the characteristics of a command economy.
2. Apply principles of economic reasoning to explain the collapse of communism in the Soviet Union.

### CONTENT STANDARDS

- Different methods can be used to allocate goods and services. People, acting individually or collectively through government, must choose which methods to use to allocate different kinds of goods and services. (NCEE Content Standard 3)
- People respond predictably to positive and negative incentives. (NCEE Content Standard 4)
- Markets exist when buyers and sellers interact. This interaction determines market prices and thereby allocates scarce goods and services. (NCEE Content Standard 7)
- Prices send signals and provide incentives to buyers and sellers. When supply or demand changes, market prices adjust, affecting incentives. (NCEE Content Standard 8)
- Institutions evolve in market economies to help individuals and groups accomplish their goals. Banks, labor unions, corporations, legal systems, and not-for-profit organizations are examples of important institutions. A different kind of institution, clearly defined and well enforced property rights, is essential to a market economy. (NCEE Content Standard 10)

### LESSON DESCRIPTION

Students examine and discuss visuals to solve an economic mystery regarding the command system of the Soviet Union.

*Time Required: 45 minutes*

### MATERIALS

- A transparency of Visuals 1, 2, 3, 4, and 5
- Activity 1

### PROCEDURE

1. Tell the class that the collapse of communism in the former Soviet Union and its satellite states was one of the most important events of the twentieth century. Explain that the purpose of this lesson is to apply economic reasoning in an effort to explain why communism collapsed.

2. Display Visual 1. Ask:

    - What was the position of the former Soviet Union for much of the twentieth century?

        *(The Soviet Union was regarded as one of two superpowers.)*

    - How was the Soviet Union opposed?

        *(In the Cold War and certain "proxy wars," including the war in Vietnam, the United States and other nations opposed the expansion of communism.)*

    - What is the mystery?

        *(Why did the Soviet Union collapse?)*

3. Display Visual 2. Ask the students to speculate about whether each statement is true or false.

# WHY DID COMMUNISM COLLAPSE?

4. Refer the students to Activity 1 and ask them to read it. Display Visual 2 again. Discuss the students' responses to the true/false questions.

   A. For much of the twentieth century, nearly one-third of the world's population lived under communism or socialism. *(True)*

   B. The Soviet Union worked from the premise that only government planners could provide for the overall economic well-being of Soviet society. *(True)*

   C. In a market economy, prices send important information to producers and consumers regarding the relative value of goods and services. *(True)*

   D. In command economies, prices are controlled by the government. *(True)*

   E. Ask the students to solve the mystery, making reference to specific principles of economic reasoning.

   *(Soviet authorities assumed that government planners had superior information, enabling them to make better economic decisions than those made by individuals acting on their own behalf. But it was nearly impossible for government planners to understand local circumstances related to the production and consumption of goods and services. Principle 4.*

   *(The rules of the Soviet economic system abolished the incentives that ordinarily encourage producers to respond to consumers. First, most private ownership was abolished. Individuals were no longer allowed to benefit economically from the property they owned or worked. Second, under communism, the government owned businesses, and government managers managed businesses to meet government goals, not to make profits. This discouraged managers from responding to the interests of consumers. Principles 3 and 4.*

   *(In any economic system, prices send valuable messages to individuals and business owners. In a communist system, prices set by the government distorted the information sent to individuals and businesses. As a result, people often made poor decisions, causing waste and environmental damage. Principles 3 and 4.)*

5. Display Visual 4. Explain the basic characteristics of a market economy.

   - Private property: Private individuals and groups are the owners of the means of production — including factories, farms, and their own labor.

   - Freedom of choice: Businesses are free to decide what products to produce, and they may purchase what they need from suppliers of their choice. Consumers are free to spend or save their income in ways they choose.

   - Self interest: People make choices they judge to be in their own interest. Adam Smith argued that in making such decisions people are led by an "invisible hand" to promote the good of society as a whole.

   - Profit motive: Businesses are free to earn profits. Profits are viewed as rewards earned by those who take the risks involved in producing goods and services for consumers.

   - Markets and prices: Most exchanges are handled through markets — local, regional, national, or international. Market prices are established through the interaction of buyers and sellers. Prices are used to allocate goods and services in the economy.

   - Competition: Market systems depend on competition to restrain participants as they engage in self-interested behavior. In competitive systems, no one business can control market prices.

   - Limited government: Market systems require a limited the role for government. The government's regulatory role is restricted by constitutional or other legal limits. Defining and enforcing property rights, however, is an important obligation of government in a market system.

6. Display Visual 5. Explain that economists use the term *command economy* to describe the characteristics of a communist system. Use Visual 5 to explain the characteristics of a command economy.

   - Public ownership: The government is the owner of the means of production, including factories, farms, and so forth.

   - Centralized decision making: A central authority such as a bureau, legislature, or government official makes the fundamental decisions about what and how much will be produced.

   - Economic planning: A central authority such as a bureau, legislature, or government official makes the fundamental decisions about how goods and services will be produced. National economic goals are often an important focus. Objectives are established for each sector of the economy. Objectives are fine-tuned to provide instructions for each farm, factory, or mine.

- Allocation by command: A central authority such as such as a bureau, legislature, or government official makes the fundamental decisions about how goods and services are distributed. Raw materials and labor are assigned to factories, farms, and other units of production according to priorities established by government.

## Closure

Review the key points of the lesson. Ask:

- What are the principles in the **Guide to Economic Reasoning?**

    1. People choose.
    2. People's choices involve costs.
    3. People respond to incentives in predictable ways.
    4. People create economic systems that influence individual choices and incentives.
    5. People gain when they trade voluntarily.
    6. People's choices have consequences that lie in the future.

- Why did communism collapse?

    *(Under communism, government was thought to have superior information, enabling it to make better economic decisions than individuals might make acting on their own behalf. The rules of the economic system abolished the incentives (including private ownership and the profit motive) that encourage producers to respond to consumers. Prices and quantities set by the government distorted the information sent to individuals and businesses.)*

- What are the characteristics of a market economy?

    *(Private property, freedom of choice, self interest, the profit motive, markets and prices, competition, limited government.)*

- What are the characteristics of a command economy?

    *(Public ownership, centralized decision making, economic planning, allocation by command.)*

## Multiple-Choice Questions

(Correct answers shown in bold)

1. Which of the following is not a characteristic of a market economy?

    A. Private ownership

    B. Freedom of choice

    C. Competition

    **D. Selfishness**

2. Which of the following is not a characteristic of a command economy?

    A. Public ownership

    **B. Competition**

    C. Allocation by command

    D. Economic planning

## Essay Question

The members of parliament in a newly independent nation are debating whether to design an economy that is primarily market- or command-oriented. Write an essay comparing the advantages and disadvantages of each type of system.

*(Market economies have several advantages. They offer people a great deal of personal economic freedom. They place most economic decisions in the hands of the people who have the best knowledge about the issues at stake. They offer incentives that encourage innovation and reward people for the production of goods and services. They are associated with relatively high standards of living.*

*(A disadvantage is that market systems place pressure on people to produce. In a market system, there is always a competitor trying to outwit you and your business partners. Markets systems are not for the faint-hearted.*

*(An advantage of command systems is that nationwide goals can be set, and resources can be focused on meeting specific goals. The Soviet Union in the 1950s and the United States during World War II provide examples of how, in the short term, command systems can achieve important objectives.*

*(Among the disadvantages of command systems: They limit the economic freedom of individuals; they are often highly inefficient, producing goods and services that consumers may not want while failing to produce goods and services that consumers do want. In this respect, command systems suffer from built-in information problems. Economic systems are highly complex. It is nearly impossible for government planners to acquire and act upon information sufficient to provide for centralized economic planning and management. Market systems, by depending on profits and market prices, convey information much more efficiently. The result is that command systems tend to waste resources, damage the environment, and provide a low standard of living for most people — while preserving privilege and status for a few.)*

# WHY DID COMMUNISM COLLAPSE?

**Unit 2, Lesson 6**
Visual 1

## WHY DID COMMUNISM COLLAPSE?

- The Soviet Union from 1945 until 1991 was regarded as a superpower.

- The Soviet Union was a potent force. The largest nation on the planet, the Soviet Union possessed a strong military force, major deposits of oil, natural gas, coal, and many strategic minerals.

- Many Western leaders feared the Soviet Union would become the dominant world power. The "Cold War" and the Vietnam War were fought to stop the spread of communist ideas.

- Yet, in 1991, the Soviet Union abruptly disappeared. In that year, Russian President Boris Yeltsin declared that the Soviet Union ceased to exist.

- *Why did the Soviet Union collapse?*

**Unit 2, Lesson 6**
Visual 2

## TRUE/FALSE CLUES

1. For much of the twentieth century, nearly one-third of the world's population lived under communism or socialism.

    True or False?

2. The Soviet Union worked from the premise that only government planners could provide for the overall economic well-being of Soviet society.

    True or False?

3. In a market economy, prices send important information to producers and consumers regarding the relative value of goods and services.

    True or False?

4. In command economies, prices are controlled by the government.

    True or False?

**Unit 2, Lesson 6**
Visual 3

## SOLUTION TO THE COLLAPSE OF COMMUNISM MYSTERY

### THE MYSTERY

Why did the Soviet Union collapse?

### THE SOLUTION

- Under communism, government was thought to have superior information, enabling it to make better economic decisions than individuals might make acting on their own behalf.

- The rules of the economic system abolished the incentives that ordinarily encourage producers to respond to consumers:
  ✓ Private ownership
  ✓ Profit motive

- Prices and quantities set by the government distorted the information sent to individuals and businesses.

**Unit 2, Lesson 6**
Visual 4

## CHARACTERISTICS OF A MARKET ECONOMY

- Private Property
- Freedom of Choice
- Self-Interest
- Profit Motive
- Markets and Prices
- Competition
- Limited Government

**Unit 2, Lesson 6**
Visual 5

## CHARACTERISTICS OF A COMMAND ECONOMY

- Public Ownership
- Centralized Decision Making
- Economic Planning
- Allocation by Command

# Unit 2 | Teacher's Guide

## Unit 2 Lesson 7

## A Silver Market

### INTRODUCTION

**Economics**  In a competitive market, prices are discovered, not set by authorities. The price in a competitive market depends on the behavior of buyers and sellers. Buyers try to buy at the lowest possible prices. Sellers try to sell at the highest possible prices. The interaction of buyers and sellers determines the equilibrium or market-clearing price. The market-clearing price reflects the forces of supply and demand.

**Reasoning**  Many students memorize a definition stating that the equilibrium price is where supply and demand cross. Unfortunately, few students understand why this happens. The market is an environment where people attempt to improve their well-being by responding to incentives to trade with others. In this lesson, students should focus on the behavior they observe and relate it to the concepts of *choice* and *incentives*, which underlie the supply and demand analysis of a market.

### CONCEPTS

- Choice
- Competition
- Consumer surplus
- Demand
- Incentives
- Market-clearing price or equilibrium price
- Markets
- Producer surplus
- Supply

### OBJECTIVES

*Students will:*

1. Participate in a market simulation.
2. Make choices as buyers and sellers.
3. Explain how the forces of supply and demand determine price and how changes in the price of a good or service affect the quantities demanded and supplied.
4. Describe how exchange creates consumer and producer surplus.
5. Show how incentives act to move a price toward equilibrium.

### CONTENT STANDARDS

- People respond predictably to positive and negative incentives. (NCEE Content Standard 4)
- Markets exist when buyers and sellers interact. This interaction determines market prices and thereby allocates scarce goods and services. (NCEE Content Standard 7)

### LESSON DESCRIPTION

Students participate in a simulation activity that shows how a competitive market works. Although most markets for goods and services are not as competitive as the silver commodity market, the example helps students gain an understanding of how prices are set in any market.

*Time Required: 75 minutes*

### MATERIALS

- Handout material (see pp. 45, 46) used to make 32 Buy cards and 32 Sell cards. Use different colors for the Buy and Sell cards. (You might laminate the cards; you might also provide arm bands to distinguish buyers and sellers.)
  Make cards in the following amounts:

| Buy Cards | | Sell Cards | |
|---|---|---|---|
| Buy Price | No. | Sell Price | No. |
| $3.50 | 2 | $3.50 | 4 |
| 3.70 | 2 | 3.70 | 6 |
| 3.90 | 2 | 3.90 | 6 |
| 4.10 | 2 | 4.10 | 4 |
| 4.30 | 4 | 4.30 | 4 |
| 4.50 | 4 | 4.50 | 2 |
| 4.70 | 4 | 4.70 | 2 |
| 4.90 | 4 | 4.90 | 2 |
| 5.10 | 4 | 5.10 | 2 |
| 5.30 | 4 | | |

- Activities 1, 2, and 3
- A transparency of Visuals 1 and 2

CAPSTONE: EXEMPLARY LESSONS FOR HIGH SCHOOL ECONOMICS @ NATIONAL COUNCIL ON ECONOMIC EDUCATION, NEW YORK, NY

# A SILVER MARKET

## PROCEDURE

1. Tell the students that they are going to take part in a market simulation called "A Silver Market."

2. Refer the students to Activity 1 and have them read it. Go over the rules of the simulation and make sure the students understand their roles as buyers and sellers.

3. You may want to designate one student to oversee the distribution of Buy and Sell cards during the simulation and another to record each transaction on the tally sheet. Buy and Sell cards should be kept in separate piles, and each pile should be shuffled between rounds. Place the piles of Buy and Sell cards at opposite ends of the desk or table to minimize the possibility of students taking cards from the wrong pile. When students return cards, the cards should be placed at the bottom of the deck.

4. Clear the center of the room and designate it as the marketplace.

5. Divide the class into two equal-sized groups. One group will be sellers, the other buyers. Explain that buyers will be buyers throughout the simulation and sellers will be sellers throughout the simulation. You could identify the sellers by having them wear arm bands or a piece of paper as a badge.

6. Refer the students to the individual score sheets (Activity 2) and explain that they should record their transactions on these sheets. Review details of the score sheet if necessary.

7. Make sure the students understand how to calculate gains or losses, as explained on their score sheets.

8. Explain that you will conduct three rounds of trading, each round lasting five minutes. Keep time and announce the time when one minute remains in each round.

9. Use Visual 1 to record transactions, as described in Activity 1. Remind the sellers to report the price of each trade.

10. After each of the trading rounds, allow time for the students to calculate their net gains and losses (gains minus losses). Before discussing the outcomes of the simulation (in Procedure 13), have the students calculate their total net gain or net loss in each round. At the end of round 3, have the students calculate the grand total by summing up the totals for rounds 1, 2, and 3.

11. Encourage the students to make as many deals as they can in the time permitted. Explain that it is permissible to take a loss in order to get a new transaction card. Try not to reveal the fact that the students who have the highest net gain are often those who engage in the most transactions. This will be discovered during the discussion following completion of the simulation.

12. During the time between trading rounds, direct the students' attention to the record of all transactions on the Class Tally Sheet (Visual 1). Point out that it contains useful information for them. Do not elaborate.

13. Conduct post-simulation discussion. Ask:

    - At what price was silver most frequently sold in each round?

      *(Have the students examine data on their score sheets and on the Class Tally Sheet.)*

    - In which round did the greatest spread in prices occur?

      *(Examine data. It is usually Round 1.)*

    - Why did the prices become more clustered in later rounds?

      *(Competition among buyers and sellers based on greater information is the most important cause. Markets tend to move toward an equilibrium price as buyers and sellers obtain information about the quantity of products available at different prices.)*

    - Did buyers or sellers determine the final market price for silver?

      *(Buyers and sellers determined the market price by their interaction in the marketplace.)*

    - How did competition among sellers and buyers influence price?

      *(Because of competition within both groups, no single buyer or seller controlled the price. Note that buyers compete with other buyers, sellers with other sellers.)*

14. Determine consumer surplus and producer surplus.

    A. Have the buyers report their cumulative profit or loss for the three rounds. (You might want to give a prize to the best buyer to motivate the students.) Add these amounts on the board or on a transparency and determine the grand total. Label it "Total Profit for Buyers."

    B. Have the sellers report their cumulative profit or loss for the three rounds. (You might want to give a prize to the best seller to motivate the students.) Add these amounts on the board or on a transparency and determine the grand total. Label it "Total Profit for Sellers."

    C. In almost all cases, there will be a positive profit for the buyers and sellers. Profit for the buyers is called consumer surplus. Profit for the sellers is called producer surplus.

D. Consumer surplus and producer surplus are the main reasons why market economies work better than command economies. In a voluntary market, both buyers and sellers gain. This is very cool.

15. Assign Activity 3 as homework. Ask the students to draw the graph and answer the questions in Activity 3.

16. Project Visual 2 and check the students' graphs. Review supply, demand, and equilibrium.

17. Review the students' answers to the questions.

    A. What is the relationship between the amount of silver people want to buy and the price?

    *(The lower the price, the more silver people want to buy. The higher the price, the less silver people want to buy. This is called the law of demand.)*

    B. What is the relationship between the amount of silver people want to sell and the price?

    *(The lower the price, the less silver people want to sell. The higher the price, the more silver people want to sell. This is called the law of supply.)*

    C. What is the equilibrium or market-clearing price on this graph?

    *($4.30)*

    What is the quantity traded at that price?

    *(24 ounces)*

    D. Were more trades made at this price in the simulation than at any other price?

    *(Hopefully, yes.)*

    E. Why do you think all trades were not made at the equilibrium or market-clearing price?

    *(Markets don't work that way. Equilibrium is a tendency. When there is a temporary surplus, prices fall. When there is a temporary shortage, prices rise. Buyers and sellers are constantly interacting as prices constantly change.)*

    F. How did prices change as you played additional rounds of the simulation?

    *(Prices were closer to equilibrium as buyers and sellers reacted to their experiences and the information displayed.)*

## CLOSURE

Review the key points learned in the simulation. Ask:

- In a market, who or what determines the equilibrium price?

  *(The interaction of buyers and sellers.)*

- Who gains and who loses when people trade in a market?

  *(Both buyers and sellers gain. There are consumer surpluses and producer surpluses.)*

## MULTIPLE-CHOICE QUESTIONS

### (CORRECT ANSWERS SHOWN IN BOLD)

1. Who sets the price of a good or service in a market economy?

   A. Mostly buyers

   B. Mostly sellers

   **C. Buyers and sellers**

   D. Government economic policies

2. According to the law of demand:

   A. The higher the price, the more of the good people want to buy.

   **B. The lower the price, the more of the good people want to buy.**

   C. The higher the price, the more of the good businesses want to sell.

   D. The lower the price, the more of the good businesses want to sell.

3. The equilibrium price is the price where:

   **A. The amount of the good offered for sale is bought.**

   B. There are more buyers than sellers.

   C. There are more sellers than buyers.

   D. The prices of all goods and services are equal.

4. What is consumer surplus?

   A. A price where there is a surplus of the good offered for sale

   **B. The difference between what the consumer is willing to pay for the good and the price of the good**

   C. A price where sellers are at a disadvantage

   D. A situation that occurs most often in a command economy

# A Silver Market

## Essay Questions

1. Why didn't all the trades in the silver market take place at the equilibrium or market-clearing price?

   *(Markets don't work that way. Equilibrium is a tendency. When there is a temporary surplus, prices fall. When there is a temporary shortage, prices rise. Prices are constantly changing but moving toward equilibrium.)*

2. Why is the consumer and producer surplus that exists in a market economy a good thing?

   *(This means that consumers bought the good for less than they were willing to pay and sellers sold the good for more than they were willing to accept. Both buyers and sellers gained.)*

# Unit 2, Lesson 7

## Handout Material

### Buy Cards

| | | |
|---|---|---|
| You are authorized to **BUY** one ounce of silver, paying as **little** as possible. If you pay more than $5.30 per ounce, you lose money. | You are authorized to **BUY** one ounce of silver, paying as **little** as possible. If you pay more than $5.10 per ounce, you lose money. | You are authorized to **BUY** one ounce of silver, paying as **little** as possible. If you pay more than $4.90 per ounce, you lose money. |
| You are authorized to **BUY** one ounce of silver, paying as **little** as possible. If you pay more than $4.70 per ounce, you lose money. | You are authorized to **BUY** one ounce of silver, paying as **little** as possible. If you pay more than $4.50 per ounce, you lose money. | You are authorized to **BUY** one ounce of silver, paying as **little** as possible. If you pay more than $4.30 per ounce, you lose money. |
| You are authorized to **BUY** one ounce of silver, paying as **little** as possible. If you pay more than $4.10 per ounce, you lose money. | You are authorized to **BUY** one ounce of silver, paying as **little** as possible. If you pay more than $3.90 per ounce, you lose money. | You are authorized to **BUY** one ounce of silver, paying as **little** as possible. If you pay more than $3.70 per ounce, you lose money. |
| | You are authorized to **BUY** one ounce of silver, paying as **little** as possible. If you pay more than $3.50 per ounce, you lose money. | |

## A Silver Market

# Unit 2, Lesson 7

## Handout Material

### Sell Cards

| You are authorized to **SELL** one ounce of silver for as **much** as possible. If you accept less than $5.10 per ounce, you lose money. | You are authorized to **SELL** one ounce of silver for as **much** as possible. If you accept less than $4.90 per ounce, you lose money. | You are authorized to **SELL** one ounce of silver for as **much** as possible. If you accept less than $4.70 per ounce, you lose money. |
|---|---|---|
| You are authorized to **SELL** one ounce of silver for as **much** as possible. If you accept less than $4.50 per ounce, you lose money. | You are authorized to **SELL** one ounce of silver for as **much** as possible. If you accept less than $4.30 per ounce, you lose money. | You are authorized to **SELL** one ounce of silver for as **much** as possible. If you accept less than $4.10 per ounce, you lose money. |
| You are authorized to **SELL** one ounce of silver for as **much** as possible. If you accept less than $3.90 per ounce, you lose money. | You are authorized to **SELL** one ounce of silver for as **much** as possible. If you accept less than $3.70 per ounce, you lose money. | You are authorized to **SELL** one ounce of silver for as **much** as possible. If you accept less than $3.50 per ounce, you lose money. |

# Unit 2 | Teacher's Guide

**Unit 2, Lesson 7**
Visual 1

## Class Tally Sheet

| Trading Price<br>1 oz. of Silver | Round 1 | Round 2 | Round 3 |
|---|---|---|---|
| 5.40 | | | |
| 5.30 | | | |
| 5.20 | | | |
| 5.10 | | | |
| 5.00 | | | |
| 4.90 | | | |
| 4.80 | | | |
| 4.70 | | | |
| 4.60 | | | |
| 4.50 | | | |
| 4.40 | | | |
| 4.30 | | | |
| 4.20 | | | |
| 4.10 | | | |
| 4.00 | | | |
| 3.90 | | | |
| 3.80 | | | |
| 3.70 | | | |
| 3.60 | | | |
| 3.50 | | | |
| 3.40 | | | |
| 3.30 | | | |

A SILVER MARKET

**Unit 2, Lesson 7**
Visual 2

## SUPPLY AND DEMAND GRAPH FOR SILVER

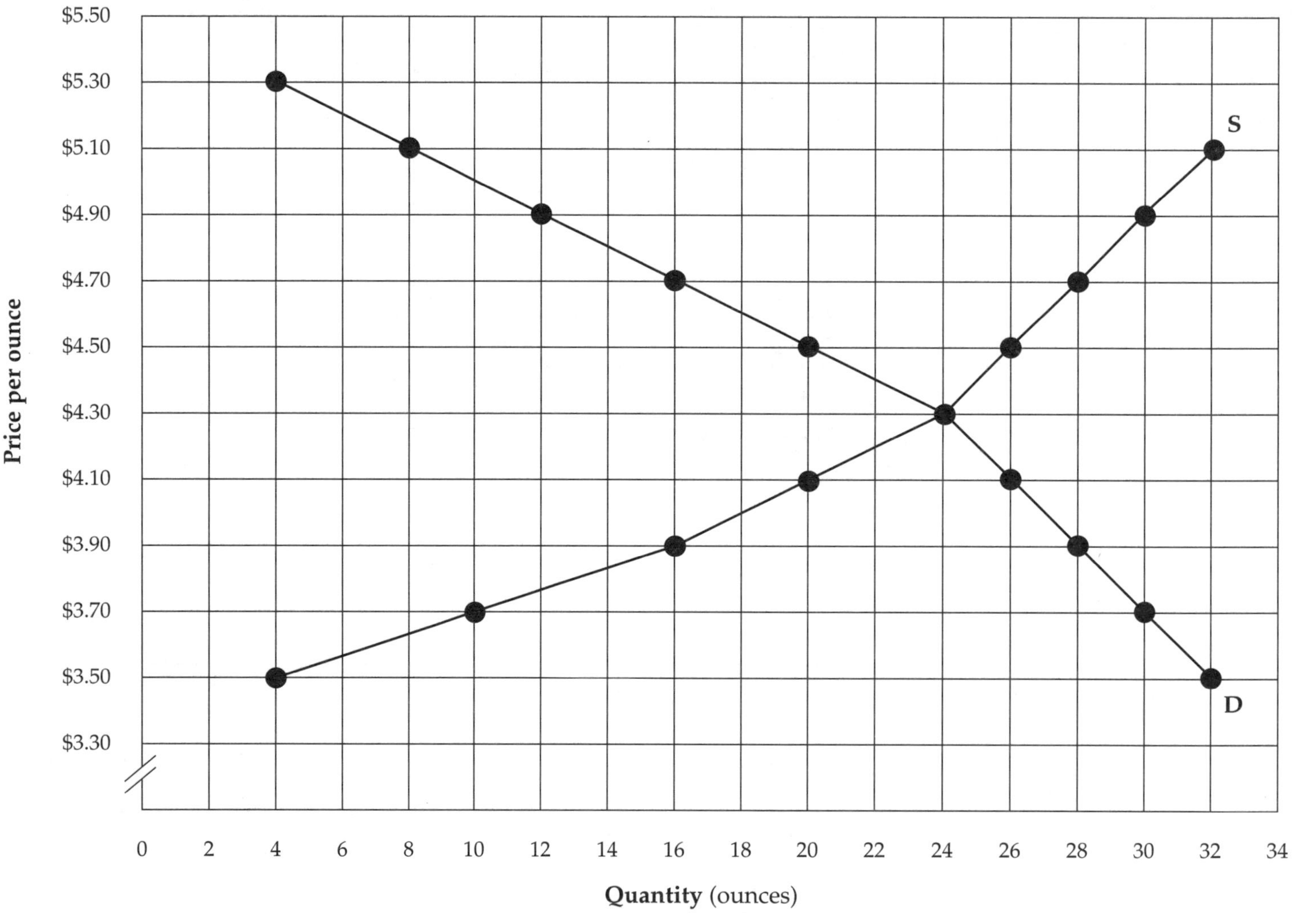

# Unit 2 | Teacher's Guide

**Unit 2 Lesson 8**

## A Picture Is Worth a Thousand Words: Demand

### Introduction

**Economics**   The choices that consumers make form a pattern and establish the basis for the law of demand. The law of demand states that consumers will tend to buy less of a good or service at higher prices and more at lower prices. As the price increases, the quantity demanded for that item falls. As the price decreases, the quantity demanded increases. These relationships demonstrate economizing behavior. When prices increase, the anticipated benefit does not change, but the value of the next-best alternative (the opportunity cost) increases; consumers respond to the changed incentives and purchase less of the product. When prices decline, the anticipated benefit remains the same, but the value of the next-best alternative (the opportunity cost) declines; therefore, consumers are rewarded if they purchase more.

**Reasoning**   The concept of demand is based on three key assumptions: that people economize, that people respond to incentives in predictable ways, and that all choices involve costs. Students can use the concept of demand and the related assumptions to explain why consumers purchase more at lower prices. Lower prices reduce costs relative to benefits for a particular purchase, while higher prices raise costs relative to benefits. Buyers seek the best deal among the alternatives available to them. Also, the concept of demand can be used to forecast what consumers will do when prices change or when variables that affect the actual demand for a product change and create a new price-quantity relationship.

### Concepts

- Demand
- Determinants of demand
- Price

### Objectives

*Students will:*

1. Explain the relationship between price changes and the quantity consumers are willing and able to buy.
2. Graph an example of a consumer demand schedule.
3. Predict how various events/conditions will shift demand.
4. Use the law of demand to predict consumer behavior in the marketplace.

### Content Standards

- People respond predictably to positive and negative incentives. (NCEE Content Standard 4)
- Prices send signals and provide incentives to buyers and sellers. When supply or demand changes, market prices adjust, affecting incentives. (NCEE Content Standard 8)

### Lesson Description

This lesson asks students to analyze the relationship between changing prices and changes in consumer behavior, to create and understand the demand schedule graph, and to identify how various determinants of demand change the relative location of the demand schedule.

*Time Required: 75 minutes*

### Materials

- One item of value to the students (a CD, tee shirt, hat, or candy bar, for example) to be used for a classroom auction
- Transparencies of Visuals 1 and 2
- Two copies for each student of Visual 2
- Handout material (see p. 53) for I.O.U.s

### Procedure

1. Explain that the purpose of this lesson is to introduce the law of demand. Pose this hypothetical problem to the class.

    *One day you are shopping with your friends, and you walk into a small greeting-card shop close to school to buy a birthday card for one of your relatives. While you are checking out the cards, you overhear the owner complaining that a certain style of card is not selling, and the display of that card is taking up precious space in the small store. "Unfortunately, I bought these cards up front and they cannot be returned," he says. "I guess I will just throw them away and use the space for something that has a better chance of selling." As the store owner looks over to you and your friends, he continues: "I learned in my economics class in high school that a person shouldn't cry over spilt milk or let costs incurred in the past influence future choices — right?" It becomes obvious that the owner is soliciting a response from you.*

# A Picture Is Worth a Thousand Words: Demand

2. Ask: Do you support the owner's view, or do you suggest an alternative course of action? Record the students' responses on the board.

   *(Possible answers: the owner is right — throw the "dogs" away; lower the price of the cards — put them on sale; place the cards in a more prominent place in the store; donate the cards to a charity; advertise the value of sending greeting cards; or be sure to recycle them.)*

3. Write the word "Sale" on the chalkboard. Ask: Why do businesses put items on sale?

   *(Possible responses: To sell more merchandise; to reduce surplus merchandise and avoid throwing away items that may still have value; to increase consumer demand. If this last answer is given, circle it and tell the students you will revisit it in a later activity. It is an incorrect answer because it refers to a change in demand caused by a price change, whereas price changes can only cause a change in quantity demanded. The incorrect response does fit into the changing demand activities that follow, however, so it will be a good motivator.)*

4. Ask: If the owner puts the cards that weren't selling on sale, will that be a good way for him to begin solving his problem of the cards that won't go away?

   *(Yes. Although the owner can't change his decision to buy the cards in the first place, getting something for the cards now is better than getting nothing, so at the very least the decision minimizes losses.)*

5. Explain that when business people put products on sale, they are attempting to predict consumer behavior. They are predicting that the number of products bought will increase at lower prices. That is not the only possible way to increase sales, of course. If the owner could change his customers' perception of value for the cards, the customers also would buy more. Changing customers' perceptions is one of the purposes of marketing through advertising.

6. Tell the students that you will now conduct an experiment to see whether such predictions of consumer behavior are correct. Announce that you found a king-sized candy bar (note: use another suitable object for the auction if you do not wish to provide candy to your students) in your lunch this morning (obviously placed there by a caring spouse or friend), but you are firmly committed to beginning your low-sugar diet today. Not wanting to waste the candy bar, you thought somebody in class might find some value in consuming it. Since you have only one candy bar and you want to make sure you get it to the consumer who values it the most, you have decided to auction the candy bar to the class.

7. Display Visual 1 and use it to keep track of the students' bids. Partially cover Visual 1, revealing only the suggested price of 10 cents. Ask how many students will buy the candy bar at this price. Record the number. Then reveal the 20-cents price and ask how many students would buy the candy bar for 20 cents. Record this number. Continue the routine, recording the quantity demanded at each price. Because you have only one candy bar to sell, continue the process by adding higher prices, if necessary, until only one person is willing to pay the highest price. Complete the transaction by providing the candy bar to the one buyer and collecting the money. Put numbers on the quantity axis after you record the numbers.

8. Discuss the results of the auction. Ask:

   - Did anyone choose not to bid on the candy bar?

     *(Usually students bid at very low prices even if they don't really want/like the item. This is because they think they might be able to sell it to somebody else later for a profit. Sometimes students don't bid even at a low price because they see no value at all in the item — they may have an allergy to chocolate, for example.)*

   - What goes through your mind before a bid is made?

     *(A calculation of the value of ownership in comparison to the cost of buying it — my opportunity cost.)*

   - Why does a higher price reduce the number of items demanded?

     *(Higher prices increase the number and value of alternative uses for the money. The alternatives may provide more satisfaction for some, and they will stop bidding. Higher prices also reduce an individual's total purchasing power.)*

   - Once a price is established in the market, do you think it stays the same for long periods?

     *(Generally not, because consumer preferences as well as other key variables change, and such changes influence demand. These changing variables actually shift the demand schedule and create a new price-quantity relationship. This shifting will be discussed following the graphing of the students' demand for the teacher's candy bar.)*

9. Tell the class that the information from the auction may be pictured on a graph. This graph illustrates the students' behavior regarding the candy bar at this time. Display Visual 2 and distribute a copy of it to each student. Get them started by first writing "price" near the vertical axis and "quantity" near the horizontal axis. Enter two quantities demanded at 10 cents and 20 cents. Ask the students to draw the additional information from the auction table on

their graphs and connect the price-quantity points making a line graph. When the students have completed their picture of demand, the teacher should complete the information on Visual 2. Ask the students to assess how well they did with their own drawings. Be sure to emphasize proper labeling of the picture: price for the vertical axis, the intersection representing the zero point, and quantity of candy bars for the horizontal axis.

10. After the graph is drawn and labeled, ask the students to summarize in their own words the information displayed on the graph. Stress the idea that as prices for goods or services rise, the quantity people are willing and able to buy declines; as prices for goods and services fall, the quantity people are willing and able to buy increases. The graph should look like this:

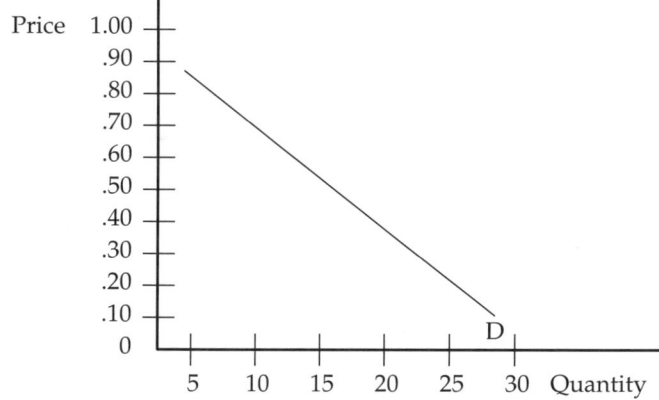

**Demand for King-Sized Candy Bars**

11. Ask the students whether they recall an earlier comment from the discussion following the auction — a comment suggesting that sometimes the demand for products actually changes when certain variables change. Explain that consumers are influenced by outside factors such as income, tastes and preferences, price of related products, expectations, and number of buyers. These are called determinants of demand.

12. To demonstrate how selected determinants of demand can change demand, conduct the following experiment: Tell the students that they are going to be given another opportunity to participate in an auction for a candy bar just like the last one (luckily, you have found another one in your lunch bag). You have just learned that a new study has revealed that… (dramatic pause) this candy bar reduces people's risk of getting cancer and having a heart attack. Many of the negative side effects people once attributed to eating chocolate have now been disproved. Announce further that you will accept I.O.U.s for purchase of the candy bar. Distribute I.O.U.s produced from the Handout Material.

13. Display a clean copy of Visual 1. Be prepared to increase the prices. Conduct a second auction, using the procedure followed earlier. Record the information on Visual 1. Distribute a second copy of Visual 2. Ask:

- How did your buying decision change after you learned more about chocolate and had the I.O.U. option?

    *(Some students may have been more interested in the candy bar because it is healthier than they expected. Some may have been more involved in the auction because the I.O.U. actually added to their available income for this experiment. Both of these variables influence some peoples' demand for products and services.)*

- How do the two graphs of demand for candy bars compare?

    *(In most cases the two graphs will be different. They will have different price-quantity pairs, although the relationship is the same. In the second auction, the demand will usually be greater [located further to the right on the coordinate system]. At any price there is a greater quantity demanded. This is because of changes in the determinants of demand — tastes, preferences, prices of related goods, and income. The shift in demand between auction 1 and 2 should look like this:*

**Shift in Demand for King-Sized Candy Bars**

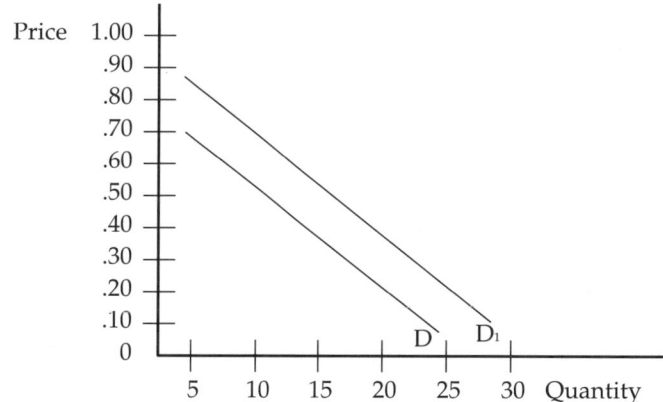

14. Ask the students to raise hands to show what will happen to demand in the following circumstances (raise the right hand to indicate a shift of the demand curve to the right; raise the left hand to indicate a shift of the demand curve to the left):

- The demand for cars when people get a tax refund *(shift right)*

- The demand for gloves after the first snow storm *(shift right)*

- The demand for hot dogs when the price of hot dog buns rises *(shift left)*

# A Picture Is Worth a Thousand Words: Demand

- The demand for gasoline today when people expect prices to fall tomorrow *(shift left)*
- The demand for ice cream when the price of ice cream drops *(no hand should go up because this is a change in quantity demanded, not a demand change)*

## Closure

Review the law of demand. Ask the students to identify a current event that they think will change either the quantity demanded or the demand for a particular good or service. List two or three examples.

## Multiple-Choice Questions

### (Correct Answers Shown in Bold)

1. The law of demand states:

   A. There is a positive relationship between price and quantity demanded.

   B. The graph of a demand curve is an upward sloping line.

   **C. People usually buy less goods and services when their price rises.**

   D. People's behavior in the marketplace is unpredictable.

2. When the price of an item changes, people will usually:

   **A. Look at how the price change influences the relative value of their alternatives.**

   B. Disregard a small change in price.

   C. Assume the item is on sale and buy more.

   D. None of the above.

3. Which of the following will usually not cause people to demand more of a good or service?

   A. Expectations

   B. Number of buyers

   **C. Price**

   D. Higher income

## Essay Question

Develop an economic rationale for the advertising marketing function. Include a graph as part of your answer.

*(Advertising when properly implemented will change some consumers' tastes and preferences for a product. With this higher valuation of the benefits associated with consumption of the product, more people will choose to buy it because the expected benefits are now higher than the expected costs. The graph should demonstrate how a demand schedule can shift to the right when the determinant of demand [tastes and preferences] has changed. With supply remaining the same, more will be purchased.)*

## Unit 2 | Teacher's Guide

# Unit 2, Lesson 8

## Handout Material for I.O.U.s

| | |
|---|---|
| Name: _____<br><br>**I.O.U.**<br><br>Amount: $ _____ | Name: _____<br><br>**I.O.U.**<br><br>Amount: $ _____ |
| Name: _____<br><br>**I.O.U.**<br><br>Amount: $ _____ | Name: _____<br><br>**I.O.U.**<br><br>Amount: $ _____ |
| Name: _____<br><br>**I.O.U.**<br><br>Amount: $ _____ | Name: _____<br><br>**I.O.U.**<br><br>Amount: $ _____ |

# A Picture Is Worth a Thousand Words: Demand

**Unit 2, Lesson 8**
Visual 1

| Candy Bars Suggested Price | Quantity Demanded |
|---|---|
| $ .10 | _____ |
| $ .20 | _____ |
| $ .30 | _____ |
| $ .40 | _____ |
| $ .50 | _____ |
| $ .60 | _____ |
| $ .70 | _____ |
| $ .80 | _____ |
| $ .90 | _____ |
| $1.00 | _____ |

# Unit 2 | Teacher's Guide

**Unit 2, Lesson 8**
Visual 2

## DEMAND FOR KING-SIZED CANDY BARS

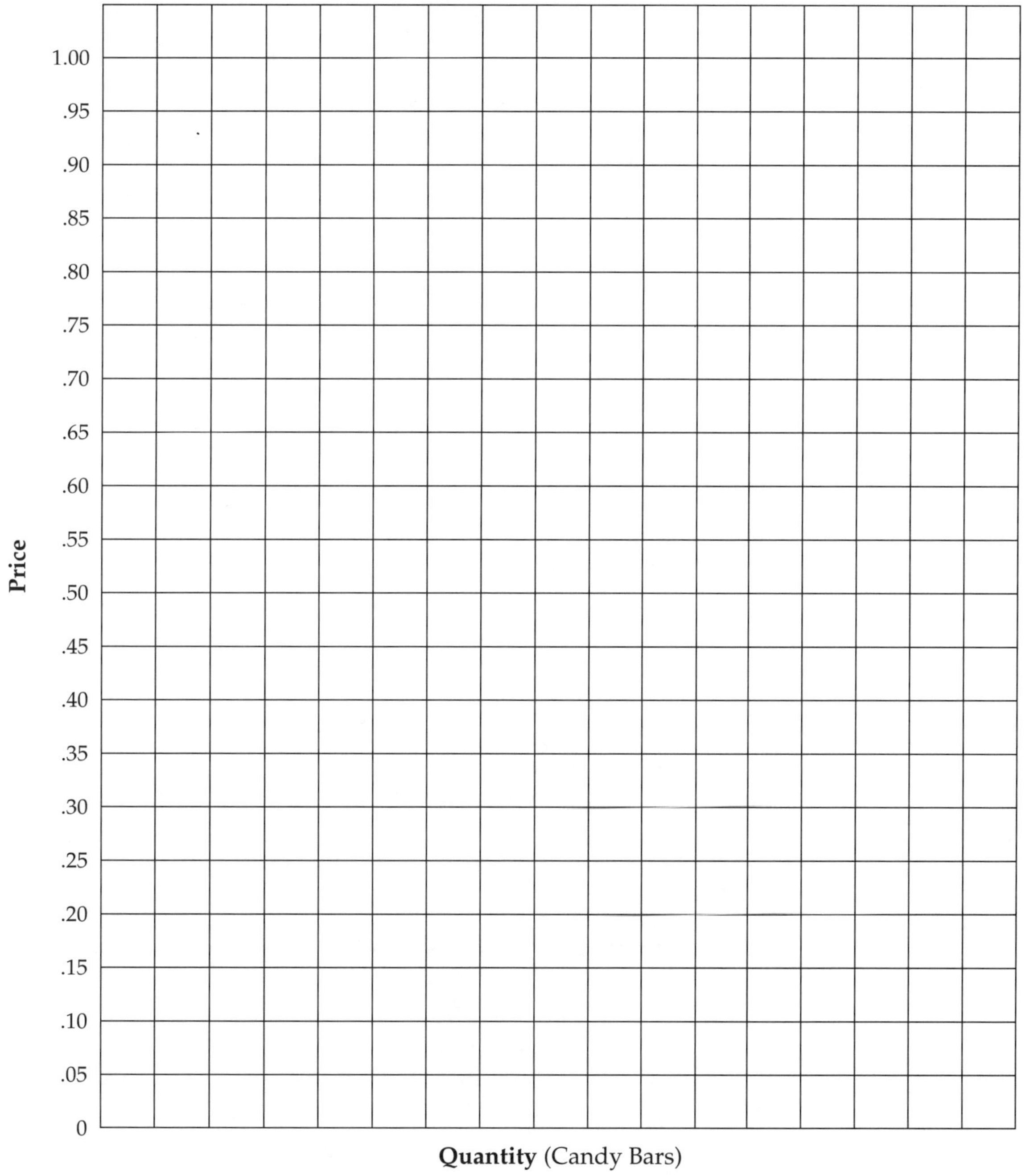

Price (y-axis): 0, .05, .10, .15, .20, .25, .30, .35, .40, .45, .50, .55, .60, .65, .70, .75, .80, .85, .90, .95, 1.00

**Quantity** (Candy Bars)

# Unit 2 | Teacher's Guide

## Unit 2 Lesson 9

## A Picture Is Worth a Thousand Words: Supply

### INTRODUCTION

**Economics**  The choices that producers make form a pattern and establish the basis for the law of supply. The law of supply states that producers will tend to supply more of a good or service as prices for the good or service increase. As prices decrease, the quantity supplied also decreases. Why? As prices increase, the anticipated benefit to producers rises; the higher price acts as an incentive, encouraging producers to move more resources into production of the higher-value good or service. When prices go down, the anticipated revenue will fall short of the opportunity cost the producers had previously considered; consequently, producers will produce less.

**Reasoning**  The concept of supply also relates to the three key assumptions we considered in studying demand: that people economize, that people respond to incentives in predictable ways, and that all choices involve costs. Students can use the concept of supply together with the related assumptions to explain why firms produce more goods and services at higher prices. Higher prices generate greater business revenue. Suppliers seek the best use of their expertise and other resources because, given a choice, they would rather earn more than less when they produce and sell goods and services. Also, students can use the concept of supply to forecast what producers will do in the market when prices change or when variables that affect supply for a given product change and create a new price-quantity relationship.

### CONCEPTS

- Determinants of supply
- Incentive
- Price
- Supply

### OBJECTIVES

*Students will:*

1. Explain how price changes affect the quantity producers are willing and able to supply.
2. Graph an example of a producer supply schedule on a coordinate axis system.
3. Predict how various events/conditions will shift producer supply.
4. Use the law of supply to predict producer behavior in the marketplace.

### CONTENT STANDARDS

- People respond predictably to positive and negative incentives. (NCEE Content Standard 4)
- Prices send signals and provide incentives to buyers and sellers. When supply or demand changes, market prices adjust, affecting incentives. (NCEE Content Standard 8)

### LESSON DESCRIPTION

Students analyze the relationship between changing prices and changes in producer behavior. They create a supply schedule graph to represent this relationship. They observe changes in determinants of supply and note the effect of those changes on the supply schedule and the corresponding price-quantity relationships.

*Time Required: 75 minutes*

### MATERIALS

- A transparency of Visuals 1 and 2
- Two copies for each student of Visual 2
- Activities 1 and 2

### PROCEDURE

1. Explain that the purpose of this lesson is to introduce the law of supply. Pose this hypothetical problem to the class.

    *The owner of the local fast-food restaurant is having trouble hiring workers for the closing shift. Although the closers have a few more responsibilities than other workers, including cleaning, the closing shift often fits best with students' schedules. The owner of the restaurant doesn't know what to do. He is angry. He says that "Young people today are just plain lazy and maybe spoiled too."*

    Ask: Is the owner right? Are there other explanations of why young people might choose not to work as closers in the fast-food restaurant?

    *(Answers should include the difficulty of the task plus the value of other ways in which young people could use the evening hours — hanging out with friends, studying, perhaps holding better jobs available elsewhere in the community.)*

# A Picture Is Worth a Thousand Words: Supply

2. Write the word *producer* on the chalkboard. Ask: Why do producers offer goods and services for sale?

   *(Typically, students will suggest that producers wish to earn money or that they take pride in providing a good or service that other people find valuable enough to buy. In discussing these responses, help the students to identify the relationship between the price a good or service sells for and the incentive producers have to produce it. This relationship between price and the quantity producers are willing to produce is depicted by a supply schedule. As the price rises, producers are willing, for most goods and services, to produce more. To help students grasp the point, encourage them to consider their own experience as producers. For example, some of them might provide babysitting services or work at a library. The time they commit to providing these services is their time — time they "own." They may use it, accordingly, to produce things of value on the job, at home, or in school, and the choices they make in this regard may well be influenced by the prices others are willing to pay for the use of their time.)*

3. Ask the students to take part in an experiment that will provide information on how producers behave in the marketplace. The information derived from the experiment will be used to reach conclusions about suppliers and to picture aspects of their behavior on a graph. Refer the students to Activity 1; tell them that you want to tabulate the number of work hours they are willing to work per week. Ask them to provide the information requested in Activity 1.

4. When the students have completed Activity 1, display Visual 1. Sample four or five members of the class, asking them to report how many hours they would be willing to work at each price. Record the numbers on Visual 1. Total the numbers. Ask:

   - What pattern do you observe in the responses on Visual 1?

     *(At low rates of pay, the quantity supplied is low. As the rates of pay increase, the quantity supplied increases.)*

   - Several students chose not supply labor at any wage rate? Why?

     *(Often students choose not to work at low wage rates. They usually enter the market when wage rates rise. Some students, however, may value other alternatives so highly that they refuse to work even at the $100 wage. At a $100 pay rate, in fact, some students might choose to work less, since they could earn a considerable amount of money at that rate in a short time.)*

   - What influences your decision to work or not to work?

     *(The expected benefits derived from work at that wage rate are equal to or greater than the next-best use of my time.)*

   - Why does a higher wage usually increase the number of hours people are willing to work?

     *(Higher wages provide positive incentives to work. These positive incentives generate benefits greater than the expected value of the next-best alternative.)*

   - Would you predict that a different group of people would fill out the questionnaire differently?

     *(People value things differently and consequently make different choices. Although the relationship between wages and number of hours worked would be the same, people might differ in the specific number of hours they would work at each wage rate.)*

5. Tell the class that the information recorded on Activity 1 can be pictured on a graph. This graph will illustrate the supply of labor in the class at that moment in time. Distribute copies of Visual 2 and display the transparency of Visual 2. Graph the labels on the visual: price near the vertical axis and quantity (of hours worked) near the horizontal axis. Explain that the labels indicate what the graph will show: the relationship between wage rates and the students' decisions about how many hours they would be willing to work.

6. The students are to add the information from the sample of the students' material created in Procedure 4. After the supply curve is drawn and labeled (as labor supply), ask the students to summarize in their own words the information displayed on the graph. Encourage them to summarize the law of supply: As prices for goods or services rise, the quantity people are willing and able to supply rises; as prices for goods and services fall, the quantity people are willing and able to supply decreases. The graph should look like this:

**Supply of Hours to Work**

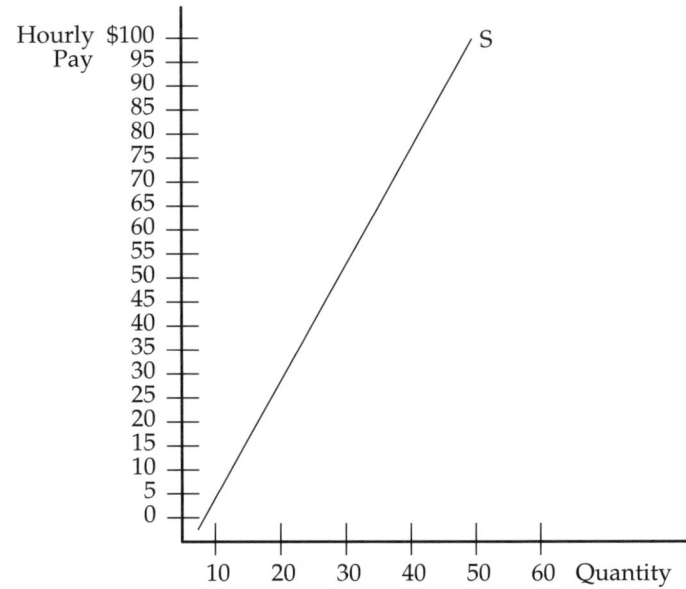

# Unit 2 | Teacher's Guide

7. Explain that the study of producers and their behavior in the marketplace goes beyond the price and quantity relationship just graphed. Inquisitive minds might want to know what causes the supply curve to locate itself as it does on the coordinate axis system. Or, to put it another way, what creates the magnitude of the price-quantity relationship or an actual supply change?

   *(In discussing students' responses, introduce the term "determinants of supply." Determinants of supply are variables other than price that can shift the supply schedule. These variables include input prices, technology, expectations, and/or the number of sellers in a given market sector.)*

8. To demonstrate how selected determinants of supply can shift the supply schedule, refer the students to Activity 2; ask them to read it and answer the questions. Discuss their responses:

   A. Why did so many farmers leave farming to go into other careers?

   *(Answers might include better alternatives, low market value for their crops, prospect of increased competition from foreign producers of food products, high equipment costs, and taxes.)*

   B. When many producers leave a market (as in the case of farming), what is likely to happen to the quantity produced at any given price?

   *(That quantity will fall. The falling quantity is pictured by a supply curve that has shifted to the left. The whole price-quantity relationship or supply curve moves on the graph. This shift occurs because one of the determinants of supply [the number of sellers] has changed. When a determinant changes, the whole supply picture changes.)*

9. Ask the students to indicate with a show of hands (raise the right hand to indicate a shift of supply to the right — an increase; raise the left hand to indicate a shift of supply to the left — a decrease) what will happen to supply in the following circumstances:

   A. The supply of cars when open-trade agreements bring in new producers.

   *(Shift right; increase in producers.)*

   B. The supply of coffee when freezing temperatures hit the major coffee-producing regions of Brazil and Costa Rica.

   *(Shift left; natural disaster decreases inputs.)*

   C. The supply of lumber when a new computer-assisted saw reduces the cost of lumber production.

   *(Shift right; new technology decreases production costs.)*

   D. The supply of gasoline today if there is an expected shortage and higher prices likely to occur next week.

   *(Shift left; sellers want higher future prices, so they will decrease their supply today.)*

## CLOSURE

Review of law of supply. Remind the students that at lower prices the quantity supplied is less and at higher prices the quantity supplied is more. Ask the students to identify a current event that they think will change either the quantity supplied or the supply for a particular good or service. List two or three examples.

## MULTIPLE-CHOICE QUESTIONS

### (CORRECT ANSWERS SHOWN IN BOLD)

1. The law of supply states:

   **A. There is a positive relationship between price and quantity supplied.**

   B. The graph of a supply curve is a downward sloping line.

   C. People usually supply fewer goods and services when their prices rise.

   D. People's behavior in the marketplace is unpredictable.

2. When the price of an item changes, producers will usually:

   **A. Look at how the price change influences the relative value of their alternatives.**

   B. Disregard a small change in price.

   C. Assume the item is on sale and produce more.

   D. None of the above.

3. Which item will not change the supply for a good or service?

   A. Expectations

   B. Number of sellers

   **C. Price**

   D. Change in technology

## ESSAY QUESTION

Develop an economic rationale for consumer support of trade agreements that will increase the number of producers for products consumers want. In your rationale, use the concepts of supply and shifts in supply.

*(An increase in the number of sellers will shift the supply curve to the right and — everything else staying the same — consumers will usually have more products to choose from at a lower price. They will be made better off.)*

# A Picture Is Worth a Thousand Words: Supply

**Unit 2, Lesson 9**
Visual 1

| Hourly pay | Hours willing to work for one week | | | | |
|---|---|---|---|---|---|
| | Student 1 | Student 2 | Student 3 | Student 4 | Total |
| $ 1.00 | _____ | _____ | _____ | _____ | _____ |
| $ 5.00 | _____ | _____ | _____ | _____ | _____ |
| $ 7.00 | _____ | _____ | _____ | _____ | _____ |
| $ 10.00 | _____ | _____ | _____ | _____ | _____ |
| $ 15.00 | _____ | _____ | _____ | _____ | _____ |
| $ 20.00 | _____ | _____ | _____ | _____ | _____ |
| $ 25.00 | _____ | _____ | _____ | _____ | _____ |
| $100.00 | _____ | _____ | _____ | _____ | _____ |

Total _____

# Unit 2 | Teacher's Guide

**Unit 2, Lesson 9**
Visual 2

## SUPPLY OF HOURS TO WORK

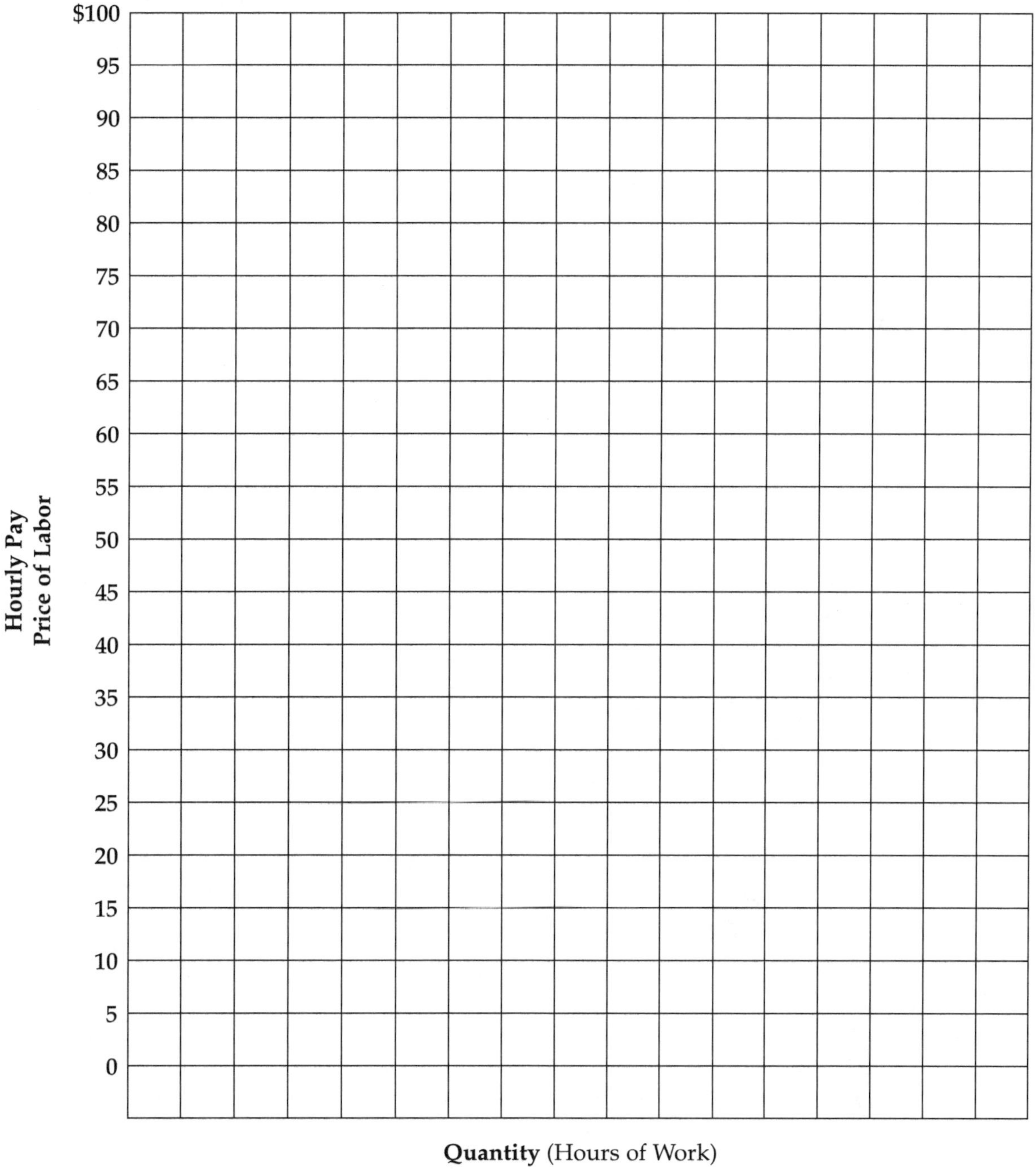

*Y-axis:* Hourly Pay Price of Labor ($0–$100)

*X-axis:* **Quantity** (Hours of Work)

# Unit 2 | Teacher's Guide

## Unit 2 Lesson 10

# Equilibrium Prices and Equilibrium Quantities

### INTRODUCTION

**Economics**  The forces of supply and demand work to establish a price at which the quantity of goods and services consumers will buy is equal to the quantity of goods and services businesses will sell. This price is called the equilibrium price or market-clearing price. It is important for students to know that the underlying conditions of supply and demand determine price. Equilibrium price is the child of supply and demand.

**Reasoning**  Students should not think of equilibrium price as a rigid point where two lines on a graph cross. Instead, they should think of it as the result of a process of mutual accommodation among buyers and sellers. Economists may seem to be obsessed about prices; if they are, it is because they know that prices provide the indispensable information and incentives that make the invisible hand of the marketplace such a powerful mechanism for coordinating economic behavior.

### CONCEPTS

- Demand
- Equilibrium price
- Quantity demanded
- Quantity supplied
- Shortage
- Supply
- Surplus

### OBJECTIVES

*Students will:*

1. Define equilibrium price and equilibrium quantity.
2. Determine the equilibrium price and equilibrium quantity when given the demand for and supply of a good or service.
3. Explain why the price of a good or service and the amount bought and sold in a competitive market will be the equilibrium price and quantity.
4. Predict the effects of changes in supply and demand on equilibrium price and quantity.

### CONTENT STANDARDS

- Markets exist when buyers and sellers interact. This interaction determines market prices and thereby allocates scarce goods and services. (NCEE Content Standard 7)

- Prices send signals and provide incentives to buyers and sellers. When supply or demand changes, market prices adjust, affecting incentives. (NCEE Content Standard 8)

### LESSON DESCRIPTION

In examining a visual about the market for yo-yos, students think through the process of mutual accommodation among buyers and sellers that results in an equilibrium price. Students then complete an activity plotting supply and demand curves in the market for Frisbees, identifying the equilibrium price and quantity under different conditions.

*Time Required: 45 minutes*

### MATERIALS

- Transparencies of Visuals 1, 2, and 3
- Activity 1

### PROCEDURE

1. Explain that the purpose of this lesson is to help the students gain a deeper understanding of equilibrium price. Explain that equilibrium is a state of balance between opposing forces. It occurs because everywhere else there is a state of imbalance or disequilibrium. In markets, equilibrium is often a temporary condition. You might illustrate this by putting a ball in a bowl. It will come to rest. Then hit the bowl, and the ball will move and come to rest again. Hitting the bowl is like a shift in demand or supply. However, the difference is that equilibrium occurs at different levels in supply and demand analysis. Each resting place is a different setting, depending on market conditions.

2. Display Visual 1 and show how markets reach equilibrium. Ask:

    A. What if the market price were $4?

    *(There would be a surplus of 800 yo-yos because the quantity demanded is 600 and the quantity supplied is 1,400.)*

    B. How would sellers get rid of the surplus?

    *(They would lower the price until all the yo-yos offered for sale were sold. The lower price is an incentive [for buyers] that increases the quantity demanded but decreases the quantity supplied. All the yo-yos would be sold at $3, the equilibrium price.)*

    C. What if the market price were $2?

    *(There would be a shortage of 800 yo-yos. Buyers would demand 800 more yo-yos than sellers are willing to sell. The quantity demanded is 1,400 and the quantity supplied is 600.)*

# Equilibrium Prices and Equilibrium Quantities

D. Which buyers will get the yo-yos?

*(The ones who will pay more. The higher price is an incentive [for sellers] that increases the quantity offered for sale. Once again, at $3 the number of yo-yos offered for sale in a time period is equal to the number of yo-yos consumers are willing and able to buy.)*

E. Explain that only at a price of $3 is the number of yo-yos sellers are willing and able to sell equal to the number of yo-yos consumers are willing and able to buy. This is why the equilibrium price of yo-yos is $3 and the equilibrium quantity of yo-yos is 1,000.

F. Explain that this is a process in which prices, incentives, shortages, and surpluses determine an equilibrium or resting place. The equilibrium price is produced by a process of mutual accommodation among buyers and sellers. Furthermore, prices in equilibrium may not remain in equilibrium for long. Any change in underlying conditions leads to a new equilibrium.

3. Refer the students to Activity 1 and ask them to complete Parts A-E. Project Visual 2 and discuss the answers to Parts A-E.

4. Now have the students complete Parts F and G. They should draw curves $S_1$ and $S_2$ on the same graph as before and answer the questions. They may need help in drawing the lines.

5. Project Visual 3 and discuss the answers to Parts F and G.

## Answers to Activity 1

A. Under these conditions, competitive market forces would tend to establish an equilibrium price of *$3.00* per Frisbee and an equilibrium quantity of *200* million Frisbees.

B. If the price currently prevailing on the market is $4.00 per Frisbee, buyers would want to buy *150* million Frisbees and sellers would want to sell *250* million Frisbees. Under these conditions, there would be a *surplus* of *100* million Frisbees. Competitive market forces would tend to cause the price to *decrease* to a price of *$3.00* per Frisbee.

C. At this new price, buyers would now want to buy *200* million Frisbees, and sellers would now want to sell *200* million Frisbees. Because of this change in *price*, the *quantity demanded* changed by *50* million Frisbees, and the *quantity supplied* changed by *50* million Frisbees.

D. If the price currently prevailing on the market is $2.00 per Frisbee, buyers would want to buy *250* million Frisbees and sellers would want to sell *150* million Frisbees. Under these conditions, there would be a *shortage* of *100* million Frisbees. Competitive market forces would tend to cause the price to *increase* to a price of *$3.00* per Frisbee.

E. At this new price, buyers would now want to buy *200* million Frisbees, and sellers would now want to sell *200* million Frisbees. Because of this change in *price*, the *quantity demanded* changed by *50* million Frisbees, and the *quantity supplied* changed by *50* million Frisbees.

F. Under these conditions, competitive market forces would tend to establish an equilibrium price of *$4.00* per Frisbee and an equilibrium quantity of *150* million Frisbees. Compared to the equilibrium price in question A., we say that, because of this change in *underlying conditions*, the *supply* changed, and both the equilibrium price and the equilibrium quantity changed. The equilibrium price *increased* and the equilibrium quantity *decreased*.

G. Under these conditions, with the supply schedule at $S_1$, competitive market forces would tend to establish an equilibrium price of *$3.00* per Frisbee and an equilibrium quantity of *100* million Frisbees. Compared to the equilibrium price in question F, because of this change in *underlying conditions*, the *demand* changed. The equilibrium price *decreased* and the equilibrium quantity *decreased*.

## Closure

Ask the students to review questions such as the following:

- Why does the price decrease if it is above equilibrium?

  *(The quantity for sale is greater than the quantity demanded, so sellers have an incentive to lower the price.)*

- Why does the price increase if it is below equilibrium?

  *(At a price below equilibrium, the quantity demanded exceeds the quantity supplied. Buyers have an incentive to offer a higher price if they want the good.)*

- For each of the following, predict the change in the equilibrium price of turkeys and explain your prediction.

  a. Turkey is called a health food by the U.S. Surgeon General.

     *(Price increases because demand increases and shifts right.)*

  b. New technology helps turkeys breed faster.

     *(Price decreases because supply increases and shifts right.)*

# Unit 2 | Teacher's Guide

c. Thanksgiving is abolished.

*(Price decreases because demand decreases and shifts left.)*

## Multiple-Choice Questions
### (Correct answers shown in bold)

1. The National Football League "blocks out" local television of football games when the game in question is not sold out in advance. The NFL supports this action because it

   **A. Increases the demand for football tickets.**

   B. Reduces the supply of football tickets.

   C. Reduces the price of football tickets.

   D. Increases the amount of money that the networks pay to televise NFL games.

*Answer questions 2 and 3 on the basis of the following diagram:*

Supply and Demand for Hot Dogs

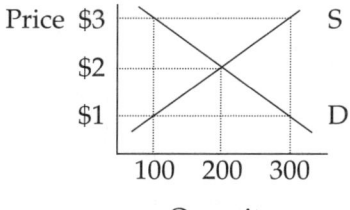

2. The equilibrium price and quantity are:

   A. $3 and 100.

   B. $3 and 300.

   **C. $2 and 200.**

   D. $1 and 100.

3. If the price were temporarily at $3.00:

   A. A shortage of 200 hot dogs would occur.

   B. The market would be in temporary equilibrium.

   **C. The price would decrease.**

   D. The quantity supplied would increase.

4. The equilibrium price is one at which:

   A. The market clears.

   B. The quantity supplied equals the quantity demanded.

   C. Neither a shortage nor a surplus exists.

   **D. All of the above occur.**

5. The function of a market-clearing price is to:

   A. Distribute income equally.

   **B. Equate quantity demanded with quantity supplied.**

   C. Encourage technological improvement.

   D. Ensure that sellers earn profits.

6. The discovery of oil in Mexico:

   A. Decreased the oil supply.

   **B. Increased the oil supply.**

   C. Decreased the oil demand.

   D. Increased the oil demand.

## Essay Questions

1. What is the difference between a change in quantity demanded and a change in demand?

   *(A movement along the demand curve is called a change in quantity demanded. Only a change in price can change quantity demanded. A shift in the position of the entire curve is called a change in demand. A change in demand for a good or service is caused by a change in the underlying conditions for that good or service.)*

2. The equilibrium price of oil has risen. Sara Green says that this must be because oil companies are cutting back on the supply. If you were her economics teacher, would you fail her or pass her? Why?

   *(You should fail her. Her explanation is possible. However, the demand for oil could also have increased. The supply of oil could have decreased but for different reasons such as an increase in the cost of producing or transporting oil. Sara has less than half of the story right, and that is an F.)*

EQUILIBRIUM PRICES AND EQUILIBRIUM QUANTITIES

**Unit 2, Lesson 10**
Visual 1

# Equilibrium

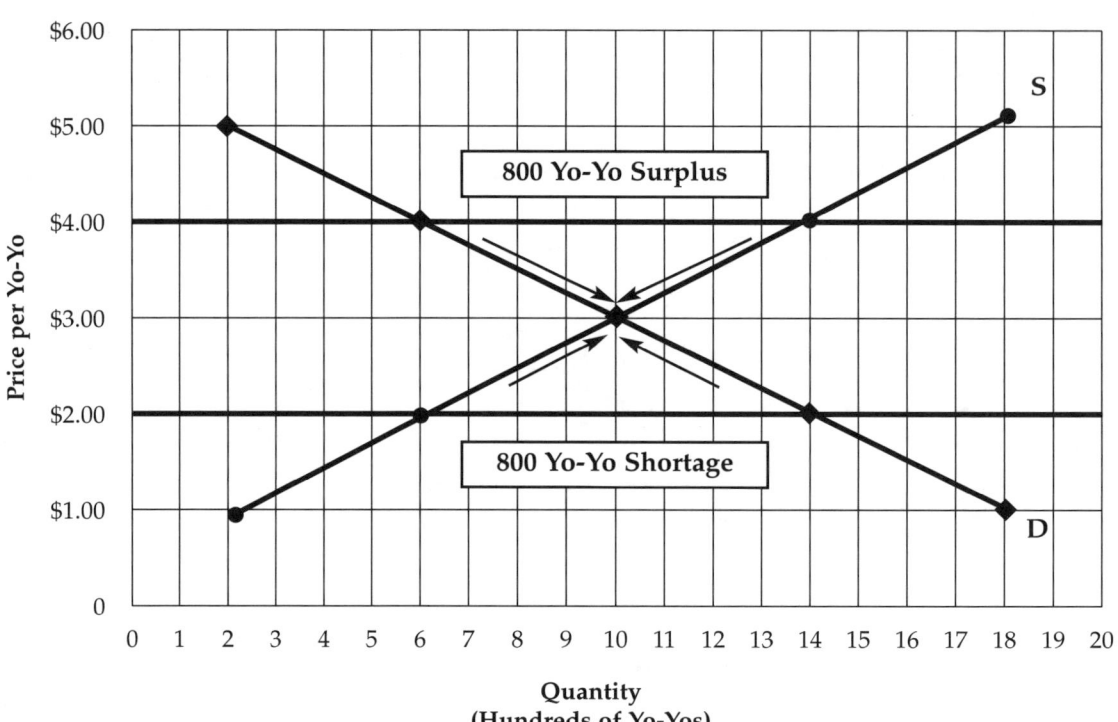

# Unit 2 | Teacher's Guide

**Unit 2, Lesson 10**
Visual 2

*Answers to Activity 1*

# PLOTTING DEMAND FOR AND SUPPLY OF FRISBEES

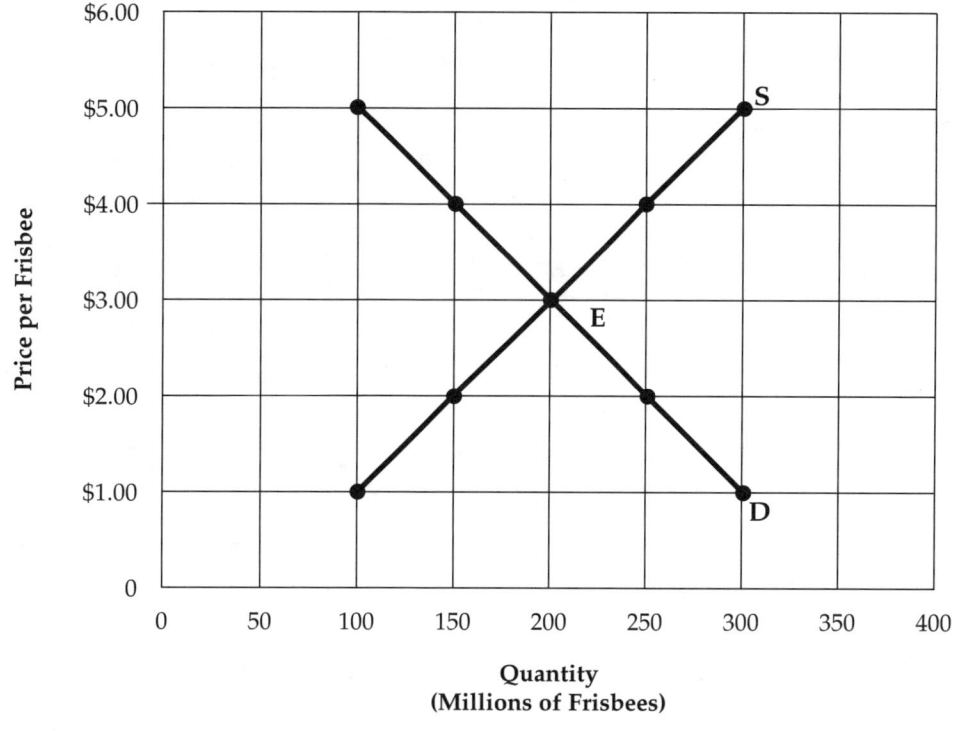

EQUILIBRIUM PRICES AND EQUILIBRIUM QUANTITIES

**Unit 2, Lesson 10**
Visual 3

*Answers to Activity 1*

# PLOTTING CHANGES IN DEMAND FOR AND SUPPLY OF FRISBEES

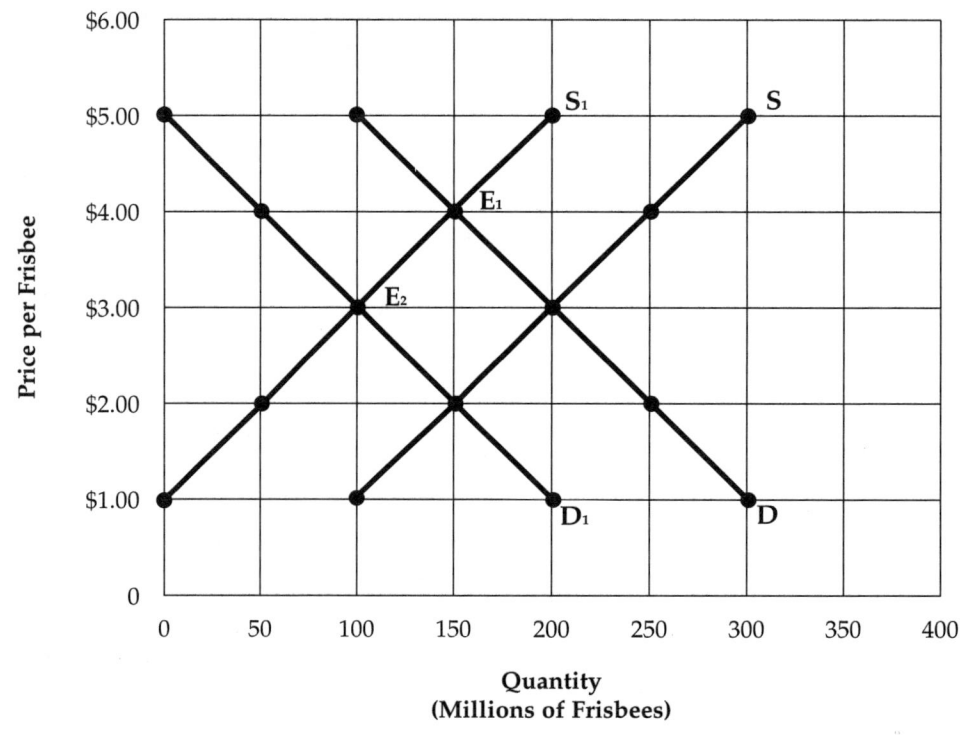

# Unit 2 | Teacher's Guide

## Unit 2 Lesson 11

## Do Prices Matter to Consumers?

### Introduction

**Economics** People try to make good choices by identifying the benefits they expect to gain and weighing those benefits against the expected costs. Prices play an important role in this process. They enable people to compare the value of one good or service to that of another and to calculate the costs and the benefits of acquiring one or the other. Price differences are a major reason why people sometimes choose not to buy what they like best. If what they like best has a very high price, and a reasonable substitute can be purchased at a lower price, people may choose not to buy the good or service they would otherwise have preferred.

**Reasoning** Students often say that they buy things because they like them. This seems to mean that they buy something when they expect to gain high benefits from the purchase. But that is not the whole story. Economists know that people also consider costs in deciding what to buy. The weighing of expected costs and expected benefits allows people to make the most of their scarce resources. In this lesson students consider expected costs and expected benefits, using price as their guide.

### Concepts

- Benefits
- Choice
- Costs
- Incentives
- Price
- Substitutes

### Objectives

*Students will:*

1. Analyze the effect of prices on choices people make in the market.
2. Make economizing choices among goods and services with different prices.
3. Identify the expected costs and expected benefits associated with various alternatives.
4. Explain why people sometimes substitute a lower-priced good or service for a higher-priced one.

### Content Standards

- Productive resources are limited. Therefore, people cannot have all the goods and services they want; as a result, they must choose some things and give up others. (NCEE Content Standard 1)
- People respond predictably to positive and negative incentives. (NCEE Content Standard 4)
- Prices send signals and provide incentives to buyers and sellers. When supply or demand changes, market prices adjust, affecting incentives. (NCEE Content Standard 8)

### Lesson Description

This lesson demonstrates how people use prices when they weigh expected costs and expected benefits in making economic decisions. It helps students see how choosing a second-best good or service can in some cases improve their overall well-being.

*Time Required: 60 minutes*

### Materials

- An inexpensive mechanical pencil
- A standard yellow pencil
- A transparency of Visual 1
- Activity 1

### Procedure

1. Tell the students that in this lesson they will sharpen their understanding of the choices people make when they buy things or choose not to buy them.

2. Hold up a standard yellow pencil, sharpened but unused. Do the same for an inexpensive mechanical pencil. Ask:

    - What are these items used for?

      *(Writing, drawing, and so forth.)*

    - Which one of these writing implements do you like best?

      *(After a few responses, ask the students to vote for the writing implement they like the most. Record the vote on the board. Note the type of pencil that comes in first in the voting.)*

3. Ask the students to explain the result: Why was the one type of pencil preferred?

    *(Students' responses will vary.)*

# Do Prices Matter to Consumers?

4. Explain that you are going to test a theory. Ask the students to assume that pencils of the preferred type will, starting now, cost $2.00 more than they have cost in the past. If the mechanical pencil was the winner, for example, price it at $2.25 and price the regular yellow pencil at $.25.

5. Ask: Given this new information about prices, how many students now would buy the mechanical pencil? How many would buy the standard pencil? Record the results.

   *(The usual result is that fewer students say they would buy the more expensive pencil, even though they previously said they preferred it. If you don't get that result at first, continue to increase the price of the more expensive pencil and conduct additional rounds of voting until a number of students do choose the cheaper pencil.)*

6. Ask for an explanation of the new results: Why have some students not remained loyal to their preferred type of pencil?

   *(The price is too high. The students can make better use of their limited resources by buying a substitute, the cheaper pencil, and using the rest of their money in another way.)*

7. Tell the students that their responses to the experiment illustrate economizing behavior. In practicing economizing behavior, they are not alone; it is what people generally try to do. Understanding economizing behavior can therefore help people predict the actions of others. This possibility can be illustrated in another simulation activity.

8. Divide the class into groups of three or four students each. Refer the students to Activity 1. Assign students in the groups the task of spending $100 for each hypothetical person described on Activity 1. The goal is to predict what that person would in fact buy if he or she went out to spend $100. The groups should use the catalog of items provided in Part 2 of the Activity as their list of possible selections. Suggest to members of each group that they should discuss the personality and likes and dislikes of each person described before deciding on the purchases to be made.

9. Upon completion of the activity, ask the groups to report on their predictions by listing on the board the items they selected for each hypothetical person. Compare the students' choices across groups; then display Visual 1, which describes the most probable purchases for each hypothetical person.

10. How well did the groups do in predicting the likely purchases of their hypothetical consumers? Ask:

    - Which person's consumer behavior was easiest to predict? Why?

    *(Usually students can predict Jessica Jones' purchases accurately because their experiences and values are similar to hers.)*

    - Why are the students' lists so different from the carpenter's list? *(Age differences and the carpenter's job requirements probably account for dramatically different values reflected in purchasing decisions.)*

    - What overall similarities or differences do you see in how the lists were created?

    *(The decision-making model seems to be the same in all cases. Everybody weighed expected costs, as measured by price, against expected benefits for each alternative and selected the combination most likely to maximize their satisfaction. Given the $100 limit on spending, people usually did not select higher-priced items if lower-priced substitutes were available.)*

    - Could the money spent on the listed items have been spent on other listed items?

    *(Of course. But in the case of items not selected, people decided that the relative benefit per dollar spent was lower than the benefit per dollar that they could gain by buying what they did.)*

    - Could people have bought different items within given categories — clothes, tools, and so on?

    *(Yes. People could have chosen to buy a brand X sweater instead of a brand-name sweater. Choices within categories were constrained by scarcity [the $100 spending limit] and by calculations about additional benefits as against additional costs. For example: If somebody needed a sweater to complete an outfit for a specific event, and the sweater wasn't going to get used much later on, then perhaps a less expensive sweater would be the best choice.)*

## Closure

Ask the students if they would like to have a new (different) mode of transportation — a new way of getting around. Most probably would, but what might their preferred new vehicle be? Assign the students to collect information about at least three interesting modes of transportation, currently on the market, that they think are very nifty. They might focus on options within a category (such as cars, used and new) or on options from different categories (such as bicycles, trucks, snowmobiles). The information can come from newspaper ads, brochures, Internet sources — whatever serves the purpose.

The students should bring their information to class by a specified time for use in creating a bulletin board: ***My Transportation Options***. Once the bulletin board is in place, ask the students to review the information it provides and select the mode of transportation they like the best, for any reasons whatsoever. Usually students will pick a cool automobile that represents the car of their dreams. Follow up by asking which item shown on the bulletin board they would actually be likely to purchase, and why? Students who take the latter two questions seriously will most likely select something other than the car or Lear jet of their dreams, simply because their dreams are unaffordable.

Pursue this line of thought by asking the students what they would have to do to in order buy their dream vehicle. "Work a lot" will be one common response. Press further: If they did work long and hard until they finally earned enough money to do so, would they in fact buy their first-choice vehicle? Some will say "yes" and others "no," with the nay-sayers probably explaining that they would rather buy something cheaper to get around in while using the rest of their money to buy other things. To put it in other words: The vehicle of their dreams would come at too high an opportunity cost, requiring that they give up too many other ways of using their money.

## MULTIPLE-CHOICE QUESTIONS

### (CORRECT ANSWERS SHOWN IN BOLD)

1. People make choices based upon:

    A. What they like best.

    **B. The economizing principle.**

    C. Durability.

    D. Color and style.

2. People often substitute lower-priced items for higher-priced items because:

    A. They are cheap.

    B. Lower priced items are of better quality.

    **C. The opportunity cost of a higher-priced item is too high.**

    D. Most people don't do this type of substitution.

3. An important function of price is to:

    A. Assist the cashier to total the amount owed.

    **B. Provide a common denominator that allows consumers to calculate relative costs and benefits.**

    C. Help government officials determine fair prices.

    D. All of the above.

## ESSAY QUESTION

Recall the last time you spent $10 or more. Explain how you made your consumer decision by identifying the expected benefits and the expected costs of your purchase.

*(Answers will vary, especially regarding benefits. Comments on cost should include some reference to the opportunity cost of the decisions about what to buy.)*

# Do Prices Matter to Consumers?

**Unit 2, Lesson 11**
Visual 1

## Probable Purchases

*Jessica Jones*
| | |
|---|---|
| Designer jeans | $46.00 |
| Shampoo | 1.50 |
| Pencils (six) | 1.50 |
| Trapper-keeper | 8.50 |
| Lipstick | 2.50 |
| Name brand sweater | 38.50 |
| Chewing gum | 1.00 |
| **Total** | **$99.00** |

*Willie Washington*
| | |
|---|---|
| Current paperback novel | $ 9.00 |
| Soup (four cans) | 3.00 |
| Cat food (six cans) | 3.00 |
| Light bulbs | 2.00 |
| Brand X sweater | 12.50 |
| Newspaper | .50 |
| Reading lamp | 19.00 |
| Shampoo | 1.50 |
| Dishwasher soap | 2.50 |
| Cat caddy | 38.50 |
| **Total** | **$92.00** |

*Harvey Hammer*
| | |
|---|---|
| Men's long underwear | $13.50 |
| 16-oz. hammer | 12.00 |
| Tape measure-50 ft. | 14.00 |
| Steel-toe insulated boots | 39.50 |
| Pencils (six) | 1.50 |
| Work gloves | 10.00 |
| Shampoo | 1.50 |
| Box of chocolates | 5.50 |
| **Total** | **$97.50** |

*Richie Mann*
| | |
|---|---|
| Men's dress shirt | $18.00 |
| Dress driving gloves | 17.50 |
| Men's dress socks | 3.50 |
| Silk necktie | 34.00 |
| Shampoo | 1.50 |
| Breath mints | 2.00 |
| Wine | 9.00 |
| Steaks (1) | 4.50 |
| Box of chocolates | 5.50 |
| **Total** | **$96.00** |

# Unit 2 | Teacher's Guide

## Unit 2 Lesson 12

## How Do Prices Influence My Behavior? Price Elasticity

### Introduction

**Economics**  The *price elasticity of demand* measures the flexibility of consumers' responses to price changes. Price elasticity can be calculated by dividing the percentage change in quantity demanded by the percentage change in price. If an increase or a decrease in price results in little change in quantity demanded, the demand for that good or service is called inelastic. When the percentage change in quantity demanded is noticeably or substantially greater than the percentage change in price, the demand is called elastic.

Price elasticity of supply is calculated by dividing the percentage change in the quantity supplied by the percentage change in price. This calculation measures the supplier's responsiveness to price changes. Suppliers' responsiveness often changes over time, especially when technology and costs change.

**Reasoning**  People choose among alternatives, seeking a favorable balance of benefits and costs. Some choices involve more alternatives or substitutes than others, and some alternatives come at a higher cost than others. The number of alternatives and their respective costs help to determine how much flexibility a consumer has when the price of a desired good or service changes. Elasticity is related to this condition. When few good alternatives exist for a very important good or service, people tend to downplay the importance of changes in price as they make their decisions.

### Concepts

- Choice
- Incentives
- Price
- Price elasticity
- Substitutes

### Objectives

*Students will:*

1. Analyze price as a factor influencing people's choices.
2. Recognize that different product characteristics, real and perceived, influence people's consumption and supply responses to price change.
3. Conclude that, in the long run, substitutes exist for almost all goods and services.
4. Recognize that suppliers' ability to respond to price changes is affected by time, technology, and costs of production.
5. Calculate the price elasticity of demand or supply, given the mid-point formula.

### Content Standards

- Productive resources are limited. Therefore, people cannot have all the goods and services they want; as a result, they must choose some things and give up others. (NCEE Content Standard 1)
- People respond predictably to positive and negative incentives. (NCEE Content Standard 4)
- Prices send signals and provide incentives to buyers and sellers. When supply or demand changes, market prices adjust, affecting incentives. (NCEE Content Standard 8)

### Lesson Description

Students review consumer and producer behavior in light of changing prices. They predict consumers' and producers' responses to changes in prices, product characteristics, costs of production, time, and technology factors.

*Time Required: 60 minutes*

### Materials

- A transparency of Visuals 1, 2, and 3
- Activity 1
- Glue, scissors (two), four different-colored crayons, a box of small paper clips, and a ream of white paper

### Procedure

1. Explain that this lesson focuses on how consumers and producers respond to changes in price. Display Visual 1. Ask:

   - For these goods and services, how do you think consumers might respond to changes in price?

     *(At least in the short run, consumers might keep buying these items even if their prices were to go up, since the items are important to many people and there are few substitutes for them.)*

   - How might consumers respond if prices were to go up for long-distance phone calls and gasoline?

     *(The impact of price changes here might be greater. Some consumers would spend less time on long-distance calls, perhaps using e-mail as a substitute, or cut back on non-essential driving.)*

# How Do Prices Influence My Behavior?
## Price Elasticity

2. Tell the students that they are on the right track. Price changes affect consumer demand more in some cases than in others. In other words, consumer demand for a given product is more or less elastic — responsive to changes in price — depending upon such factors as how important the product is to the consumer and how easy or hard it is to find a lower-cost substitute. The rest of the lesson elaborates on this general point.

3. Explain that it is possible to be precise about elasticity of demand. Given certain information about market circumstances, we can calculate price elasticity. To do so, we divide the percentage change in quantity demanded by the percentage change in price. This relationship can also be shown graphically when demand and supply pictures are placed on a coordinate axis system. Refer the students to Activity 1 and display the corresponding Visual 2. Ask the students to identify the market demand picture that they think is the best example of a good or service where price does not influence consumers' buying behavior very much. Ask them to use the same logic to identify the picture of demand where price seems to be very influential on consumer behavior. Direct them to label two pictures with products or services that represent this type of behavior. The picture of demand that is close to a vertical line demonstrates a small price effect on consumption. These products are said to have an inelastic demand (a good example would be insulin for a diabetic). As the demand schedule becomes more horizontal, price changes influence quantities bought a great deal. An example of this type of product would be a specific brand of orange juice.

4. Calculate the price elasticity of demand using the following formula:

$$\text{Price elasticity of demand} = \frac{(Q_2-Q_1)/[(Q_1+Q_2)/2]}{(P_2-P_1)/[(P_1+P_2)/2]}$$

(Q1 is equal to the quantity consumers demand at the initial price, Q2 is the quantity demanded at the new price, P1 is the initial price, and P2 is the new price.)

Have the students calculate price elasticity of demand for insulin using this information:

Q1 = 12 injections per week
Q2 = 14 injections per week
P1 = $20.00 per injection
P2 = $10.00 per injection

The resulting price elasticity of demand of -.23 is read without the negative sign, or just .23. This calculation confirms what common sense would predict. The price elasticity of demand for insulin is inelastic because it is less than one. People usually don't change the quantity that they demand very much for products or services that have few substitutes and are considered necessary. Also, a good will generally be price-inelastic if it accounts for only a small portion of a consumer's budget, like shoelaces or pepper.

5. Have the students calculate the price elasticity of demand for a specific brand of orange juice, using this information:

Q1 = 1 quart per week
Q2 = 3 quarts per week
P1 = $2.50 per quart
P2 = $2.25 per quart

The resulting price elasticity of demand of -9.52 is read without the negative sign, or just 9.52. This calculation also confirms what common sense would predict. The price elasticity of demand for a specific brand of orange juice is elastic — greater than one. People usually will change their buying behavior for a specific brand of orange juice a great deal because they can buy other brands or substitute other juices, fruits, or vitamin C tablets.

6. Inform the students that they can use this same formula for determining price elasticity of supply. To demonstrate how the concept of elasticity helps to explain the behavior of suppliers, divide the class into two manufacturing businesses. Inform each group that it is to manufacture paper airplanes.

   - Company A must design an airplane made of an 8.5 x 11-inch piece of paper with no name, number, or required weight; no tools should be used to construct the airplane, and it is not necessary that the airplane be able to fly.

   - Company B must design an airplane that is made of two pieces of 8.5 x 11-inch paper, has a name and number written in two colors, is constructed by use of a scissors, glue, and a paper clip. In addition, the plane must be able to fly a minimum of six feet.

7. Once the planes have been designed, have each group show its plane to the class. Inform the class that you are the purchasing agent for a major airline and will be making contracts with the airplane manufacturers. In this capacity, you must know how responsive each company is to contract requests. Ask each group the following questions:

   A. How many planes can you make in five minutes?
   
   *(An experiment will be necessary to determine this answer.)*

   B. How many resources are used in the manufacturer of your airplane?
   
   *(Each company will list its resources.)*

C. How many more airplanes can you make for me if I triple the amount I am willing to pay for the airplanes?

*(Company B will forecast fewer than Company A because of more production complexity and its need for more resources.)*

D. Why is it difficult for Company B to respond quickly to changes in prices?

*(Company B needs to gather many more resources; without easy access to the resources, its production numbers won't change much no matter what the reward. It will take Company B more time to adjust production numbers.)*

8. Explain that suppliers whose products take a long time to produce, or who depend upon techniques, materials, or human skills that are hard to find or difficult to adjust, cannot increase production rapidly and therefore cannot respond rapidly to changes in market prices. These products tend to be inelastic as prices change. Products that tend to be elastic as prices change are usually easy to produce, require no special skill or technology, and use easily acquired resources.

## Closure

Display Visual 3 or write out the material on the board, being sure that students do not see the estimated price elasticity of demand calculations. Ask the students to guess the price elasticity of demand for the goods and services listed. Have them raise their hands to provide their guesses and give their reasons. Remind the students that inelastic products have a price elasticity calculation less than one (for price-elastic products, greater than one). How much less or greater describes the degree of responsiveness.

After students have made guesses for all goods and services listed, show or write the real elasticities. Discuss the students' responses to the real calculations.

## Multiple-Choice Questions

### (Correct Answers Shown in Bold)

1. A price elasticity of demand of .45 for certain goods suggests:

    A. They are cheap.

    B. They are luxuries with many substitutes.

    **C. They are necessary items with few substitutes.**

    D. Most people want them.

2. The most important factor determining price elasticity for supply is:

    **A. Time.**

    B. Price.

    C. Whether it is a good or service.

    D. None of the above.

## Essay Question

Identify a good or service that you buy that is highly inelastic, and explain why it is inelastic.

*(Answers will vary. Goods and services that are inelastic are considered to be necessities with few low-cost substitutes. For a teenager who depends on a car to travel to school and work, repairing a malfunctioning starter or battery might be considered inelastic.)*

# How Do Prices Influence My Behavior?
## Price Elasticity

**Unit 2, Lesson 12**
Visual 1

What do you think the relationship is between the price of these goods and services and consumers' behavior?

- Prescription eyewear
- Car battery
- Dental care
- Pain medication
- Gasoline
- Long-distance phone calls

# Unit 2 | Teacher's Guide

**Unit 2, Lesson 12**
Visual 2 (also Activity 1 in the Student Book)

## PICTURING AND CALCULATING ELASTICITY

Pictures of market demand:

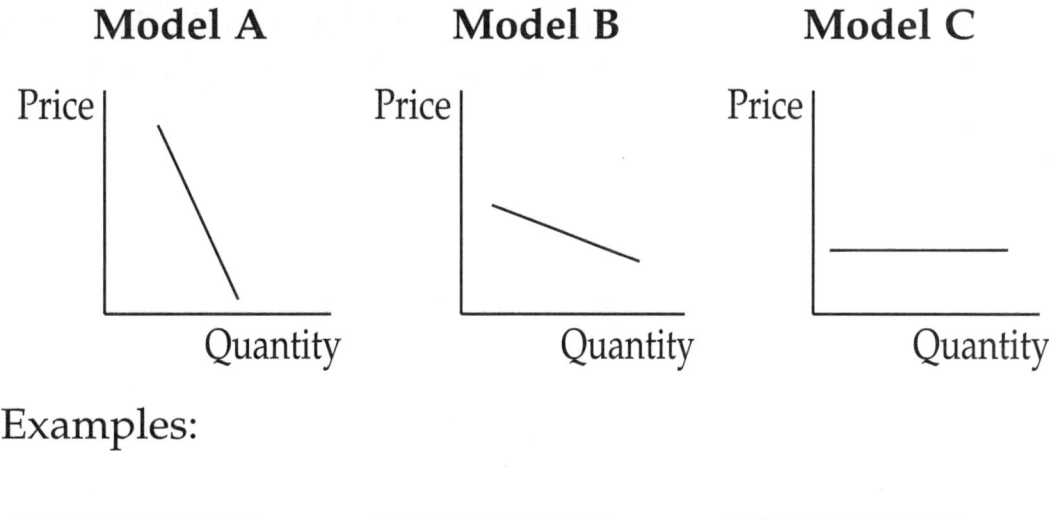

Examples:

_____    _____    _____


Using the following formula, calculate the price elasticity of demand for each product.

$$\text{Price elasticity of demand} = \frac{(Q2-Q1)/[(Q1+Q2)/2]}{(P2-P1)/[(P1+P2)/2]}$$

Price elasticity of demand for insulin:_____

Price elasticity of demand for a brand of orange juice:_____

# How Do Prices Influence My Behavior?
## Price Elasticity

**Unit 2, Lesson 12**
Visual 3

## ELASTICITY PREDICTIONS

*Directions:* Estimate the price elasticity of demand calculation for each of the following, using numbers greater than zero and less than 5. Decimals are appropriate.

| Item | Prediction | Actual |
|---|---|---|
| Salt | _____ | 0.10 |
| Toothpicks | _____ | 0.10 |
| Fresh tomatoes | _____ | 4.60 |
| Movie tickets | _____ | 2.50 |
| Automobiles | _____ | 1.20 |
| Chevrolet automobiles | _____ | 4.00 |
| Housing | _____ | 0.90 |
| Physician services | _____ | 0.60 |
| Cigarettes | _____ | 0.35 |
| China and tableware | _____ | 1.10 |
| Gasoline | _____ | 0.20 |
| Coffee | _____ | 0.25 |
| Electricity | _____ | 0.10 |

# Unit 2 | Teacher's Guide

## Unit 2 Lesson 13

## How Markets Allocate Resources

### INTRODUCTION

**Economics** Supply and demand analysis is a useful tool to show the impact of market changes on equilibrium price and quantity. Furthermore, supply and demand analysis illustrates how markets are interdependent and how a change in one market can affect the equilibrium prices and quantities in other markets. This interaction of markets is the famous "invisible hand of the marketplace" identified by Adam Smith. The invisible hand leads to what F.A. Hayek called a "spontaneous order" that allocates resources in the most efficient way.

**Reasoning** Economic thinking is subtle, not simplistic. A simple mind concludes that conscious government planning must be more effective than the invisible hand of the marketplace. The subtle economic thinker knows otherwise. No central planner can know all the details of a transaction or how best to reconcile the interests of every individual with other individuals. Market prices, however, convey information to everyone and create incentives that cause people to make mutual adjustments in their best interest.

These mutual adjustments mean that every action causes secondary effects. Frederic Bastiat, a nineteenth-century economist, stated that "the difference between a good and a bad economist is that the bad economist considers only the immediate, visible effects whereas the good economist is also aware of the secondary effects, effects that are indirectly related to the initial policy and whose influence might only be seen or felt with the passage of time." Because of secondary effects, government policies can have consequences far different from those the planners imagined.

### CONCEPTS

- Complements
- Invisible hand of the marketplace
- Markets and prices
- Secondary effects
- Substitutes
- Supply and demand

### OBJECTIVES

*Students will:*

1. Analyze the effect of changes in determinants of supply and demand on market prices and quantities exchanged.

2. Analyze the effect of changes in one market on changes in other markets.

3. Analyze the secondary effects of government policies.

4. Explain why the invisible hand of the market brings about spontaneous order.

### CONTENT STANDARDS

- Markets exist when buyers and sellers interact. This interaction determines market prices and thereby allocates scarce goods and services. (NCEE Content Standard 7)

- Prices send signals and provide incentives to buyers and sellers. When supply or demand changes, market prices adjust, affecting incentives. (NCEE Content Standard 8)

### LESSON DESCRIPTION

Students read *I, Pencil*, by Leonard Read, to gain an understanding of Adam Smith's concept of the invisible hand of the marketplace. Students see that a system of market prices brings about cooperation without coercion. Then students use supply and demand analysis to explain how a change in one market tends to affect related markets.

*Time Required: 90 minutes*

### MATERIALS

- A transparency of Visual 1
- Activities 1 and 2

### PROCEDURE

1. Begin the lesson by holding up a pencil. Using facts provided in Activity 1 (which you have read in advance), discuss the number of people who made the pencil. Explain briefly that thousands of people made the pencil, yet no one ordered them to do it. Point out that these people lived in different countries, spoke different languages, practiced different religions, and in many cases never communicated with one another. (And if they had communicated, they might not even have liked one another.) Yet none of these differences kept them from cooperating to produce a pencil. This is an illustration of the power of the market.

2. Assign the students to read Activity 1. It will elaborate on your brief opening remarks. Also assign the students to answer the questions at the end of the reading.

3. Discuss the answers to the questions in Activity 1. Ask:

    A. How many people does it take to make a simple pencil?

*(Thousands; you might elaborate on all the tasks.)*

B. Why would all these people cooperate in making a pencil?

*(Each person expected to benefit from his or her part in the process.)*

C. What or who organizes all these people to make a pencil?

*(No one person organizes this process. Instead, it is organized and moved forward by the invisible hand of the marketplace — market prices, profits, and wages.)*

D. What is meant by the "invisible hand of the marketplace"?

*(The invisible hand analogy was used by Adam Smith to explain how economic order can emerge from the unintended consequences of people voluntarily making decisions in their own interest.)*

E. Is it easier and more efficient for a pencil to be made by voluntary exchanges in the marketplace or by government rules?

*(Voluntary exchange — this is even more so as products become more complex.)*

F. What role do prices play in the making of a pencil?

*(Prices play the key role. The prices that emerge from voluntary trades among buyers and sellers coordinate economic activity.)*

4. Reinforce the key points by summarizing as follows: Notice how complicated it is to make a pencil. Yet producing most other goods and services is even more complex. Imagine how hard it would be for any central planner to replicate the information and cooperation involved in a marketplace.

5. Tell the students that they are going to see how the invisible hand of the marketplace really works. They may find the activity difficult, but real markets are even more complex. That is why markets work better than central planning.

6. Explain that to understand changes in markets, it is useful to know the distinction between complements and substitutes. Display Visual 1 and explain the differences.

7. Refer the students to Activity 2. Explain the ground rules for the activity. The activity shows how markets allocate resources. It illustrates how the apparently chaotic billions of individual choices that are made in a market result in an orderly allocation of scarce resources. In this activity, students should decide whether the goods are complements or substitutes. They should ignore "feedback" effects, which means they should shift only one curve in each market. Long-run supply curves are shown, so the supply curve shifts only if there are changes in underlying conditions. A change in the equilibrium price and quantity in one market may shift demand or supply in another market. The changes in the other markets are assumed not to feed back on Market 1 in this time period. Emphasize changes in equilibrium quantity as well as changes in equilibrium price. Quantity changes will differ depending on what caused the price change, and quantity changes affect the demand for substitute and complementary goods.

8. Go over the first problem with the class as a group, and draw the graph on the board or on a transparency. Very carefully, explain that improvements in technology increase the supply of DVDs, lower the price, and increase the quantity demanded. Draw a new supply curve showing a shift to the right. VCRs are a substitute good for DVDs, so demand decreases, price decreases, and equilibrium quantity supplied decreases. Draw a new demand curve showing a shift to the left. The demand increases for DVD disks because they are a complementary good for DVDs. The demand for VCR tapes decreases because they are a complementary good for VCRs. Draw a new demand curve showing a shift to the left.

*Answers to Activity 2, Market 1*

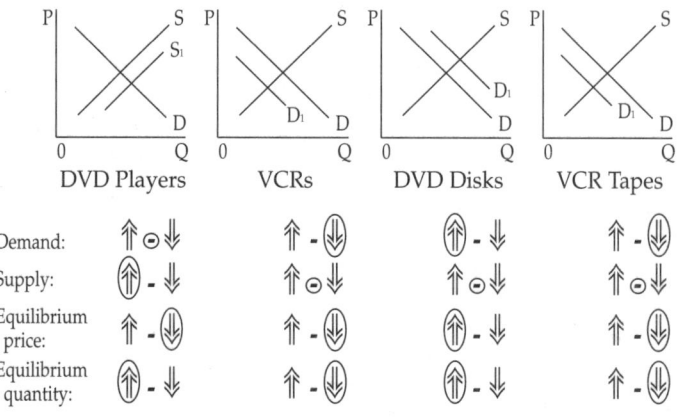

9. Divide the class into small groups and assign the groups to answer the other questions. Have a representative from each group draw one of its graphs on the board. Here is the logic that underlies each case.

*Market 2.* The destruction of the coffee crop is a reduction in supply. Tea and coffee are probably substitutes for many consumers, so the higher equilibrium price and smaller equilibrium quantity of coffee will increase the demand for tea. Assuming that more cream is used in coffee than in tea, this will reduce the demand for cream and automatic coffeemakers, as well as their price and quantity.

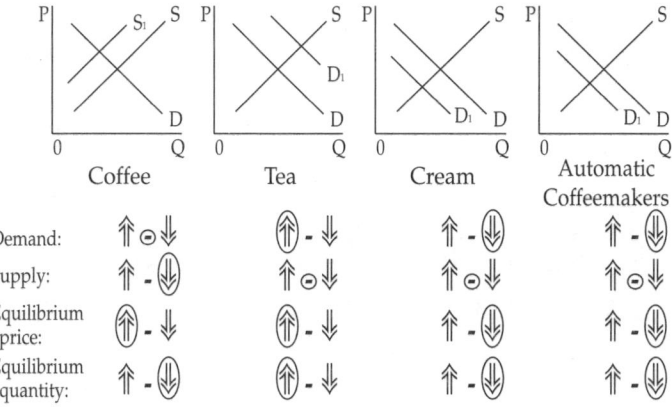

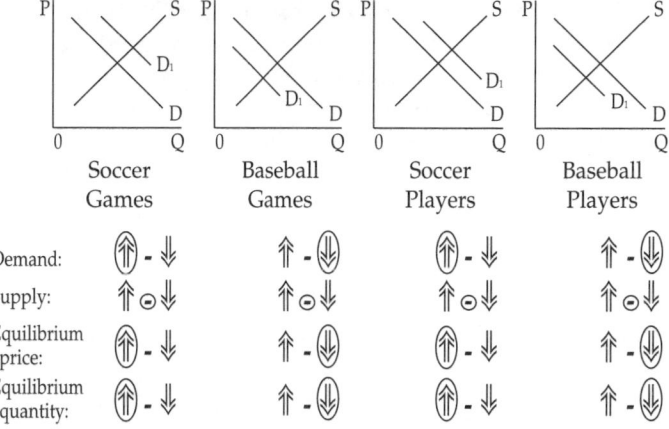

*Market 3.* The environmental regulations increase the cost of producing electricity in California; the increased cost decreases supply, increases the equilibrium price, and decreases the equilibrium quantity. This development increases the demand by Californians for electricity produced in other states, a substitute good. Other consumers substitute gas heat for electric heat, increasing the demand for natural gas. Higher energy costs increase the demand for energy-efficient furnaces.

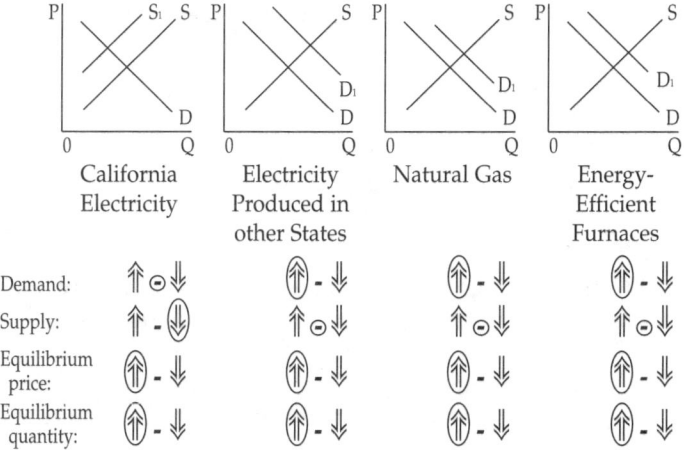

*Market 4.* The demand for soccer games increases; increased demand increases both the equilibrium price and the quantity supplied. Demand for baseball games, a substitute good, decreases. The demand for soccer players increases, thus increasing the number hired and their wages. The demand for labor is derived from the demand for the good. Wages are the price of labor. Salaries of baseball players and the number hired decrease because the demand for baseball players decreases.

*Market 5.* The cost of making yachts increases; the increased cost decreases supply, increases the equilibrium price, and lowers the equilibrium quantity. A tax is a cost of production. This development increases the demand for luxury cars, a substitute good for yachts. The demand for boat marinas decreases because they are a complementary good for yachts. Because yachts are produced at lower numbers, the demand for yacht workers decreases, lowering the number hired and their wages. This is an actual example; the U.S. yacht industry almost completely shut down a few years ago, before the tax was repealed. The goal was to tax the rich, but the unintended consequence was that middle-class yacht workers lost their jobs. The rich just bought other luxury items instead of yachts.

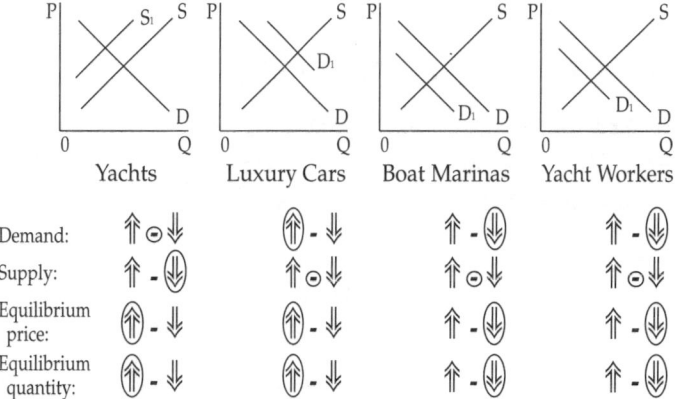

*Market 6.* The tariff or tax increases the cost of producing foreign steel because a tax is a cost. The cost of foreign steel increases; the cost increase decreases supply, increases equilibrium price, and lowers equilibrium quantity. Firms use a steel substitute (U.S.-produced steel), increasing the price and quantity. In the short run, such policies may help the U.S. steel industry and its workers. But now consider the unintended consequences in the long run. The cost of producing autos increases, decreasing supply,

# How Markets Allocate Resources

increasing prices, and decreasing the equilibrium quantity demanded. If fewer autos are produced, the demand for autoworkers decreases, causing a decrease in wages. One group has gained at the expense at another, and consumers pay higher prices for autos and everything else made from steel.

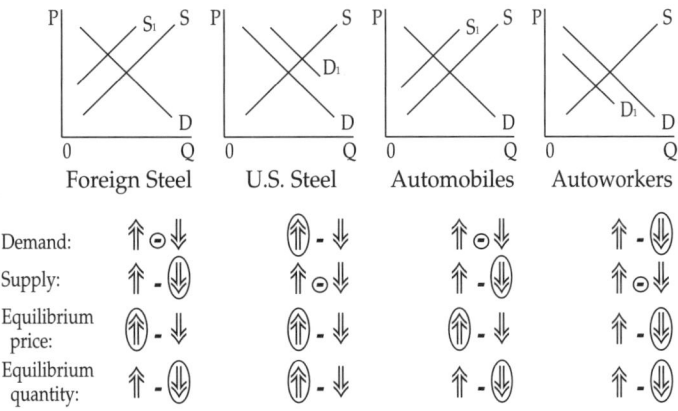

## Closure

1. Have the students add additional markets to each of the scenarios in Activity 2. For example, you could add VCR workers and DVD workers to Question 1. How would video games be affected by less expensive DVD technology?

2. Have the students locate newspaper articles that show how a change in one market affects changes in other markets. Then have them construct a series of interrelated graphs to represent these changes.

## Multiple-Choice Questions

(correct answers shown in bold)

*Questions 1-3 are based on the following graphs dealing with automobiles:*

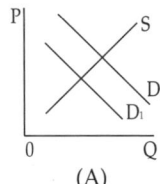
(A)

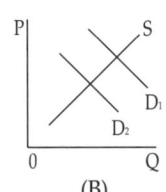
(B)

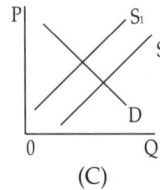
(C)

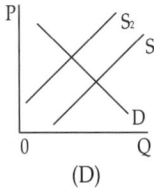
(D)

1. Which graph illustrates the effects of high gasoline prices on the auto market?
   A. Graph A
   **B. Graph B**
   C. Graph C
   D. Graph D

2. A tariff is a tax on imports. Which graph illustrates the effects of a government tariff on foreign automobiles imported into the United States?
   A. Graph A
   B. Graph B
   C. Graph C
   **D. Graph D**

3. Which graph illustrates the effects of an auto manufacturer's use of new robots to produce autos more efficiently?
   A. Graph A
   B. Graph B
   **C. Graph C**
   D. Graph D

4. We observe a market in which the price has risen and the quantity sold has risen as well. This could be caused only by:
   **A. An increase in demand.**
   B. An increase in supply.
   C. A decrease in demand.
   D. A decrease in supply.

5. If marijuana is legalized and the risk previously associated with buying and selling it is thereby eliminated, there is likely to be an effect on its demand and its supply. This will most likely affect equilibrium price and equilibrium quantity in which of the following ways?
   A. Effect on equilibrium quantity uncertain; price will definitely rise.
   B. Effect on equilibrium quantity uncertain; price will definitely fall.
   **C. Effect on equilibrium price uncertain; quantity will definitely increase.**
   D. Effect on equilibrium price uncertain; quantity will definitely decrease.

## Unit 2 | Teacher's Guide

ESSAY QUESTIONS

1. A letter to the editor says, "America is producing stuff today that we could not even have dreamed of 10 years ago. People are buying millions of different goods, and those same people are working at millions of different jobs. Yet we rely on individual choice to get this done. This will lead to disaster. Clearly, the government must move to organize our chaotic economy." Do you agree or disagree with the letter writer? Why?

   *(Disagree. If you agree, you fail economics. Only a decentralized market can organize such a complex economy. If people act in their self-interest, an invisible hand will organize the economy. Supply, demand, and prices provide the signals that make that possible.)*

2. Assume that the U.S. government decides that it will not allow oil drilling in Alaska. What will be the effect on price for each of the following, and why? Draw a graph for each product.

   A. Gasoline

   B. Small, fuel-efficient cars

   C. Natural gas

   D. Home insulation products

   *(A. The supply of oil will decrease, which will decrease the supply of gasoline, increasing the equilibrium price and decreasing quantity demanded. B. The demand for small, fuel-efficient cars will increase, which will increase equilibrium price and quantity supplied. C. Natural gas is a substitute for oil. The demand for natural gas will increase, which will increase the equilibrium price and quantity supplied. D. Home insulation reduces fuel costs. The demand for home insulation products will increase, which will increase the equilibrium price and quantity supplied.)*

**Unit 2, Lesson 13**
Visual 1

## COMPLEMENTS AND SUBSTITUTES

- Complements: Goods or services that are consumed together — for example, left and right socks, or tennis rackets and tennis lessons.

- Substitutes: Goods or services that may be used in place of other goods or services — for example, shoes and sandals, or movies and concerts.

# Unit 2 | Teacher's Guide

## Unit 2 Lesson 14

## Secondary Effects: Price Ceilings and Floors

### INTRODUCTION

**Economics**  Not all markets are ones in which price is allowed to move freely. Governments may set some prices by rule, and prices set in this way may differ from the market-clearing price. When a price set by rule differs from the market-clearing price, the result will be a shortage or a surplus in the market. A shortage of products occurs when the price is set lower than the market-clearing price. A surplus occurs when the price is set higher than the market-clearing price.

**Reasoning**  Rules establishing prices do not change the basic economizing behavior of individuals. People continue to make their best choices as they respond to anticipated costs and benefits. But new rules may alter the available options, thus prompting consumers to make choices different from those they would have made in the absence of the rules. By using economic reasoning students should be able to predict the consequences that price-setting rules will have on people's choices.

### CONCEPTS

- Price ceiling
- Price floor
- Secondary effects
- Shortages
- Surpluses

### OBJECTIVES

*Students will:*

1. Define *price ceilings* and *price floors.*
2. Analyze the consequences of price controls regarding market behavior, shortages, and surpluses.
3. Anticipate secondary effects of price controls in different markets for goods and services.

### CONTENT STANDARDS

- Markets exist when buyers and sellers interact. This interaction determines market prices and thereby allocates scarce goods and services. (NCEE Content Standard 7)
- Prices send signals and provide incentives to buyers and sellers. When supply or demand changes, market prices adjust, affecting incentives. (NCEE Content Standard 8.)

### LESSON DESCRIPTION

Students investigate the consequences of price controls in markets for silver, rock concerts, automobiles, razor clams, and school textbooks. (It would be best to use this lesson after students have participated in the silver market game [Unit 2, Lesson 7].)

*Time Required: 90 minutes*

### MATERIALS

- Activities 1, 2, and 3 from Unit 2, Lesson 7
- A transparency of Visual 1 from Unit 2, Lesson 7
- A transparency of Visual 1
- Activity 1

### PROCEDURE

1. Explain to the class that not all markets are ones in which prices are set by demand and supply. Governments sometimes, with the best of intentions, set prices that are different from the market prices. Tell the students that this lesson will focus on the importance of anticipating consequences that follow from such economic policies. Specifically, the lesson focuses on secondary effects of price controls.

2. Distribute the silver market game (from Lesson 7). Explain that you plan to play one more round of the game. But this time you want to make the game fairer. Clearly the consumers got ripped off, you say, in the prior rounds. In today's version of the game, all the rules will stay the same — except that no price can go higher than $3.00. The purpose of this new rule is to make it easier for people to obtain silver.

3. As the students play the game, remind sellers that they have to make only one sale. They do not have to continue making deals, which causes them to lose money.

4. Record the transactions on Visual 1 from Lesson 7. After the round is completed, have the students explain what happened.

   *(The round may end before time is up. Sellers may get tired of selling at such bad prices and boycott the market. They also might make illegal deals—prices above $3.00.)*

   The following comments should surface:

   - There were more buyers trying to buy than there were sellers trying to sell.
   - We couldn't find any sellers.
   - All the buyers liked the market until the sellers quit selling.

CAPSTONE: EXEMPLARY LESSONS FOR HIGH SCHOOL ECONOMICS @ NATIONAL COUNCIL ON ECONOMIC EDUCATION, NEW YORK, NY     85

## Secondary Effects: Price Ceilings and Floors

- We made some deals for more than $3.00. What happens if you catch us?
- In the end, the market wasn't working very well.

5. Ask:
   - How did the original market-clearing price (established the first time this game was played) compare to the $3.00 price in this game? Was it lower or higher?

   *(The original market-clearing price [$4.30] was higher. The lower price [$3.00] this time around explains why the sellers were not very interested in participating. Sellers in this game faced a price ceiling: a price set below the equilibrium price. Price ceilings lead to shortages, as in this case.)*

   - What would happen if the price were set above the original market-clearing price of $4.30?

   *(More sellers would make products available for sale, and fewer buyers would be willing to buy. Buyers would face a price floor: a price set above the equilibrium price. Price floors lead to surpluses.)*

6. Refer the students to Activity 1. Ask them to answer the questions and anticipate the consequences implied in each question.

### Answers to Activity 1

A. A very popular singer is coming to a town to perform a concert in a concert hall that seats 10,000 people. The ticket price for the concert is $30.00 per person. There are 30,000 fans in the area who are willing to pay $80.00 per seat to listen to the concert. What will happen? Shortage of seats __X__ Surplus of seats_____

B. A very popular singer is coming to town to perform a concert in a concert hall that seats 10,000 people. The ticket price for the concert is $30,000 per person. There are 3,000 fans in the area who are willing to pay $80.00 to listen to the concert. What will happen? Shortage of seats_____ Surplus of seats __X__

C. The Ford Motor Company has designed a new car that resembles a Ford model that was popular 40 years ago. Ford plans to produce 100,000 of the new-old cars each year. Ford will price these cars at $24,000 and require dealers not to change that price. There are 200,000 people per year who wish to buy the car. What will happen? Shortage of cars __X__ Surplus of cars_____

D. The Fish and Wildlife Department in a West Coast state decides to allow people to dig for razor clams on the ocean beaches three days each year. There is a small charge ($10) for a license to dig these clams. Millions of people enjoy eating razor clams. During most of the year they buy razor clams from fishmarkets for $20 to $30 a dozen. What will happen on the days when people can dig clams for themselves? Shortage of clams __X__ Surplus of clams_____

E. Schools ask students to take good care of their textbooks during the year and to return them to the school on the last day of school. Often students turn back the books in poor condition. In an effort to encourage students to take better care of the books, the School Board offers to pay students $2,000 for any textbook returned in good condition. What will happen? Shortage of textbooks_____ Surplus of textbooks __X__

F. Display Visual 1. Remind the students that they have learned how supply and demand analysis works. Now they can look at the graph and anticipate what will happen in this market for cars. How many cars per week will be sold at $25,000?

*(120 cars will be offered for sale, and 120 will be purchased.)*

G. What happens to sales if a price ceiling is set at $15,000?

*(About 60 cars will be offered for sale, and consumers will try to purchase 160 cars. There will be a shortage of 100 cars on the market.)*

H. What happens to sales if a price floor is set at $40,000?

*(About 180 cars will be offered for sale, and about 60 will be purchased by consumers. There will be a surplus of 120 cars on the market.)*

### Closure

- Ask the students to review the main ideas in this exercise by applying them in an analysis of the parking lot at the high school.

*(When the price for a good or service is set above or below the market-clearing price, surpluses or shortages will result. In the case of the school parking lot, the price is probably zero — i.e., below the market-clearing price. There is probably a surplus of cars in the parking lot.)*

- Have the students consider what would happen if the school allowed students to bid for the right to park at school. What would the market-clearing price be?

*(Something greater than zero.)*

# Unit 2 | Teacher's Guide

## Multiple-Choice Questions

(correct answers shown in bold)

1. A shortage of new DVD players has occurred in the stores during the Christmas shopping season. All companies set their prices before the Christmas season begins. What explains this shortage?

   A. The price of DVD players was set higher than the market-clearing price.

   **B. The price of DVD players was set lower than the market-clearing price.**

   C. The price of DVD players was set at the same level as the market-clearing price.

   D. The IQ of the manager who set the price of the DVD players was lower than the market-clearing price.

2. During dry years, many cities experience water shortages and encourage citizens to conserve on water, reducing water usage for lawns, showers, and washing clothes and cars. What might be an alternative way to help reduce the water shortage problem during a drought?

   **A. Raise the price of water to the market-clearing price.**

   B. Drop the price of water below the market-clearing price.

   C. Raise the price of water above the market-clearing price.

   D. Raise the price of bottled water sold in the grocery stores.

3. Most airports charge airplanes a landing fee for using the airport runways. What would happen if airports charged all airplanes the same fee and did not change the fee for several years?

   **A. Airports would get very crowded, with many airplanes using the facilities.**

   B. Airports would see a decrease in big airplanes using the facilities.

   C. Airports would see a decrease in little airplanes using the facilities.

   D. Airports would soon be empty.

## Essay Question

A U.S senator has just announced a proposal to help reduce gasoline costs for all consumers. That proposal would set gasoline prices nationwide at $2.00 or less, regardless of supply and demand conditions in the market. Use the concepts of shortages and surpluses to explain the consequences of this policy if (a) it were to hold prices below the market-clearing price, and (b) it were to hold prices above the market-clearing price.

*(If the set price was lower than the market-clearing price, customers would face a shortage; they would find themselves scrambling to buy more gas than there was gas available. If the set price was higher than the market-clearing price, there would be a surplus of gasoline. If the price matched the market-clearing price, no change would be observed in the market for gasoline.)*

# Secondary Effects: Price Ceilings and Floors

**Unit 2, Lesson 14**
Visual 1

## The Market for Automobiles: Price Floors and Ceilings

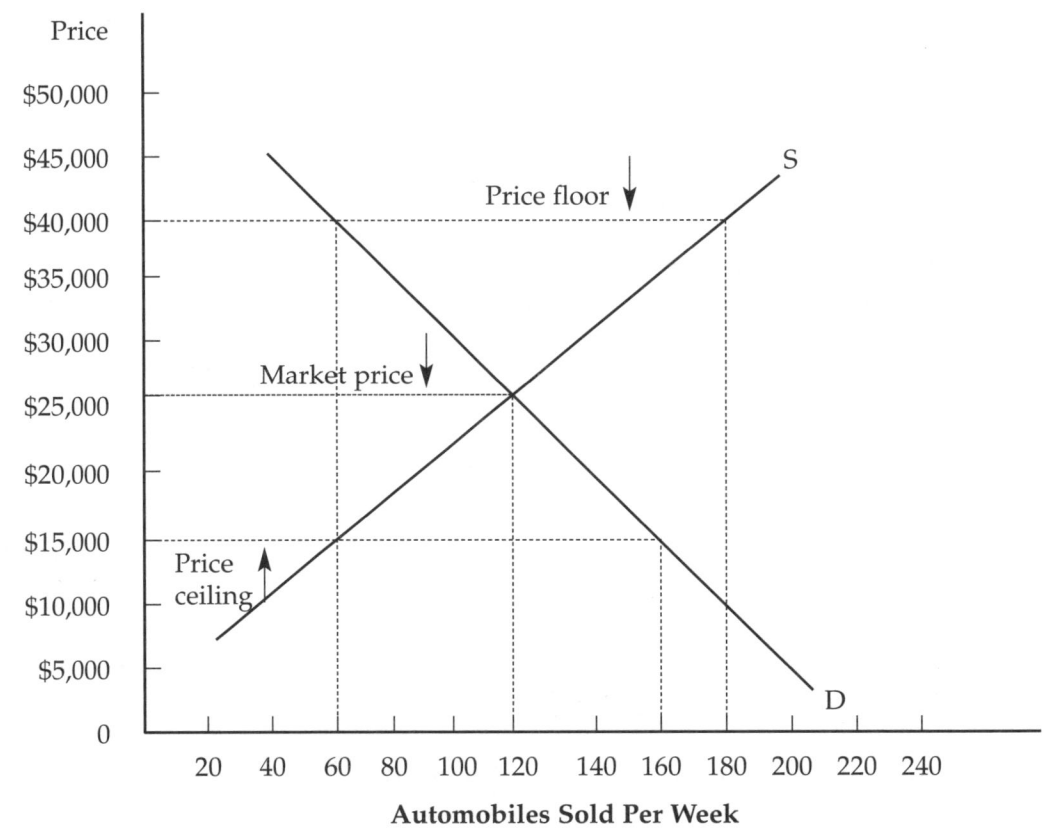

CAPSTONE

## UNIT 3

# HOW YOU CAN PROSPER IN A MARKET ECONOMY

Lesson 15   Why Do Some People Earn More Than Others?

Lesson 16   Making Choices about Saving and Investing

Lesson 17   Creating and Using a Budget

Lesson 18   Credit Management

Lesson 19   Earning an Income

# Unit 3 | Teacher's Guide

## Unit 3 Lesson 15

# Why Do Some People Earn More Than Others?

## INTRODUCTION

**Economics**  Human capital refers to the health, education, training, and skills that potential workers bring to the marketplace. Developing human capital requires spending resources now in order to increase productivity in the future. In this respect human capital is like physical capital (goods such as plants and equipment), in which people also make an up-front investment in order to benefit later. Some investment in human capital is targeted to groups — displaced workers served by publicly funded job training programs, for example. But investment in human capital can also be an individual or family venture. Young people can enhance their individual human capital by investing in their own futures.

**Reasoning**  Investments in human capital are tied closely to incentives. Labor markets are governed by the laws of supply and demand. Employers are willing to pay more to hire highly educated workers because highly educated workers increase the amount of output employers obtain from an additional unit of labor. Many workers are willing to pay the cost of becoming educated because there is a reward for doing so. One reward is increased income. College graduates in the United States, for example, earn 65 percent more than workers who hold only a high school diploma.

## CONCEPTS

- Choice
- Economic system
- Future consequences
- Human capital
- Incentives
- Opportunity cost
- Voluntary trade

## OBJECTIVES

*Students will:*

1. Analyze the problem of why some people earn more income than others.
2. Apply principles of economic reasoning to explain differences in income.

## CONTENT STANDARDS

- Effective decision making requires comparing the additional costs with the additional benefits. Most choices involve doing a little more or a little less of something; few choices are all-or-nothing decisions. (NCEE Content Standard 2)

- Different methods can be used to allocate goods and services. People, acting individually or collectively through government, must choose which methods to use to allocate different kinds of goods and services. (NCEE Content Standard 3)

- People respond predictably to positive and negative incentives. (NCEE Content Standard 4)

- Voluntary exchange occurs only when all participating parties expect to gain. This is true for trade among individuals or organizations within a nation, and among individuals or organizations in different nations. (NCEE Content Standard 5)

- Income for most people is determined by the market value of the productive resources they sell. What workers earn depends, primarily, on the market value of what they produce and how productive they are. (NCEE Content Standard 13)

- Investment in factories, machinery, new technology, and the health, education, and training of people can raise future standards of living. (NCEE Content Standard 15)

## LESSON DESCRIPTION

Students examine and discuss visuals to identify an economic mystery regarding differences in income. They use the **Guide to Economic Reasoning** to analyze the problem and reach a tentative solution.

*Time Required: 45 minutes*

## MATERIALS

- A transparency of Visuals 1, 2, and 3
- Activity 1

## PROCEDURE

1. Tell the class that people often complain, sometimes bitterly, about why some people earn more income than others. They complain that "the rich get richer" and "the poor get poorer." They suggest that the system is unfair. It must be! How else could it be that professional golfers earn more income than professional nurses? Explain that the purpose of this lesson is to apply economic reasoning in an effort to explain why some people make more income than others.

# Why Do Some People Earn More than Others?

2. Display Visual 1. Ask:

   - Can you identify some Americans who earn large incomes?

     *(Students may identify celebrities like Katie Couric, Tom Cruise, Tiger Woods.)*

   - Which Americans earn less than the celebrities listed in Visual 1?

     *(Among many possibilities: Nurses, teachers, social workers, electricians, retail clerks.)*

   - What is the mystery?

     *(Why is it that people in diverse occupations, occupations that contribute in very different ways to the social good, earn such different incomes?)*

3. Display Visual 2. Ask the students to speculate about whether each statement is true or false.

   A. People with more formal education earn less on average than to people with less formal education. *(False)*

   B. The laws of demand and supply do not apply to wages and salaries. *(False)*

   C. Natural ability and willingness to work hard contribute little to earning more income. *(False)*

4. Display Visual 3. Explain that some of the variation in income derives from what economists call investments in human capital. Explain that *human capital* refers to the health, education, training, and skills potential workers bring to the marketplace.

5. Refer the students to Activity 1; ask them to read the activity sheet and answer the questions. Review and discuss the students' answers:

   A. Describe the relationship between level of education and median income.

      *(Higher levels of formal education are associated with higher median incomes.)*

   B. In 2000, how much more would a college graduate have earned per year than a high school graduate?

      *($16,736 more)*

   C. Assuming a 40-year work life and no pay increases along the way, how much more might a college graduate expect to earn than a high school graduate?

      *($669,440 more)*

   D. Solve the mystery: Why is it that people in diverse occupations, occupations that contribute in very different ways to the social good, earn such different incomes?

      *(People make choices regarding their occupations. These choices are influenced by several factors including natural abilities, levels of education, training, health, and interests. Businesses, to earn profits, must attract people to produce goods and services. Businesses must offer wages, salaries, and benefits sufficient to attract workers willing to work for them. The wage or salary paid to a worker is a reflection of the market price for labor in that market.)*

   E. Why do celebrities seem to earn so much income?

      *(The market for celebrities is influenced by many of the same factors that influence other markets, including the laws of supply and demand. However, technological changes [in television, movies, and other media] now permit entertainers to provide millions of fans with entertainment services at relatively low prices. For a few successful celebrities, this results in large incomes. The same can be said of large, successful businesses that earn high profits by selling millions of products.)*

## Closure

Review the key points of the lesson. Ask:

- What are the principles in the **Guide to Economic Reasoning**?

  *(People choose. People's choices involve costs. People respond to incentives in predictable ways. People create economic systems that influence individual choices and incentives. People gain when they trade voluntarily. People's choices have consequences that lie in the future.)*

- Why do some people earn more income than others?

  *(The income people earn depends in part on supply and demand. Businesses want to hire [i.e., they demand] skilled, productive workers. They are willing to pay higher wages to workers who seem likely to be skilled and productive. In response to this demand, some prospective employees invest in their own human capital, obtaining the education and experience they need to become skilled and productive. Those who become skilled and productive in a high demand/low supply field ordinarily earn more than those who enter a high supply/low demand field. The wage or salary paid, in other words, reflects the market price for labor in the labor market in question.)*

# Unit 3 | Teacher's Guide

MULTIPLE-CHOICE QUESTIONS

(CORRECT ANSWERS SHOWN IN BOLD)

1. On average, who in this group is likely to earn the largest income?

   A. A person who completes high school

   B. A person who completes college

   C. A person who earns a Master's degree

   **D. A person who earns a professional degree**

2. In a market system, the price of labor is set by:

   A. The U.S. Department of Labor.

   **B. Supply and demand.**

   C. Employers.

   D. Workers.

ESSAY QUESTION

Barry Stocks, a professional baseball player, recently signed a multi-million dollar contract. Your friend says, "This is outrageous! Nobody who plays a kid's game should make that much money." Explain how you, a practitioner of the **Guide to Economic Reasoning**, might disagree.

*(While the demand is high for professional athletes, the supply is low. Few people have the necessary talent, physical endowments, work ethic, drive, and tolerance for risk — or whatever else it takes to become a celebrity in sports or entertainment. The market for star athletes and celebrities operates in much the same way as other markets. People offer their talents in return for compensation from their customers. However, technology has changed a great deal over the past 50 years. Athletes and celebrities are now able to deliver their services to millions of fans by way of television, movies, and other media. Thus, the equilibrium price of their labor is likely to be at a high level. Through technology, athletes and celebrities are able to sell their services to millions of consumers at a relatively low cost.)*

**Unit 3, Lesson 15**
Visual 1

## WHY DO SOME PEOPLE EARN MORE THAN OTHERS?

- Many Americans are delighted to learn that their favorite celebrities earn large incomes.
    - ✓ In 2002, Katie Couric signed a contract with NBC for $65 million for 4.5 years.
    - ✓ Tom Cruise made $43.2 million in 2001.
    - ✓ Tiger Woods made $53 million in 2001.

- People in other occupations make much less.
    - ✓ The median annual income of a hospital registered nurse was $45,780 in 2001.
    - ✓ The median annual income of a hospital social worker was $33,150 in 2001.

- *Why is it that people in diverse occupations, occupations that contribute in very different ways to the social good, earn such different incomes?*

# Unit 3 | Teacher's Guide

**Unit 3, Lesson 15**
Visual 2

## True/False Clues

A. People with more formal education earn less on average than people with less formal education.

True or False?

B. The laws of demand and supply do not apply to wages and salaries.

True or False?

C. Natural ability and willingness to work hard contribute little to earning more income.

True or False?

**Unit 3, Lesson 15**
Visual 3

# HUMAN CAPITAL

- Human Capital: The health, education, training, and skills potential workers bring to the marketplace.

- Benefits in the future: Like all forms of capital, human capital is attained by people who spend resources now in order to raise productivity in the future.

- Education: People who have more education are likely to have greater abilities than others to read, do math, and solve problems. As a result, they are likely to produce more than people with less education.

- Training: People with more training, often obtained on the job, are likely to produce more than those with less training.

- Health: People who have better health are less likely to miss work and usually are able to produce more than people in poor health.

# Unit 3 | Teacher's Guide

## Unit 3 Lesson 16

## Making Choices about Saving and Investing

### Introduction

**Economics** When people choose to retain some of their income after paying for consumption and taxes, they are saving. There are many reasons to save. People might wish to save for a big purchase at a later date, or enjoy the security of knowing that their savings are available for use during bad times, or watch their savings grow from compounding interest. People's individual decisions about saving also affect the economy as a whole. The decision to save provides more money to the loanable funds market, making it easier for those who want to invest in growth-producing capital to do so.

Saving and investment are two different things, though people often confuse one with the other and use the terms *saving* and *investment* interchangeably. Savings is the unspent income that people place in banks or other financial institutions, or use to buy bonds or stocks. When people have income left after they pay for consumption and taxes, the leftover amount adds to the nation's savings or loanable funds totals. The typical error is to describe the placing of these leftover dollars into savings accounts or stock portfolios as investing. In economics, investing is the purchase of capital that is used for production of goods and services. When businesses buy trucks or buildings, for example, they are investing the dollars they obtain (through loans) from the savers.

As is the case with other consumption decisions, people should weigh expected costs and expected benefits when they think about saving. Sometimes the scale tips in favor of saving and sometimes it does not. In every case, the price of money is an important consideration. When the price of money is low, the return to savings is small. When the price of money is high, the return to savings is high. Interest rates determine the price of money. Of course, the real interest rate — the rate adjusted for price-level changes — is the price that must be considered.

**Reasoning** In considering whether to save, people must decide if the expected benefits of saving outweigh the expected costs. A choice to save means giving up the benefit of consuming today in order to gain an increased potential for consumption at a later date. A choice to buy now means giving up the increased potential for buying later, as well the potential for money saved to grow in value. When savings grow a great deal in real value over time, it usually pays to save. When savings grow only a little or not at all in real terms, the cost of saving is high relative to the benefit.

### Concepts

- Choice
- Inflation
- Interest
- Investment
- Loanable funds market
- Purchasing power
- Real interest
- Savings

### Objectives

*Students will:*

1. Predict how real interest rates influence savings decisions.
2. Distinguish between saving and investment.
3. Determine how consumer preferences vary with an individual life's circumstances and how such circumstances influence decisions to save or not to save.
4. Use the Rule of 72.
5. Explain when saving is and is not a good idea.

### Content Standards

- Effective decision making requires comparing the additional costs of alternatives with the additional benefits. Most choices involve doing a little more or a little less of something; few choices are all-or-nothing decisions. (NCEE Content Standard 2)

- Interest rates, adjusted for inflation, rise and fall to balance the amount saved with the amount borrowed, thus affecting the allocation of scarce resources between present and future uses. (NCEE Content Standard 12)

### Lesson Description

This lesson introduces the distinction between savings and investment. It demonstrates how the price of money — the interest rate — is critical to making the right savings and investment choices. It explains when, under various conditions, it is or is not in people's best interest to save.

*Time Required: 90 minutes*

### Materials

- A transparency of Visual 1 and Visual 2
- Activity 1
- A $5 bill
- A blank piece of 8.5 x 11-inch paper
- A facial tissue

# MAKING CHOICES ABOUT SAVING AND INVESTING

## PROCEDURE

1. Tell the class that this lesson provides an overview of basic knowledge regarding saving and investing. To introduce several of the concepts, give the class a short true-or-false quiz. Display Visual 1, read the questions, and call for student responses. When the students have answered all the questions, explain that the correct answer to all the questions is *false*.

2. Discuss why the answers are false.

    A. When people buy U.S. Savings Bonds with their extra income, they are making an economic investment.

    *(False. Personal investing means placing savings in instruments such as U.S. Savings Bonds or savings accounts, or purchasing stocks. Economic investing refers to the purchase of capital that is used to increase the production of goods and services. When businesses buy trucks or buildings, for example, they are investing dollars they have obtained from savers.)*

    B. Money does not have a price.

    *(False. The price of money is the interest rate.)*

    C. Overall, it is always beneficial to save.

    *(False. Savers should weigh the expected benefits and costs of saving. There may be times when saving is not worth the sacrifice. In periods of high inflation, for example, it is expensive to save.)*

    D. Overall price-level changes do not relate to saving or investment decisions.

    *(False. Inflation influences the value of money over time.)*

    E. People should choose to save when the interest rate on savings is 3 percent and the cost of living is rising by 4.5 percent.

    *(False. In such a case, inflation exceeds the return on savings, making it unwise to save.)*

    F. The rule of 72 refers to the amount of time it takes to save enough money to buy a 1972 Corvette.

    *(False. The rule of 72 provides a method for calculating how long it takes for savings to double.)*

    G. The more money people save, the less money there is available for investments.

    *(False. When people save, they make more money available in the loanable funds market. This means more dollars will be available for borrowing and lending.)*

3. Explain that in deciding whether to save or consume, people ought to weigh the expected costs against expected benefits. It is important to consider real numbers — adjusted for price-level changes — in making such decisions. Hold up a $5 bill. Ask whether anyone wants this piece of paper. Most students will be willing to take this piece of paper off your hands. Hold up a blank 8.5 x 11-inch piece of paper. Ask whether anybody wants that piece of paper. Some students may want it, but most probably will not. Then hold up a facial tissue. Blow your nose, using the tissue. Ask whether anybody wants the tissue. Class clowns aside, no one will. There must be some interesting differences between one piece of paper and another.

4. Follow up on the question of differences. Ask:

    - Why are some pieces of paper more valuable than others?

        *(The $5 bill is more than a piece of paper; it represents purchasing power — the ability to obtain valuable goods and services in the marketplace. It is this purchasing power that gives the $5 bill its value.)*

    - Do dollars ever lose their purchasing power? How might inflation influence the value of money?

        *(Explain that inflation [a sustained period of rising price levels] erodes the value of money. Inflation therefore has an important bearing on decisions about whether to save or spend.)*

5. Tell the students to imagine that they have a friend named Jackie who is thinking about buying a used car for $3,500. Refer the students to Activity 1 and ask them to complete Part 1.

### Answers to Activity 1, Part 1

Savings account

| | |
|---|---:|
| Deposit | $3,500.00 |
| Add interest earned ($3,500 x .03) | 105.00 |
| Total | 3,605.00 |

Price of the used car

| | |
|---|---:|
| Price | $3,500.00 |
| Add inflation ($3,500 x .05) | 175.00 |
| New price at year's end | 3,675.00 |

What do you think Jackie should do?

*(She should buy the car now. If she waits, she will lose money on purchasing the car because inflation is growing faster than the interest she can earn on her savings.)*

6. Tell the class to read another story about Jackie and her decision about buying a car. This time, they are going to learn about compounding and the Rule of 72, which they can use to calculate how long it takes for money saved to double. Ask the students to complete Part 2 of Activity 1.

## Unit 3 | Teacher's Guide

*Answers to Activity 1, Part 2*

| Form of savings | Real interest or rate of return | Years to double |
|---|---|---|
| Passbook savings | 2% | 36 |
| Money market account | 5% | 14.40 |
| U.S. Treasury Bond | 6% | 12 |
| Stock market | 10% | 7.20 |

7. Explain that individuals' decisions to save or not to save can have widespread implications. What is good (or bad) for the individual might also be good (or bad) for the economy generally. To see why, ask the students to read Part 3 of Activity 1 and respond to the questions.

   A. What is the loanable funds market?

   *(The loanable funds market is the market that brings together the people who want to supply funds [savers] and the people who want to demand funds [borrowers].)*

   B. How does increasing savings cause interest rates to decrease?

   *(Adding money into the loanable funds market increases the supply of savings dollars. This shifts the supply curve for dollars to the right, causing the price [interest rate] to fall.)*

   C. How does reducing savings cause interest rates to increase?

   *(Reducing the amount of money in the loanable funds market decreases the supply of savings dollars and shifts the supply curve for dollars to the left, causing the price [interest rate] to increase.)*

8. Display Visual 2 to demonstrate this change and reinforce the ideas that the loanable funds market looks like other markets when supply, demand, and equilibrium price are considered.

## Closure

Review the key points of the lesson. Display Visual 1 and review why the answer to each question is false.

## Multiple-Choice Questions
(Correct answers shown in bold)

1. The price of money is:
   A. Constantly rising.
   B. The interest rate.
   C. Determined by the market.
   **D. Both B and C are correct.**

2. It is a good idea to save when:
   A. The expected benefits are greater that the expected costs.
   B. Real interest rates are positive.
   C. Economic growth is a desirable goal.
   **D. All of the above.**

3. Savings are particularly important to young people because:
   **A. Compounding increases the return.**
   B. They need to buy so many things.
   C. They are usually poor money managers.
   D. They usually earn a minimum wage.

## Essay Question

Jackie is giving advice to her friend Joanna. Joanna says, "I hear all this talk about saving and investing. It seems to me to be focused on greed. How much will I get if I do this? How much if I do that? It's all about greed, right, Jackie?" How might Jackie respond?

*(Jackie might explain that the money people save goes into the market for loanable funds. When people add dollars to the loanable funds market, more funds become available for borrowing and lending. Businesses, for example, borrow money from the loanable funds market to expand their businesses — perhaps by buying new equipment, hiring new employees, or providing new training programs for employees. Actions of this sort result in more jobs, more production, better goods and services, and a higher standard of living. Saving can help others in the economy while it also helps individual savers.)*

MAKING CHOICES ABOUT SAVING AND INVESTING

**Unit 3, Lesson 16**
Visual 1

## SAVINGS AND INVESTING QUIZ

ANSWER EACH QUESTION BELOW BY CIRCLING TRUE OR FALSE.

A. When people buy U.S. Savings Bonds with their extra income, they are making an economic investment.   True   False

B. Money does not have a price.   True   False

C. Overall, it is always beneficial to save.

   True   False

D. Overall price-level changes do not relate to saving or investment decisions.   True   False

E. People should choose to save when the interest rate on savings is 3 percent and the cost of living is rising by 4.5 percent.   True   False

F. The rule of 72 refers to the amount of time it takes to save enough money to buy a 1972 Corvette.

   True   False

G. The more money people save, the less money there is available for investments.   True   False

# Unit 3 | Teacher's Guide

**Unit 3, Lesson 16**
Visual 2

## LOANABLE FUNDS: A MARKET

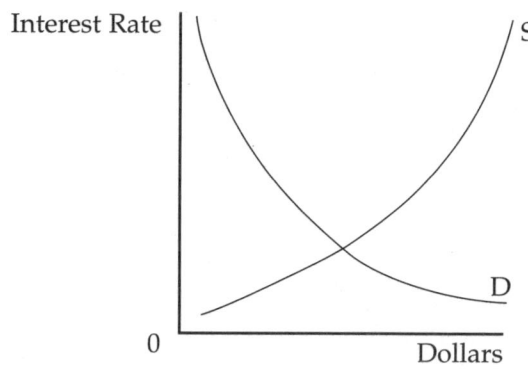

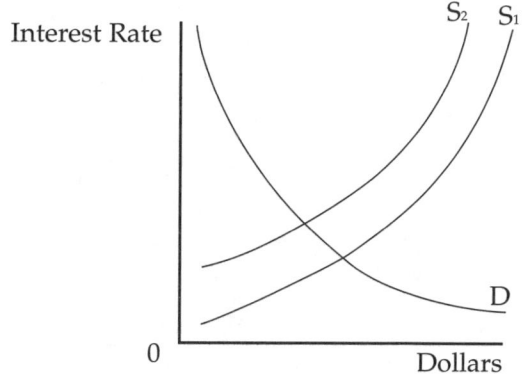

# Unit 3 | Teacher's Guide

## Unit 3 Lesson 17

## Creating and Using a Budget

### Introduction

**Economics**  The fundamentals of budgeting include knowing what one considers important in life and knowing the level and stability of one's income and spending patterns. Attention to these fundamentals, and to price information, enables people to weigh the benefits and costs associated with decisions related to personal finance.

Because consumption and savings decisions are seldom all-or-nothing, creating and using a budget ordinarily requires marginal analysis. People trying to live within a budget, or working to modify one, find themselves asking, for example, whether to spend a bit more money on food or a bit more on clothing or entertainment, given the added or marginal costs and the marginal gains they expect to realize from each of the alternative possibilities.

**Reasoning**  Successful financial planners economize, knowing that resources are scarce. They try to make decisions that will increase their benefits and minimize their costs. They pay attention to prices, using them to identify the opportunity cost of choosing one product or service as opposed to another. They pay attention to changes — in prices and in their own preferences — and reassess the costs and benefits of forthcoming decisions as necessary, given the new information. Knowing that key variables including prices, income, and preferences change constantly, they review and revise their financial plans or budgets continually.

### Concepts

- Budget
- Choice
- Diminishing marginal utility
- Income
- Marginal analysis
- Price
- Substitute
- Utility

### Objectives

*Students will:*

1. Use principles of financial planning to create budgets.
2. Predict and take account of diversity in consumer preferences.
3. Use marginal analysis to adjust budget decisions when prices and preferences change.

### Content Standards

- Productive resources are limited. Therefore, people cannot have all the goods and services they want; as a result, they must choose some things and give up others. (NCEE Content Standard 1)

- Effective decision making requires comparing the additional costs of alternatives with the additional benefits. Most choices involve doing a little more or a little less of something; few choices are all-or-nothing decisions. (NCEE Content Standard 2)

- Prices send signals and provide incentives to buyers and sellers. When supply or demand changes, market prices adjust, affecting incentives. (NCEE Content Standard 8)

### Lesson Description

This lesson focuses on using budgeting to maximize consumer satisfaction. It describes a flexible view of budgets, linking them to markets and market information, and demonstrates how and why budgets should be reviewed and modified often.

*Time required: 90 minutes*

### Materials

- A transparency of Visual 1

- Three copies of Activity 1 (from the Student book) for each student

- Four-to-six copies of Handout Material 1 (see p. 106-107; make enough copies for one role card per student)

- Two or three copies of Handout Material 2 (see p. 108; make enough copies for one or two changing-events strips per student)

### Procedure

1. Tell the class that the people who benefit most from a financial plan are often the ones who feel they don't need one. The best time to begin using financial planning is when you are young and have a small income — before adult responsibilities begin to introduce burdens and complexities that may interfere with experimentation and learning.

2. Introduce two main principles of financial planning: It requires collecting information about goals, income, and expenditures. And it requires organizing this information in an effective manner, so that you can review it and revise it easily when market conditions change, as they most assuredly will. What might such an organized collection of information look like?

# Creating and Using a Budget

3. Distribute one copy of Activity 1 to each student and project Visual 1 on an overhead. The Activity and the Visual show what a financial planning document might look like. Discuss the components of the document. Explain that people use budget forms (or income and expense statements) of this sort to keep track of their finances and to plan.

4. Tell the students that they will use the financial planning form in three exercises. Initially they will use it in a role-playing activity, making decisions and plans according to their assigned roles. Then they will review and modify their plans in light of changing market conditions. Finally, they will construct financial plans for themselves.

5. Ask each student to pick a card from the deck of role-description cards provided by copies of Handout Material 1. Tell them that they will participate in a financial planning task as if they were the persons identified on their role cards. The components of the financial plan they must complete include an identification of the lifestyle goals of the planner, plus his or her sources of income and projected expenditures. Determining what is important helps the planner to set priorities and make choices regarding what to purchase and what to avoid. Knowing the prices of goods and services also helps planners weigh expected benefits in comparison with expected costs. Some people will pay more for an item than others, simply because they receive more satisfaction from it than others do.

6. Get the students started on their (role-determined) planning. Explain that the biographical sketches provided on the role cards highlight certain aspects of the characters listed. In some cases the sketches may seem incomplete. When that is the case, the students will need to add information — about income and expenses, for example — to complete the description. To obtain additional information, the students might interview real people whose lifestyles are similar to the lifestyle of the character in question. Also explain that all income figures provided on the cards are for income before taxes. Tax rates vary with income levels, ranging from 15 to 36 percent. As the students proceed, they should list goals first and then move on to the source-of-income and expenditures columns — always striving to reflect their roles.

7. When the students have finished this round of financial planning, conduct a discussion about the roles and their bearing on the planning procedure. Ask:

    - What determines how people value things?

    *(Students may identify the influence of family, friends, and religion. These influences often shape people's goals and the value judgments they make about careers, family life, other relationships, and what they do for fun.)*

    - How is income related to expenditure decisions?

    *(Income acts as a constraint on expenditure decisions. Even students who assume the role of upper-income persons will find that they cannot have it all: choices have to be made.)*

    - If income is a constraint for everyone, how does one make the hard choices about how much to spend and what to spend it on?

    *(Students should indicate that they sought to make expenditure choices that would provide them with the greatest satisfaction at the lowest cost, given the alternatives available. They may have started by planning to buy items they needed to survive; then, if they could afford to do so, they may have turned to the luxury items that are most consistent with their stated goals and lifestyle.)*

    - What are the pros and cons of completing a financial plan using this format?

    *(This process encourages a thoughtful weighing of expected costs and benefits. It is frustrating to realize that you can't have it all, but knowing what you value and what you want out of life makes foolish expenditures less likely.)*

8. Write on the board the statement, "One thing is for sure, nothing is for sure." Discuss the statement with the class. Stress the point that change is occurring all the time, especially in the marketplace, where price changes reflect changing conditions in the world. People's wants change; income changes; resources become more or less abundant; new technology is developed; new inventions are invented — all this and more make change prominent in day-to-day life. When prices change for items we have decided to buy or not to buy, a new decision-making environment is established, prompting us to reexamine expected benefits as compared to expected costs. More financial planning may be necessary.

9. Make copies of Handout Material 2 — enough so that each student can have at least one changing-events strip — and distribute them. When all the students have their change strips, ask them to review the financial planning documents they produced in the role-play activity. What might need to be changed, given the information on the changing-events strips? Distribute another copy of Activity 1. Ask the students to redo their plans, taking account of the new information.

10. Once the students have completed their revised plans, ask selected students to present their plans to the class, or to present them in small groups, highlighting the changes they made in light of the new information. Ask:

- Do you consider your change to be positive or negative?

    *(Answers will vary.)*

- Explain how a price increase for a particular item changed your plan.

    *(Price increases usually reduce the amount people are willing or able to buy; the increase means that the opportunity cost of the purchase also rises, so that buying the item in question would imply giving something else up.)*

- When financial plans are changed to account for income or price changes, are the changes of an all-or-nothing type?

    *(Usually not. People usually change the amount they spend within a category. As the price of entertainment falls, for example, one additional movie may be added to the list, not several. This calculation of additional costs and additional benefits demonstrates how important marginal analysis is in financial plans.)*

- Why do most people make small adjustments to their budget when a price changes?

    *(Lower prices will usually cause people to want more, but when people consume more of a single item the satisfaction derived from the additional consumption is less than before. The third glass of cold water on a hot day isn't as satisfying as the first or the second. Getting tired of consuming a particular good or service as you consume more of it demonstrates diminishing marginal utility.)*

11. Distribute another copy of Activity 1 to every student. Tell the students that this time around they will complete a financial plan for themselves. They should use their own goals and lifestyle information, their current income levels, and the basic constraints associated with being a high school student.

## CLOSURE

Assign the students the task of creating a changing event of their own that will force them to review and modify their financial plan. Ask them to write a short paper describing the event and how they think it will affect their plan.

*(Accept a variety of answers. Some examples of events might be obtaining a scholarship for college, acquiring a lot of credit card debt, becoming seriously ill with no health insurance, or failing to make a car payment.)*

## MULTIPLE-CHOICE QUESTIONS
## (CORRECT ANSWERS SHOWN IN BOLD)

1. The primary goal of financial planning is to:
    A. Set goals.
    **B. Maximize satisfaction.**
    C. Put information on paper.
    D. All of the above.

2. Financial plans:
    A. Are more useful for high-income people.
    B. Are usually stable.
    **C. Need to be reviewed and revised often.**
    D. Focus on needs more than wants.

3. Financial plans use price information for:
    A. A comparison of expected benefits and costs.
    B. A determination of how consumption can change to increase satisfaction.
    C. Marginal analysis.
    **D. All of the above.**

## ESSAY QUESTION

Explain why it is important for many people to complete a financial plan that lists goals and lifestyle choices, income sources, and expenditure choices.

*(Financial planning helps individuals anticipate the costs and benefits of financial decisions. Changing events, new goals, and new prices all underscore the importance of financial planning.)*

# CREATING AND USING A BUDGET

# Unit 3, Lesson 17

## Handout Material 1

### Role Cards
(cards to be duplicated and cut)

#### DUSTY LONER

DL is a 16-year-old who stays to himself. He is not concerned about his image or basic hygiene. He likes to read and sketch outdoor scenes.

DL works part-time for his uncle as a house painter, earning $30 per week. This seems to be more than enough for DL, as he lives with his parents and doesn't want a flashy lifestyle. DL travels by bus.

Looking forward to getting out of school so he can spend more time drawing, DL hopes to have a successful art show some day and earn just enough live a modest life and continue to draw.

#### BULKY BODY

BB is 17-year-old athlete who works hard to look good. He is popular with girls. He works 30 hours per week at a local health club, earning $6.00 per hour.

BB's parents both work. They make sure their son has food in the refrigerator, but he pays for his own restaurant purchases and any clothing items that go beyond the basics.

Any entertainment is BB's responsibility as well. To assist BB with all this, his parents provide him with an allowance of $50 per month. BB has an old car that costs him a total of $200 per month for gas and insurance.

BB plans to go to college, win an athletic scholarship, and eventually play in the NFL. If he attains this goal, BB will buy the big house he wants, host big parties, marry the woman of his dreams and have three children.

#### CANDY SWEET

CS is a 17-year-old girl who is often called Barbie by her classmates.

CS always looks good and dresses in the latest, most expensive clothes. She is a good student and loves to get better grades than her friends. To ensure that she will get good grades, she regularly buys books and computer hardware and software. Her parents have told her that schoolwork is her job, and they do not permit her to work.

CS's parents provide her with an allowance of $250 per month, and she also has $75 per month in income from a trust fund. Using this money, CS buys her own clothes and pays her own expenses for personal care, entertainment, and school supplies. CS has no car, but when she needs one she can borrow her mother's. In these cases she pays for the gas she uses.

CS wants to be a clothes buyer for a major retail chain after she completes a college degree in business. She worries about college, however, because her father reminds her often that both he and her mother paid their own way through school.

#### DONALD DROPOUT

DD dropped out of school two years ago at the age of 17. He didn't want any more formal schooling, he said, because he wouldn't need it, given his goal of starting up a deli sandwich shop in the mall.

His parents objected strongly to DD's plans, and when he would not reconsider, they kicked him out of the house. He then began working full-time at Plainway, a sub sandwich shop. He is now an assistant manager and earns $175 per week.

DD lives in a small studio apartment, for which he pays $275 per month in rent. He takes the bus to work, at a cost of $2.00 for a round trip.

Although DD is not a fashion plate, he must be clean and neat for work. He has met a girl he likes, and she loves to go to movies and eat pizza.

DD dreams of owning his own place. He tries to put money away every month to help make his dreams come true. Living on his own and being responsible for all his expenses has placed a great deal of pressure on DD to plan carefully.

# Unit 3 | Teacher's Guide

## NED WORTH

NW is a 24-year-old who has a job that pays $4,000 per month. He receives gifts from his wealthy family, with an average value of $300 per month, and he earns savings-account interest of $25 per month.

NW is on the fast track in his company; most people in the firm think that he is just getting started on an upward career path.

NW is married to Gloria Gogetter. He and Gloria have a two-year-old daughter and another child on the way. Gloria is the household manager; she allocates $1,000 per month to cover expenses for food, clothing, and the credit card bill, which usually comes to $300 per month. The Worths live in a big house with a big mortgage: $1,500 per month. Property taxes are included in the $1,500 total, but the yearly insurance bill of $500 is not.

Two cars requiring monthly payments of $185 and $250, respectively, plus $1,200 per year in insurance bills, add to the Worths' living expenses.

Gloria does not intend to work only at home. She wants to get a college degree before long and begin her outside-the-home career.

## RETIRING RHONDA

RR has just retired after a career as a college professor. She lives alone in a modest house that she has paid for. Her monthly expenses for property taxes, utilities, and insurance now come to $400.

RR drives a 1995 four-door Buick; it costs her about $100 per month for maintenance, gas and oil, and insurance. She knows this old car will need to be replaced soon.

RR is an avid reader, so she buys books often. She also loves to travel and spends more than $250 per month on trips. Traveling increases her monthly food and clothing expenses above the level that is normal for most retirees.

RR receives $987 per month from Social Security, plus $1,575 per month from a teachers' retirement program. She has a supplemental health insurance policy that costs her $300 per month.

CREATING AND USING A BUDGET

# Unit 3, Lesson 17

## Handout Material 2

### Changing-Events Strips
*Note to the teacher: Duplicate these events strips as necessary to provide one or two strips per student.*

---

If you own an automobile, you are picked up for speeding and must pay a $300 fine.

---

Income increases by 20 percent.

---

Food prices decline by $50 per month.

---

Insurance prices rise by 25 percent.

---

Clothes are now $100 more per month.

---

Interest earned on savings increases monthly income by $15.

---

Illness costs add $50 in monthly medical bills for a year.

---

Entertainment expenses fall by 50 percent.

---

Your car breaks down--add an additional monthly payment of $195 to your budget.

---

Your Aunt Tillie establishes a trust in your name, providing you with income of $200 per month.

---

Your income tax burden is reduced by 20 percent.

---

Prices for personal care products skyrocket--add costs of $25 per month.

---

Interest rates on savings triple--change interest earned on savings by this amount, if you have savings.

---

# Unit 3 | Teacher's Guide

**Unit 3, Lesson 17**
Visual 1

# Financial Planning Document

Name of planner _____ Date _____

## Part 1: Goal Statements

List short-term goals:

_____

_____

_____


List medium-term goals:

_____

_____

_____


List long-term goals:

_____

_____

_____

# CREATING AND USING A BUDGET

**Unit 3, Lesson 17**
Visual 1

## PART 2: INCOME INFORMATION

Complete the following, using monthly figures:

| Sources of income | Amount of income |
|---|---|
| Wages | _____ |
| Gifts | _____ |
| Allowance | _____ |
| Interest on savings | _____ |
| Sales | _____ |
| Other | _____ |
| Total | $_____ |

# Unit 3 | Teacher's Guide

**Unit 3, Lesson 17**
Visual 1

## Part 3: Expenditures

Complete the following, using monthly figures:

| Expenditures | Amount of expenditure |
|---|---|
| Housing | _____ |
| Food | _____ |
| Clothing | _____ |
| School supplies | _____ |
| Job equipment | _____ |
| Car payment | _____ |
| Gas and oil | _____ |
| Car maintenance | _____ |
| Car insurance | _____ |
| Medical care | _____ |
| Entertainment | _____ |
| Taxes | _____ |
| Personal care | _____ |
| Gifts | _____ |
| Savings | _____ |
| Credit cards | _____ |
| Other | _____ |
| Total | $_____ |

CREATING AND USING A BUDGET

**Unit 3, Lesson 17**
Visual 1

## PART 4: WHAT DO THE NUMBERS TELL YOU?

Calculate your discretionary income by subtracting your total monthly expenses from your total monthly income.

Total monthly income:    $_____

Total monthly expenses:  $_____

Discretionary income:    $_____

Given your monthly income, monthly expenses, and discretionary income, evaluate your ability to attain the goals and live the lifestyle you have selected. Are your short-, medium-, and/or long-term goals being met? Will you be able to meet them in the future, given your financial condition and plan? Write your evaluative statement below.

_____

_____

_____

_____

_____

# Unit 3 | Teacher's Guide

## Unit 3 Lesson 18

# Credit Management

### INTRODUCTION

**Economics**  Credit transactions are important to buyers and sellers. Sellers usually are not concerned about whether buyers use ready cash or borrowed money to pay for goods or services. Buyers need to be concerned about credit, however, because borrowed money is costly, and the costs vary depending upon the type of credit instrument used.

**Reasoning**  Credit enables consumers to "buy now and pay later." It is a popular option. According to the Federal Reserve System, as of August 2002, consumer debt in the United States totaled about $1.73 trillion. That is a large sum, obviously, but by itself it does not mean that buying on credit is a bad thing. For some consumers in some cases, the advantages of the credit option outweigh the added costs. For others, however, the decision to buy on credit is shortsighted. Consumers who understand various credit instruments and the real costs that come with them are more likely to use credit well and avoid shortsighted decisions.

### CONCEPTS

- Choice
- Debt
- Economic wants
- Income
- Interest
- Secured debt
- Unsecured debt

### OBJECTIVES

*Students will:*

1. Include the cost of credit in weighing the expected costs and benefits of a purchase.
2. Calculate and use the real interest rate in determining the cost of credit.
3. Identify possible credit alternatives for use in purchasing goods and services.
4. Integrate short- and long-term perspectives and goals in credit purchase decisions.
5. Appreciate the benefits of financial freedom.

### CONTENT STANDARDS

- Effective decision making requires comparing the additional costs of alternatives with the additional benefits. Most choices involve doing a little more or a little less of something; few choices are all-or-nothing decisions. (NCEE Content Standard 2)
- People respond predictably to positive and negative incentives. (NCEE Content Standard 4)
- Prices send signals and provide incentives to buyers and sellers. When supply or demand changes, market prices adjust, affecting incentives. (NCEE Content Standard 8)
- Money makes it easier to trade, borrow, save, invest, and compare the value of goods and services. (NCEE Content Standard 11)

### LESSON DESCRIPTION

This lesson is designed to help students make good consumer-credit decisions. Although using credit is beneficial at times, it often carries higher costs than many people realize. This lesson discusses the costs of credit in a manner that helps students calculate those costs and integrate them in short- and long-term decisions.

*Time required: 60 minutes*

### MATERIALS

- A transparency of Visuals 1, 2, and 3
- Activity 1

### PROCEDURE

1. Tell the students that the main purpose of this lesson is to help them think clearly and act prudently when they use credit. Display Visual 1, but reveal only the words *advantages* and *disadvantages*. Tell the students that you want to discuss their thoughts about buying goods and services on credit. (Credit in this exercise includes borrowing money with collateral [i.e., secured credit, such as a car loan] or using credit cards [i.e., unsecured credit].) After noting the students' comments, reveal and discuss all the points on Visual 1.

2. Display Visual 2. Ask the students to comment on the information it provides. Discuss their responses.

3. Remind the students that people who make good choices attempt to weigh the expected costs of a decision against expected benefits. Consumer choices regarding credit should include consideration of the cost of credit. Tell the students that they are about to make recommendations to various people as to whether they should buy a desired good or service now, wait and buy it later, or not buy it at all.

# CREDIT MANAGEMENT

4. Refer the students to Activity 1. It describes three people making purchasing decisions. Each student's task is to identify the costs and benefits of the listed alternatives and to make a recommendation. Once individual students have completed the activity, direct them to pair up with a neighbor and discuss each other's recommendations. Have each pair answer one basic credit-management question: When is the use of credit an appropriate way to pay for a purchase? Discuss the teams' answers.

   *(The general answer is a simple one. Credit is appropriate when the expected costs are less than the expected benefits. Reinforce the idea that using credit provides both benefits and costs. Decisions about the costs and benefits involved should include a time frame that includes the longer term.)*

**Possible answers to Activity 1:**

*Case One*

*Katie has a difficult choice to make. As is so often the case, the benefits of looking good don't come without costs. Even at 50 percent off, the skirt will cost $137.50. This translates into $62.50 coming out of Katie's savings. Remember that she is saving for college — the source, potentially, of a huge long-term benefit. If Katie opens a credit-card account at the store, she will reduce her out-of-pocket expenditure to $123.75 minus $75.00, or $48.75. She would have to pay this amount out of her savings when the bill arrives — or pay a minimum payment plus an interest charge. The usual 5 percent minimum payment or $10 (whichever is larger) would mean that next month she will have a 68 cent interest charge. If she misses the payment deadline, she will also incur a $35 late fee.*

*Case Two*

*Willie's situation would probably be familiar to many new college graduates. Being close to graduation is very much like being graduated, and few college grads believe they will fail to find employment. Walking away from the situation would certainly solve the money issue for the moment, but remember that Willie expects to buy a car very soon anyway. If he waits, he might forfeit a good deal and have to pay more later. If he buys the expensive Honda, he gains the benefits of the rebate and will have a smaller out-of-pocket cost in the long run. A major issue is whether he will get a job that pays enough to cover the new car — plus his student loans and his basic living expenses. The more expensive car's real cost is calculated by subtracting the rebate of $2,500 and the $500 discount (leaving $26,500) and adding 6 percent, or $1,590, plus an average $150 license fee. The total is $28,240. The cheaper car would cost $20,661. Note that these figures do not include effects related to the duration of the loan selected. Real interest needs to be considered as a benefit, since inflation allows purchasers to use cheaper dollars in paying off their debts. The real interest rate for the first year of the 48-month contract is –1.1 percent; for the 60-month contract it is +3.9 percent.*

*Case Three*

*With a new child, Mr. and Mrs. Jones will find it very helpful to have a washer and dryer. But the new child also will cause a reduction in income for a period of time. If Mrs. Jones goes back to work outside the home, child-care expenses will add to the financial burden. If Mr. and Mrs. Jones buy the $579 combo, their first payment will be approximately $29; after that they will pay 21 percent interest on the unpaid balance. The first payment on the $849 combo will be approximately $43, and the interest rate on the unpaid balance will be 21 percent. The extended warranty may reduce future repair costs, but that is an unknown. The silver service sounds like a nice extra, but Mr. and Mrs. Jones need to decide whether they would ever really use it.*

5. Display Visual 3. Discuss each of the guidelines. Ask the students to look back at the recommendations they made in Activity 1. In arriving at those recommendations, did they use some or all of these guidelines? Will they be able to use the guidelines in future decisions of their own? Why or why not?

## CLOSURE

Assign the students the task of describing the personal benefits associated with achieving financial freedom. Television advertisements, talk-show topics, and magazine articles often address the problems caused by using too much borrowed money. These discussions refer to objective problems that may follow from the overuse of credit, such as losing one's home or car, and to less tangible problems including the embarrassment or emotional trauma that sometimes accompanies steep debt or bankruptcy. Financial freedom can help people to avoid such problems. But what is financial freedom? Is it simply being rich? Students should consider their own understanding of the concept; they also should seek other people's opinions about it and do additional research about the benefits of using credit wisely or being free of debt altogether. Then the students should write a one-page essay describing how it feels to be in a good financial position.

*(The purpose of this essay is to help young people grasp the point that financial self-restraint — including not buying, in some cases, and thus not going into debt — does have advantages.)*

# Unit 3 | Teacher's Guide

## Multiple-Choice Questions
(correct answers shown in bold)

1. People should avoid buying too many goods or services on credit because:

    A. High interest charges increase the item's price.

    B. Credit-card debt reduces discretionary income levels.

    C. High credit use reduces one's opportunity to get an automobile or home loan.

    **D. All of the above.**

2. Current information about the use of credit suggests that:

    A. People are beginning to reduce their use of credit.

    **B. Many people actually have a negative savings rate.**

    C. Credit delinquency rates are falling.

    D. American Express holds the largest consumer debt.

3. People who use credit wisely will borrow money to:

    A. Deal with an emergency.

    B. Take advantage of a very low price on an item they plan to buy in the very near future.

    C. Take advantage of a low interest rate in comparison to price-level changes.

    **D. All of the above.**

## Essay Question

Write a two-part answer describing, first, a situation in which it would be a sound economic decision to use a credit-card loan at a 15 percent interest rate, and, second, a situation in which using a credit-card loan at a 15 percent interest rate would be a poor economic decision.

*(Using a credit-card loan in an emergency — perhaps to handle an unexpected car repair — is probably a good economic decision. Using a credit card loan to purchase frivolous items — soda and chips for a party — or for impulse purchases is probably not a good economic decision.)*

CREDIT MANAGEMENT

**Unit 3, Lesson 18**
Visual 1

# WHY USE CREDIT?

ADVANTAGES

- Use a good or service today and pay for it later.

- Acquire assets such as a college education or a home.

- Help with an emergency.

- Take advantage of a unique opportunity to buy.

- Pay back with cheaper dollars in a time of inflation.

DISADVANTAGES

- Loans have to be repaid with interest.

- Convenient credit might encourage impulse buying.

- People may use too much credit in relationship to their income.

- Poor credit use can harm credit ratings and make credit more expensive in the future.

# Unit 3 | Teacher's Guide

**Unit 3, Lesson 18**
Visual 2

## CONSUMER CREDIT INFORMATION

The following information about consumer credit will help people to make better decisions regarding its use:

- Credit cards enable people to obtain instant loans from banks, gasoline companies, department stores, and other retail businesses.
- Most credit cards come with limits as to how much a person can borrow.
- Most credit cards allow for cash advances, and most charge a fee (*up to 4 percent*) for cash advances.
- Interest charges on credit-card debt can be as high as 26 percent.
- The owner of a credit card is liable for up to $50 for unauthorized charges.
- Credit cards are usually valid for a period of 12 to 36 months.
- Most credit cards offer unsecured loans; the issuer relies on the credit user's promise to pay.
- Affinity cards connect credit-card use to special benefits such as frequent-flyer miles or automobile discounts.
- The real interest rate being charged credit users is the posted rate minus the inflation rate.
- The average delinquency rate for credit-card debt is on the rise.
- According to a recent issue of *U.S. News and World Report*, the typical American has between one and three credit cards and owes credit-card balances of approximately $8,000.
- Most Americans save very little, if any, of their disposable income.
- The credit-card debt of low-income families continues to rise.

CREDIT MANAGEMENT

**Unit 3, Lesson 18**
Visual 3

## CONSUMER CREDIT GUIDELINES

- Don't think you will save money by borrowing more.
- Don't impulse buy.
- Pay off high-interest credit-card balances.
- Start an emergency fund savings plan.
- Avoid joint obligations with people who have questionable spending habits.
- Charge only those items you can reasonably afford with your basic income.
- Create a realistic budget and stick to it.
- Find alternatives to spending money.
- Realize that the over-spending culprit is YOU.
- Calculate the cost of using credit before you decide to buy.
- Ask: "Can I pay for this credit purchase if I lose my job?"
- Ask: "What will happen if I don't make my credit payment on time?"
- Ask in each case: "All things considered, do the expected benefits from a credit purchase outweigh the costs?"

# Unit 3 | Teacher's Guide

## Unit 3 Lesson 19

## Earning an Income

### INTRODUCTION

**Economics**  Earning an income is what enables most people to participate in the economy. To earn an income, many people sell their time for wages. In other words, they work. The labor market seeks out the most productive people willing to work for the lowest wage rate. People also earn income by means of other income-producing resources including land (rent), capital (interest), and entrepreneurship (profit). Market forces also channel these resources to their most productive uses.

Most young people who earn an income do so by supplying their labor for some productive purpose. After-school and weekend jobs are common; they often pay a wage at or above the minimum wage. Some young people earn income from other sources — drawing interest from savings, for example, or renting things they own to others, or running a small business such as a lawn service or babysitting service. Payments from all these sources can add to individual income.

**Reasoning**  Income-generating decisions are important to nearly everyone. In their underlying form — choosing to earn income now or later, responding to incentives, evaluating market forces, trading dollars for goods and services, and evaluating alternatives by reference to future consequences — these decisions embody several important principles of economic reasoning. Wages and profits are the rewards offered by our economy for productive work.

The value of productive resources, including labor resources, changes as market conditions change. Employers hire workers based upon the perceived value workers bring to the business. The additional revenue a worker produces influences wage levels. In addition, increased on-the-job training and increased levels of formal education can increase the value of an employee to a business.

### CONCEPTS

- Capital
- Entrepreneurship
- Human capital
- Income
- Labor
- Land
- Profit

### OBJECTIVES

*Students will:*

1. Identify ways in which they can earn an income.
2. Explain how wages are determined.
3. Predict the benefits of education in the labor market.
4. Describe the role of entrepreneurs in the marketplace.
5. Compare themselves to entrepreneurs, by reference to selected entrepreneurial traits.

### CONTENT STANDARDS

- People respond predictably to positive and negative incentives. (NCEE Content Standard 4)

- Competition among sellers lowers costs and prices, and encourages producers to produce more of what consumers are willing and able to buy. Competition among buyers increases prices and allocates goods and services to those people who are willing and able to pay the most for them. (NCEE Content Standard 9)

- Income for most people is determined by the market value of the productive resources they sell. What workers earn depends, primarily, on the market value of what they produce and how productive they are. (NCEE Content Standard 13)

- Entrepreneurs are people who take the risks of organizing productive resources to make goods and services. Profit is an important incentive that leads entrepreneurs to accept risks of business failures. (NCEE Content Standard 14)

### LESSON DESCRIPTION

Students examine the concept of income. They identify factors that generate income, including entrepreneurial traits and changing conditions in labor markets. In learning how income is generated, students plan and make choices to enhance their own income-generating capacity.

*Time Required: 75 minutes*

### MATERIALS

- Activity 1 (for half the students in the class)
- Activity 2 (for half the students in the class)
- Transparencies of Visuals 1, 2, 3, and 4

# Earning an Income

## Procedure

1. Explain that the purpose of this lesson is to describe how people earn income. Ask for a show of hands to determine how many students have a paying job. Display Visual 1. Ask the students to indicate which of the pay ranges they fall into, given their current jobs. Discuss the results:

   - Why are so many students bunched in the lower pay ranges?

     *(Part-time jobs often pay only the minimum wage or something close to it. Low pay among high school students probably reflects the students' lack of experience, education, or skills. Given their obligation to attend school during most of the work week, low pay might also reflect the students' restricted availability for long, steady work, or for flexible hours.)*

   - Still, some students earn more than others. Why is that?

     *(These students might have special training, experience, or education. Stress the connection between the wage rate and the value of the employee's contribution to the products or services in question. Introduce the concept of human capital and explain that more human capital [training, experience, or education] ordinarily enhances a worker's ability to produce more and better things on the job.)*

2. Display Visual 2. Explain that most people obtain income primarily from wages. However, people who are successful financially often have multiple income sources.

3. Divide the class into two research teams to explore information related to earning income. The research information will be in two categories: information about changes in the labor market and information about the characteristics of people who start their own businesses. Direct half the students to Activity 1; direct the other half to Activity 2. After the students have completed their research, discuss their answers to the questions, beginning with Activity 1.

   A. Is the manufacturing or service sector likely to expand more?

      *(Employment in the service sector is likely to increase more than employment in manufacturing.)*

   B. What are some of the fastest-growing sectors?

      *(Health services, business services, social services, engineering, management, information technology, professional and other service occupations.)*

   C. What occupations are projected to grow more slowly?

      *(Office and administrative support occupations.)*

   D. How are education and training important?

      *(Occupations that generally require a college degree or other post-secondary training are projected to grow faster than the average across all sectors.)*

   E. How is the labor force likely to change?

      *(The labor force is likely to become somewhat older as the baby boomers age; it is also likely to include more women and more Asian, Hispanic, and African American workers.)*

4. Discuss the students' answers to the questions in Activity 2.

   A. What traits to do entrepreneurs like Mr. Lam, Mr. Atick, and Ms. Guadarrama seem to have in common?

      *(They provide new goods and services that are in high demand by consumers. They work hard, are focused on their customers, and are willing to take risks.)*

   B. How do entrepreneurs like Mr. Lam, Mr. Atick, and Ms. Guadarrama benefit our economy?

      *(They create jobs and supply new goods and services.)*

   C. How do entrepreneurs help other people to earn income?

      *(They create jobs for themselves and for their employees.)*

5. Stress the point that entrepreneurs are key players in the economy, creating jobs and improving the quality of life for many people. Display Visual 3. Ask the students whether the traits identified there can be learned. They should take notes on the discussion, listing the traits discussed and marking an asterisk next to the traits they think they possess. Give special emphasis to the entrepreneur's ability to learn from failure. This will be an important concept for the next procedure.

6. An important ability of the entrepreneur is to work aggressively with an idea in order to turn it into a business venture. Early on, the entrepreneur cannot be sure that the venture will succeed. That determination will be made in the market by consumers who do or do not find the good or service worthwhile.

7. Display Visual 4. Ask the students to comment on the slogans and explain why these are good descriptions of the entrepreneur. Ask them also to come up with new entrepreneurial slogans they think should be to be added to the list.

# Unit 3 | Teacher's Guide

## CLOSURE

Review the key points of the lesson. Ask:

- What changes does the Bureau of Labor Statistics predict will occur in the labor markets by 2010?

    *(Employment in services is expanding. Occupations requiring post-secondary education are projected to grow faster on average across all sectors.)*

- How might these changes influence people's education and career plans?

    *(People face incentives to seek careers in service occupations and to go to school after high school.)*

- What are some of the key traits of entrepreneurs?

    *(Confidence, willingness to sacrifice, high level of energy, creativity, and so forth.)*

## MULTIPLE-CHOICE QUESTIONS

### (CORRECT ANSWERS SHOWN IN BOLD)

1. Which is not a trait of an entrepreneur?
    - A. Self-confidence
    - B. High level of energy
    - **C. Interested in long-term management**
    - D. Willingness to accept failure

2. Most people's primary income source is:
    - **A. Wages.**
    - B. Interest.
    - C. Rent.
    - D. Profit.

3. Education increases workers' ability to earn more income because of:
    - A. Networking.
    - **B. Increased productivity.**
    - C. Age.
    - D. Respect.

## ESSAY QUESTION

Assume it is now the year 2010. Explain how you earn income. Also, by listing and commenting on key decisions you have made over the past 10 years, explain how you have put yourself into this income-generating position.

*(Responses will vary, but students should stress that the service-producing sector will continue to be the dominant producer of employment in the economy. Jobs in manufacturing are expected to decline by 2010. Health services, business services, social services, engineering, and management and related services are expected to account for growth. Education beyond high school and including college will become increasingly important.)*

EARNING AN INCOME

**Unit 3, Lesson 19**
Visual 1

## WHAT DO YOU EARN?

| HOURLY WAGE | NUMBER OF STUDENTS |
|---|---|
| $5.00- $7.00 | _____ |
| $7.01- $9.00 | _____ |
| $9.01- $12.00 | _____ |
| $12.01- $15.00 | _____ |
| $15.01- $25.00 | _____ |
| $25.01-$50.00 | _____ |
| $50.01- $75.00 | _____ |
| $75.01- $99.00 | _____ |
| $100 and over | _____ |

# Unit 3 | Teacher's Guide

**Unit 3, Lesson 19**
Visual 2

## Factors of Production and the Factor Payments

| Factors | Payments |
|---|---|
| Labor | Wages |
| Capital | Interest |
| Land | Rent |
| Entrepreneurship | Profit |

EARNING AN INCOME

**Unit 3, Lesson 19**
Visual 3

## TRAITS OF THE ENTREPRENEUR

1. Shows self-confidence.
2. Is willing to sacrifice.
3. Is an aggressive decision maker.
4. Can identify opportunities or niches.
5. Can keep cool through bad times.
6. Shows a high level of stamina and energy.
7. Remains focused even when distracted.
8. Keeps the spirit of creative change alive.
9. Thrives on the sense of accomplishment.
10. Opts for opportunity, not money.
11. Accepts and learns from failure.
12. Prefers innovation to status quo.

# Unit 3 | Teacher's Guide

**Unit 3, Lesson 19**
Visual 4

## ENTREPRENEURSHIP SLOGANS

- Ask not who will employ you, but whom you will employ.
- Always mess with success.
- A friend in need is a customer.
- Be distinguished or be extinguished.
- Plan on changing your plans.
- Failure is a good place to start.
- Playing it safe is dangerous.
- Look for the second right answer.
- Problems are opportunities in disguise.

# Unit 4
# The Business of Doing Business

Lesson 20   Why Helping Yourself Helps Others

Lesson 21   Productivity, Diminishing Marginal Returns, and the Demand for Labor

Lesson 22   How Competitive Is the Industry?

Lesson 23   Make a Profit: Do the Math

# Unit 4 | Teacher's Guide

## Unit 4 Lesson 20

# Why Helping Yourself Helps Others

### INTRODUCTION

**Economics**  One remarkable feature of a market economy is that the actions of self-interested individuals result in general prosperity for the society. *Unrestricted* self-interested behavior might result in undesirable outcomes. As a result, market economies rely on competition to provide the necessary discipline for producers as well as consumers.

**Reasoning**  People often think that good outcomes can result only from a well-planned, orderly system. In many contexts, this seems to be a sensible rule to follow. But economists emphasize a different view when it comes to producing goods and services that are desired by consumers. They note that economic behavior is complex. It is difficult to know, and costly to find out, what goods and services consumers want, and how much they are willing to pay. It is equally daunting to determine how best to organize resources to produce the goods and services consumers want to have. Market systems solve these problems by providing incentives to individuals to make these decisions. The incentives take the form of the profit motive and self-interested behavior.

### CONCEPTS

- Choice
- Competition
- Economic system
- Future consequences
- Incentives
- Market economy
- Opportunity cost
- Voluntary trade

### OBJECTIVES

*Students will:*

1. Distinguish between selfishness and self-interest.
2. Apply principles of economic reasoning to explain why self-interested behavior can have positive outcomes for a society.

### CONTENT STANDARDS

- Effective decision making requires comparing the additional costs of alternatives with the additional benefits. Most choices involve doing a little more or a little less of something; few choices are all-or-nothing decisions. (NCEE Content Standard 2)

- Different methods can be used to allocate goods and services. People acting individually or collectively through government, must choose which methods to use to allocate different kinds of goods and services. (NCEE Content Standard 3)

- People respond predictably to positive and negative incentives. (NCEE Content Standard 4)

- Prices send signals and provide incentives to buyers and sellers. When supply or demand changes, market prices adjust, affecting incentives. (NCEE Content Standard 8)

- Competition among sellers lowers costs and prices, and encourages producers to produce more of what consumers are willing and able to buy. Competition among buyers increases prices and allocates goods and services to those people who are willing and able to pay the most for them. (NCEE Content Standard 9)

- Voluntary exchange occurs only when all participating parties expect to gain. This is true for trade among individuals or organizations within a nation, and among individuals or organizations in different nations. (NCEE Content Standard 15)

### LESSON DESCRIPTION

Students examine and discuss visuals to identify an economic mystery regarding greed and self-interest. They use economic reasoning to analyze the mystery and reach a tentative explanation.

*Time Required: 45 minutes*

### MATERIALS

- A transparency of Visuals 1, 2, 3, 4, and 5
- Activity 1

### PROCEDURE

1. Tell the class that people often complain about the greed and selfishness they observe in others. They point to high prices for health care or medicine as examples. Some people regard market systems as the problem in these cases. They say that market systems foster unseemly values such as selfishness, greed, and a winner-take-all attitude. Economists take a far different view, asserting that market systems foster values that we generally cherish, including individual freedom, cooperation, and prosperity. Explain that the purpose of this lesson is to apply economic reasoning to show why self-interested behavior fosters positive economic and social outcomes.

2. Display Visual 1. Ask:

# Why Helping Yourself Helps Others

- Why might people of skeptical market systems?

    *(Answers will vary. Students are likely to stress concerns about greed, competition, profits, the environment, and so forth.)*

- What is the mystery?

    *(How can people acting in their own self-interest contribute to the social good?)*

3. Display Visual 2. Ask the students to speculate about whether each statement is true or false.

    A. People tend to act in their own self-interest. *(True)*

    B. Self-interested behavior rarely results in good things for others. *(False)*

    C. Market systems tend to reward virtues like honesty and tolerance. *(True)*

4. Refer the students to Activity 1. Explain to the students that they are going to participate in a simulated panel discussion. In the discussion, some students will play the roles of distinguished economists and other scholars from different historical periods. These time travelers will pose questions to Adam Smith, the founder of modern economics. Assign students to the roles of moderator, Smith (the starring role), David Hume, Voltaire, Friedrich von Hayek, Walter Heller, John Maynard Keynes, Karl Marx, John Locke, David Ricardo, and Jean-Baptiste Say. Assign roles to the students and ask them to read the dialogue in Activity 1. Discuss the questions that follow the panel session.

    A. Who was Adam Smith?

    *(Adam Smith was an 18th-century philosopher, now regarded as the founder of modern economic thought. In a book titled* The Wealth of Nations, *he offered an extensive description of the principles of a market economy.)*

    B. What is the difference between self-interest and selfishness?

    *(While some people are selfish, all people act in their own self-interest. Self-interest for some might mean seeking money; for others it might imply different priorities. Being interested in money need not mean that a person is selfish or greedy. It could just as well mean that he or she wants money in order to obtain an education or care for a family or contribute to environmental causes, and so on.)*

    C. What virtues are encouraged in market systems, according to Professor Smith?

    *(Honesty, cooperation, courtesy, and enterprise.)*

    D. Why are market prices important?

    *(Market prices reflect the value of a good to society and the cost to society of making the good. Households and businesses use prices in making decisions about what and when to buy and what and when to sell.)*

    E. Solve the mystery: How can people acting in their own self-interest contribute to the social good?

    *(The incentives established by market systems encourage people unknowingly to act in ways that help others by providing them with the goods and services they wish to have at market prices that reflect the value of goods to the society. For example, competition to make sales and earn profits encourages sellers to produce quality goods.)*

5. Display Visual 3. Ask: What motive — caring or self-interest — does Smith think is more likely to encourage people to provide for one another? Do you agree?

    *(Smith thinks that self-interest is more likely than caring to encourage people to provide for one another.)*

6. Display Visual 4. Ask: What is the invisible hand?

    *(When people pursue their own interests, they frequently and unknowingly benefit others.)*

7. Display Visual 5. Use it to explain the difference between values encouraged in market systems and values encouraged in non-market (command or traditional) systems. The following are some points you might consider making.

# Unit 3 | TEACHER'S GUIDE

## MARKET VALUES VERSUS NON-MARKET VALUES

| *Market Values* | *Non-Market Values* |
|---|---|
| ***Discipline:*** By stressing self-interested behavior, market systems encourage individuals to discipline themselves to produce the goods and services others want. Producing the goods and services demanded by others is rewarded. | ***Discipline:*** Non-market systems depend on tradition or force to encourage individuals to produce the goods and services others want. Failure to produce can lead to loss of respect or to misery. |
| ***Honesty and trustworthiness:*** While market systems are susceptible to occasional scams and schemes, most business people recognize that being honest and trustworthy with their customers will benefit the business over the long term. Customers will not continue to buy goods and services from people who cheat and lie to them. | ***Honesty and trustworthiness:*** Non-market systems rely on tradition or force to encourage individuals to be honest and trustworthy. Tradition and force often prove to be unsatisfactory, and over the long term people become inclined to trust only family members and friends. It is hard to maintain business relationships in such a setting, where no sanctions are enforced by consumers. |
| ***Tolerance:*** Market systems tend to reward people who make good business decisions rather than decisions based race, religion, gender, sexual orientation, and so forth. Judging employees on merit and selling to all customers who wish to buy are practices that are rewarded in the marketplace. | ***Tolerance:*** Non-market systems rely on tradition or force to encourage individuals to be tolerant — if they encourage tolerance at all. Here, too, tradition and force often prove to be inadequate, or worse. Tradition and force may be employed in support of hatred, or hatred may be unleashed as soon as external constraints are relaxed. |
| ***Cooperation:*** Cooperation is seldom identified as a basic characteristic of market systems. But market systems require cooperation in vast amounts to produce the extraordinary achievements that we regard as ordinary. For example, how does a car with parts from 10 countries, hundreds of suppliers, and thousands of distributors come to be sold in towns the size of cornfields? The act of producing and distributing cars (and other goods) requires extensive cooperation among strangers. | ***Cooperation:*** Non-market systems rely on tradition or force to encourage individuals to work together. Chairman Joseph Stalin, for example, deliberately distributed various manufacturing and agricultural enterprises across the former Soviet Union in a manner calculated to force people from diverse ethnic backgrounds to cooperate with one another. As soon as the threat of force was removed under Chairman Gorbachev, it all collapsed. Cooperation brought about through coercion lasted for several decades, but it could not be sustained. |
| ***Courtesy:*** Market systems encourage people to be courteous because it is in their self-interest to be courteous. Customers, for example, do not like to deal with business people who are rude or disrespectful. Some are rude or disrespectful anyway, of course — so long, at least, as they can hold on to their jobs or keep their businesses afloat. But over the long term, markets reward civil behavior, and business people seek those rewards. | ***Courtesy:*** Non-market systems depend on tradition or force to encourage individuals to produce the goods and services desired by others. In this context, indifference or antipathy toward consumers is a persistent problem. Security guards in the former Soviet Union were often assigned to each floor of Moscow's department stores. The guards were not there to protect the stores against thieves. The guards were there to protect the store clerks from customers who often became outraged by the clerks' surly, hostile attitudes. |
| ***Enterprise:*** Market systems provide large rewards for inventive and innovative business leaders. People who are unafraid of change and willing to take risks are materially rewarded. As a result, new goods and services appear continually. | ***Enterprise:*** Non-market systems tend to reward people for keeping in line with the rules. "Follow the manual" might be the motto. Following the manual rarely results in new inventions or innovations. |
| ***Responsibility:*** Market systems — with their emphasis on self-interested behavior — tend to focus on the individual and individual actions. The threat of individual failure is sobering, and it tends to encourage people to act responsibly. | ***Responsibility:*** Non-market systems depend on tradition or force to encourage individuals to act responsibly. Shirking and cheating are often respected. People who get caught may be faulted merely for not having been smart enough shirk and cheat and get away with it. |

# Why Helping Yourself Helps Others

## Closure

Review the key points of the lesson. Ask:

- Who was Adam Smith?

  *(Adam Smith was an 18th-century philosopher, now regarded as the founder of modern economic thought. In a book titled* The Wealth of Nations, *he offered an extensive description of the principles of a market economy.)*

- What is the difference between self-interest and selfishness?

  *(While some people are selfish, all people act in their own self-interest. Self-interest for some might mean seeking money; for others it might imply other priorities. Being interested in money need not mean that a person is selfish or greedy. It could just as well mean that he or she wants money in order to obtain an education or care for a family or contribute to environmental causes, and so on.)*

- What values are encouraged in a market system?

  *(The values of the market include discipline, honesty, trustworthiness, tolerance, cooperation, courtesy, and enterprise.)*

- Why are market prices important?

  *(Market prices reflect the value of a good to society and the cost to society of making the good. Households and businesses use prices in making decisions about what and when to buy and what and when to sell.)*

- How can people acting in their own self-interest contribute to the social good?

  *(The incentives established in market systems encourage people unknowingly to act in ways that help others by providing them with the goods and services they wish to have at market prices that reflect the value of goods to the society.)*

## Multiple-Choice Questions
(Correct answers shown in bold)

Adam Smith recognized that the "invisible hand" works by:

A. Government rules forcing businesses to act responsibly.

B. People living by the golden rule.

**C. Individuals acting in their own self-interest.**

D. Charitable contributions to worthy causes.

Adam Smith recognized that in market economies self-interested behavior is controlled by:

**A. Competition.**

B. Government regulations.

C. Labor unions.

D. Greed.

## Essay Question

In non-market systems, it is difficult to depend on strangers to be honest. In market economies, people depend on strangers all the time. Why the difference?

*(Non-market systems rely on tradition or force to encourage individuals to be honest. But tradition and force often prove to be inadequate means of ensuring honesty, and over the long term people become inclined to trust only their family members and friends. It is hard to maintain business relationships in such a setting, where there are no sanctions enforced by consumers. While market systems are vulnerable to occasional scams and schemes, most business people recognize that being honest with their customers will benefit their businesses over the long term. Customers will not continue to buy goods and services from people who cheat and lie to them.)*

# Unit 4 | Teacher's Guide

**Unit 4, Lesson 20**
Visual 1

## WHY HELPING YOURSELF HELPS OTHERS

- Many people are skeptical of market systems.

- They fear that market systems foster greed on the part of unrestrained business people.

- Yet, many economists argue that markets are good.

- They say that self-interested behavior contributes to the social good, not to evil.

- *How can people acting in their own self-interest contribute to the social good?*

# Why Helping Yourself Helps Others

**Unit 4, Lesson 20**
Visual 2

## True/False Clues

People tend to act in their own self-interest.

True or False?

Self-interested behavior rarely results in good things for others.

True or False?

Market systems tend to reward virtues like honesty and tolerance.

True or False?

**Unit 4, Lesson 20**
Visual 3

## ADAM SMITH ON SELF-INTEREST

It is not from the benevolence of the butcher, the brewer, or the baker, that we expect our dinner, but from their regard to their own interest. We address ourselves, not to their humanity but to their self-love, and never talk to them of our own necessities but of their advantages. Nobody but a beggar chooses to depend chiefly upon the benevolence of his fellow citizens.

*An Inquiry into the Nature and Causes of the Wealth of Nations.* 1776. Reprinted: University of Chicago Press, 1976, p. 18.

**Unit 4, Lesson 20**
Visual 4

## ADAM SMITH ON THE INVISIBLE HAND

Every individual…neither intends to promote the public interest, nor knows how much he is promoting it.… He intends only his own gain, and he is in this, as in many other cases, led by an invisible hand to promote an end which was not part of his intention. Nor is it always the worse for the society that it has no part in it. By pursuing his own interest he frequently promotes that of the society more effectually than when he really intends to promote it.

*An Inquiry into the Nature and Causes of the Wealth of Nations.* 1776. Reprinted: University of Chicago Press, 1976, p. 477.

**Unit 4, Lesson 20**
Visual 5

## VALUES ENCOURAGED IN MARKET SYSTEMS

Discipline

Honesty and Trustworthiness

Tolerance

Cooperation

Courtesy

Enterprise

**Unit 4 Lesson 21**

# Productivity, Diminishing Marginal Returns, and the Demand for Labor

## INTRODUCTION

**Economics** *Productivity* is defined as the ratio of output per unit of input, for a given period of time. A high level of productivity is necessary for economic efficiency and economic growth. This lesson focuses on labor productivity, or the output per worker in a given time period. Many factors affect labor productivity, including the education, skills, and training of the workers, the availability of capital goods for workers to use, and the level of technology.

When capital resources are fixed, the law of diminishing marginal returns predicts that the productivity of labor will eventually fall as additional workers are used in the production process. Businesses rationally make decisions about how many workers to hire based on the value that an additional worker brings to the firm, compared to what the worker costs the firm.

**Reasoning** Marginal analysis is an important part of the economic way of thinking and economic decision making. Applying marginal analysis to the production process leads to the law of diminishing marginal returns. If the amount of capital goods is fixed, and more and more workers are added to a production process, eventually there is not enough capital to go around, so workers are less productive on average. "Thinking at the margin" requires weighing the additional benefits of doing something against the additional costs. Logically, the productivity of workers is taken into consideration when hiring decisions are made.

## CONCEPTS

- Law of diminishing marginal returns
- Productivity
- Specialization

## OBJECTIVES

*Students will:*

1. Participate in a production activity with fixed resources and variable resources.
2. Discuss factors affecting worker productivity.
3. Explain the law of diminishing marginal returns.
4. Apply marginal analysis to decide how many workers to hire.

## CONTENT STANDARDS

- Productive resources are limited. Therefore, people cannot have all the goods and services they want; as a result, they must choose some things and give up others. (NCEE Content Standard 1)
- Effective decision making requires comparing the additional costs of alternatives with the additional benefits. Most choices involve doing a little more or a little less of something; few choices are all-or-nothing decisions. (NCEE Content Standard 2)

## LESSON DESCRIPTION

Students produce greeting cards with a fixed number of scissors and markers, and a variable number of workers. They discuss factors affecting worker productivity and the law of diminishing marginal returns. With a partner, they use marginal analysis to solve a problem about how many workers a firm should hire.

*Time Required: 60 minutes*

## MATERIALS

- A supply of 8.5 by 11-inch scrap paper
- A pair of scissors, or one for each group
- Two different-colored markers or pens (e.g., one red and one black), or two for each group
- One transparency of Visual 1, or one transparency and one copy per group
- Activity 1
- A transparency of Visual 2

## PROCEDURE

1. Explain that in this lesson the students will gain a more complete understanding of the concept of labor productivity. Define labor productivity as the amount of output a worker produces during a certain time period.

2. Procedure steps 3-7 may be conducted in one of two ways. You may bring the students to the front of the room and have other students observe what is occurring, or you may divide the class into groups of eight to ten and have each group follow the instructions at the same time. The procedures are written assuming that one group of students will do the activity while the other students observe.

3. Tell the students that today is National Economics Day, a little-known but very important day of celebration. To commemorate this important occasion, they will make greeting cards to give to family members and friends, or perhaps to sell.

# PRODUCTIVITY, DIMINISHING MARGINAL RETURNS, AND THE DEMAND FOR LABOR

Demonstrate how to make a greeting card:

- First fold and then cut a piece of 8.5 by 11-inch paper into quarters. It is important that the pieces are equal in size and cut evenly. Tearing the paper without using scissors is not acceptable for a National Economics Day card.

- Take one of the quarters of paper and fold it in half to make a card. On the front of the card, write "Happy Economics Day!" with the black marker. Then draw a happy face above the word "Happy," using the red marker. On the back of the card at the bottom center, write the current year in numbers, using the red marker. Now the card is finished. Admire your finished card, noting that the inside is left blank for personal economics messages. Ask if there are any questions about how to make a card.

4. Round 1: Select a volunteer card maker to come to the front of the room. (If the students are in groups, each group should choose one card maker.) Also move a small table or desk to the front, and place a supply of paper, a scissors, and two markers on the desk. Tell the student that he or she will have two minutes to finish as many high-quality cards as possible. Appoint a very reliable timekeeper, and tell the student to begin. Tell the timekeeper to say "STOP!" at the end of two minutes.

5. After two minutes, appoint a quality control inspector to look at the finished cards and count how many cards pass inspection. (She or he shouldn't be too picky, and should count all cards that are finished and accurate.) Display Visual 1 and record the numbers for Round 1 (or appoint a student record keeper to do this).

   *(For example, if the student made four cards, write the number 4 in the second column. The labor productivity or output per worker during the two minutes would be four cards divided by one worker [4/1], or 4. Write the number 4 in the third column.)*

6. Round 2: Announce that now you will observe what happens when there are two workers using the same resources (the scissors, markers, and the same small table). Choose a volunteer to be the second worker. Clear away any unfinished cards, and provide a supply of paper. Begin the second round. Have the timekeeper indicate when the round is over, and have the quality-control inspector count the number of cards that pass inspection. Have the record keeper fill in columns 2 and 3 on Visual 1 for two workers.

   *(For example, if 10 cards were finished, write the number 10 in column 2. The output per worker or labor productivity would be 5 (10/2), so you would write 5 in column 3.)*

7. Repeat Procedure 6 for several more rounds, adding one person each round — until it is clear that crowding has set in and the workers are complaining about not having enough markers or scissors to go around. Be sure to clear away the unfinished cards after each round, and make sure that each round is two minutes long. Tell the students that you will now discuss what has occurred by inspecting the numbers on Visual 2.

8. Discuss the definition of labor productivity from the bottom of Visual 1, and discuss reasons for the changes in productivity shown on Visual 1.

   *(Answers will vary. Most likely labor productivity at first increased as more workers were hired. For example, when there were two workers instead of one, workers could specialize in one task. Later, as more workers were hired but the amount of resources remained the same, productivity probably fell because there were not enough resources to go around.)*

9. Ask the students what things would have made the workers more productive.

   *(Answers will vary, but the students should mention that the workers needed more capital — scissors and markers — to be more productive. Factors affecting labor productivity in general include having more and better resources to work with, having a more educated and skilled workforce, and better technology.)*

10. Emphasize the point that improvements in productivity are important for economic growth, and lead to higher living standards in an economy.

11. Refer the students to Activity 1. Tell them to pick a partner and complete the activity together. Walk around the room to answer questions and check the answers. When pairs of students complete the assignment correctly, ask them to help other pairs of students.

12. When most of the students have finished, display Visual 2. Call on students to explain the answers, and write the correct answers on the transparency.

*Answers to Activity 1 (and Visual 2):* Marginal product of labor: 4, 5, 6, 5, 4, 2, 1, 0. Value of marginal product: $8, $10, $12, $10, $8, $4, $2, $0. Diminishing marginal returns first occur with the fourth worker (because the marginal product of the fourth worker is 5, which is less than 6, the marginal product of the third worker). If the wage rate were $5, the business would hire 5 workers. The firm wouldn't hire a sixth worker because that worker would bring in only $4 in revenue, but would cost the firm $5 in wages. Note that the firm didn't stop hiring when it reached the point of diminishing marginal returns. The hiring decision is based on comparing marginal benefits and marginal costs. Also, the firm didn't hire only three workers, although the value of the marginal product was highest for the third worker. The fourth and fifth workers were also profitable for the firm.

# Unit 4 | Teacher's Guide

## Closure

Review the factors affecting productivity including education and training, improved capital goods, and better technology. Explain that U.S. agriculture has been successful in terms of productivity growth. Ask the students to describe factors that might have influenced improvements in agricultural productivity.

*(Factors that have improved agricultural productivity include better education and training for farmers, improved farm machinery and equipment, and new technology. These factors have led to higher yielding crop varieties, better practices for breeding livestock, and improved pesticides and fertilizers. Students may also mention that many farms are larger today than in the past, and that increased farm size may lead to more efficient production.)*

## Multiple-Choice Questions

### (Correct Answers Shown in Bold)

1. Which of the following is an example of the law of diminishing marginal returns?

    **A. The tenth worker hired to work on an assembly line contributes less to the total output of the assembly line than the ninth worker.**

    B. When making lemonade, it is important to choose the correct amount of lemons and the correct amount of sugar in order to make the most profit.

    C. A company should continue to hire workers as long as the workers are willing to work hard and don't call in sick too often.

    D. When the margins on a piece of paper are diminishing in size, the paper should be returned to the store for a full refund.

2. Maria Sanchez is trying to decide whether or not to hire a new worker at her day care center. The salary, benefits, and other costs of hiring the worker are $2,000 per month. Maria should hire the worker if:

    A. Hiring the worker would allow Maria to bring in less than $2,000 in extra revenues per month.

    **B. Hiring the worker would allow Maria to bring in more than $2,000 in extra revenues per month.**

    C. The marginal costs of hiring the worker are greater than the marginal benefits.

    D. The worker is willing to work at a job — such as staffing the day care cafeteria — located on the outside or margins of the day-care property.

## Essay Question

Define *labor productivity*. Describe factors that can make workers more productive.

*(Labor productivity is the amount of output that a worker produces during a given time period, such as an hour or a year. Some factors affecting labor productivity [mentioned in the lesson] are education and training, more and better capital goods to work with, and better technology.)*

# PRODUCTIVITY, DIMINISHING MARGINAL RETURNS, AND THE DEMAND FOR LABOR

**Unit 4, Lesson 21**
Visual 1

## NATIONAL ECONOMICS DAY GREETING CARD PRODUCTIVITY DATA

| 1. Number of Workers | 2. Number of Cards Produced (in two minutes) | 3. Labor Productivity (# of cards produced in two minutes divided by # of workers) |
|---|---|---|
| 1 | | |
| 2 | | |
| 3 | | |
| 4 | | |
| 5 | | |
| 6 | | |
| 7 | | |
| 8 | | |

**Labor Productivity:** The amount of output per worker during a certain time period.

(In the example above, the output was greeting cards and the time period was two minutes.)

# Unit 4 | Teacher's Guide

**Unit 4, Lesson 21**
Visual 2

## DIMINISHING MARGINAL RETURNS AND THE DEMAND FOR LABOR

The law of diminishing marginal returns states that:

*As more of a variable resource is added to a fixed resource, the marginal (additional) output from the variable resource will eventually decline.*

Example:  Output: greeting cards
Variable resource: workers
Fixed resources: 1 scissors, 2 markers

| 1. Number of Workers | 2. Number of Cards Produced | 3. Marginal Product of Labor | 4. Value of Marginal Product (Price = $2) |
|---|---|---|---|
| 0 | 0 | — | — |
| 1 | 4 | 4 | $8 |
| 2 | 9 | 5 | $10 |
| 3 | 15 | | |
| 4 | 20 | | |
| 5 | 24 | | |
| 6 | 26 | | |
| 7 | 27 | | |
| 8 | 27 | | |

Diminishing marginal returns first occurs with the _____ worker.

The selling price of each card is $2.00.

The only cost the business has is paying each worker $5.

How many workers would the business be willing to hire? _____

# Unit 4 | Teacher's Guide

## Unit 4 Lesson 22

## How Competitive Is the Industry?

### INTRODUCTION

**Economics** Competition is an important characteristic of market economies because it leads to lower prices, better quality in goods and services, and efficient allocation of resources. Even though competitive markets dominate the U.S. economy, some industries are clearly more competitive than others. Economists find it useful to categorize industries according to the degree and type of competition that takes place in each industry. Although in reality market structures take many different forms, they are often divided into four models: pure competition, monopolistic competition, oligopoly, and monopoly.

**Reasoning** The degree of competition in an industry affects the decisions made by firms in the industry. Purely competitive firms are so small relative to the total market that their output decisions cannot affect overall prices. Pure monopolies, on the other hand, face no competition and can charge the highest prices the market will bear. Although it is difficult, if not impossible, to find realistic examples of these "pure" models, understanding the concepts enables students to view outcomes of competition in terms of resource allocation. Studying these models provides a basis for understanding how businesses make decisions about how much to produce and what prices to charge, and leads to conclusions about the efficiency of markets.

### CONCEPTS

- Barriers to entry
- Collusion
- Competition
- Concentration ratio
- Monopoly
- Monopolistic competition
- Non-price competition
- Oligopoly

### OBJECTIVES

*Students will:*

1. Participate in a discussion about the benefits of competition.
2. Analyze examples of pure competition, monopolistic competition, oligopoly, and monopoly.
3. Work in small groups to identify the characteristics of these four types of market structure.

### CONTENT STANDARD

- Competition among sellers lowers costs and prices, and encourages producers to produce more of what consumers are willing and able to buy. (NCEE Content Standard 9)

### LESSON DESCRIPTION

Using a local example, students discuss the benefits of competition. In small groups they read descriptions of the markets for cucumbers, haircuts, cereal, and diamonds (prior to 2000). They use this information to fill in a chart that summarizes characteristics of competition, monopolistic competition, oligopoly and monopoly.

*Time Required: 45 minutes*

### MATERIALS

- Activities 1 and 2
- A transparency of Activity 2 (optional)

### PROCEDURE

1. Tell the class that this lesson focuses on competition. Market systems depend on competition to lower prices, encourage better quality, and force businesses to be efficient. Ask the students to give several examples of local businesses that have a lot of competition. Choose one of the examples (such as fast-food hamburger restaurants) and ask them how competition affects prices, quality, and the availability of goods.

   *(Competition generally leads to lower prices, improved quality, and increased quantities of goods available.)*

2. Announce to the students that they will take part in an activity to see how economists classify industries in terms of how competitive they are. Divide the students into groups of four; refer the students to Activity 1 and Activity 2.

3. Explain that one student in each group should assume responsibility for one of the cases in Activity 1 (cucumbers, haircuts, cereals, or diamonds). This student should read the case to the group and lead the group in filling in the corresponding row on the chart in Activity 2.

4. When groups have finished this activity, call on students to summarize their group's results to the class as a whole. (Optional: use a transparency of Activity 2 to record and display the correct answers.)

*Answers to Activity 2:*

- Pure Competition: *Many firms, identical products, no control over prices, easy to enter, no non-price competition. Examples: agriculture, stocks, and foreign exchange.*

# How Competitive Is the Industry?

- Monopolistic Competition: *Many firms, different products, some control over prices, fairly easy to enter, a lot of non-price competition. Examples: gas stations, fast-food restaurants, and dry cleaners.*

- Oligopoly: *Few firms, similar or different products, significant control over prices, difficult to enter, a lot of non-price competition if products are differentiated. Examples: soaps, cars, airlines, copper, and glass.*

- Monopoly: *One firm, a unique (different) product, significant control over prices, difficult to enter, non-price competition may exist. Examples: companies with patents and regulated public utilities.*

## Closure

Review the major concepts of the lesson by setting up a simple quiz-game. Divide the class into halves and tell the students to clear their desks. Ask a student on one side of the room a question from Activity 2, such as "Under pure competition, do firms produce similar or differentiated products?" If the student answers correctly, award that team one point. Alternate teams and continue until all the concepts in Activity 2, as well as definitions for *non-price competition, collusion, barriers to entry,* and *concentration ratio* have been covered.

## Multiple-Choice Questions

### (Correct Answers Shown in Bold)

1. A certain industry is made up of only a few large firms. These firms keep close watch on one another's prices and business strategies. They compete in part by doing a lot of advertising. This industry would be described as:

   A. Perfect competition.

   B. Monopolistic competition.

   **C. Oligopoly.**

   D. Monopoly.

2. Under perfect competition:

   A. New firms have a great deal of trouble entering the industry.

   B. Firms charge vastly different prices.

   C. Each firm's product is very different from the products of the other firms.

   **D. No one producer is able to influence the price of the product.**

## Essay Question

Economists agree that it is better to have competitive industries in an economy than monopolies. Think of a competitive industry in your area, such as fast food. (Technically the fast-food industry would fall under monopolistic competition rather than pure competition.) What are some of the advantages of having competition in the fast-food industry? In your answer, discuss prices, quality, and amounts of goods available.

*(Competition generally leads to lower prices, higher quality in goods, and more goods available. In order to survive in a competitive industry, businesses must produce high quality goods at prices close to those of their competitors, or they will go out of business. When there is competition, more goods are produced and sold at lower prices, as compared to monopolies. Consumers benefit from competition.)*

# Unit 4 | Teacher's Guide

## Unit 4 Lesson 23

## Make a Profit: Do the Math

### INTRODUCTION

**Economics**  The desire to earn profits provides incentives for people to start and operate businesses. A firm makes profit if its total revenues are greater than its total costs. Profit is thus the money left over to the business owners or entrepreneurs after they have paid the costs of their natural resources, human resources, and capital goods. In properly functioning market economies, competition prevents both profits and prices from being excessive.

Economists and accountants measure profits in different ways. In figuring profits, accountants subtract only the total dollar costs of the resources used from total revenues. In figuring economic profits, economists subtract the opportunity costs of all resources, including the best alternative income for the entrepreneur, from total revenue.

**Reasoning**  Marginal analysis is a critically important part of the economic way of thinking. In economics, *marginal* refers to one more unit of something. It is important to "think at the margin" because doing so allows us to analyze the effects of making changes. For example, if a firm is considering hiring one more worker, or a dance studio is thinking about offering one more ballet class, how will the added hire or class affect their profits? The answer to this question, and the determination of maximum profits in general, requires comparing marginal revenues to marginal costs. If, for example, the marginal revenue of offering one more ballet class is greater than the marginal cost, the dance studio should offer it. If the marginal cost is greater than the marginal revenue, the dance studio should not offer it.

### CONCEPTS

- Incentive
- Marginal analysis
- Marginal cost
- Marginal revenue
- Profit
- Total cost
- Total revenue

### OBJECTIVES

*Students will:*

1. Explain and use the concepts of profit, total revenue, total cost, marginal revenue, and marginal cost.

2. Work teams to determine the profit-maximizing quantity of output for a firm.

3. Apply principles of marginal analysis to decision making.

### CONTENT STANDARDS

- Effective decision making requires comparing the additional costs of alternatives with the additional benefits. Most choices involve doing a little more or a little less of something; few choices are all-or-nothing decisions. (NCEE Content Standard 2)

- Entrepreneurs are people who take the risks of organizing productive resources to make goods and services. Profit is an important incentive that leads entrepreneurs to accept the risks of business failure. (NCEE Content Standard 14)

### LESSON DESCRIPTION

Working as consultant teams, students use basic math to compute fixed costs, total costs, marginal costs, total revenues, marginal revenues, and profits (or losses) for a business. They determine the profit-maximizing quantity of output for the business, and analyze their results in terms of marginal revenues and marginal costs.

*Time Required: 60 minutes*

### MATERIALS

- Activities 1 and 2
- A transparency of Activity 2

### PROCEDURE

1. Pose this situation to the class and ask the students to respond to it: "A successful local restaurant is currently open for lunch from 11 a.m. to 4 p.m. The restaurant owners are considering whether or not to stay open longer, and to serve dinners also. What factors should they consider in making their decision?" Discuss the responses.

2. Write out several responses on the board, listing everything that would be considered a cost on one side of the board and everything that would be considered a benefit on the other side. Tell the students that in making this decision, the restaurant owners should compare the marginal benefits (i.e., the additional revenue they might obtain by staying open to serve dinners) to the marginal costs (i.e., the additional costs of the food, workers, and utilities). If the marginal (additional) benefits are greater than the marginal costs, the restaurant should serve dinners. If the marginal (additional) costs are greater than the marginal benefits, the restaurant should not

# MAKE A PROFIT: DO THE MATH

serve dinners. Tell the students that economists use the term *marginal analysis* for this process of comparing additional benefits to additional costs.

3. Refer the students to Activity 1. Read the description of Andrea's Software Business together. Use the information in Activity 1 (and the relevant definitions in the glossary) to discuss fixed cost, variable cost, total cost, marginal cost, total revenue, marginal revenue, and profit. Tell the students that they will now use this information to help Andrea figure out how to maximize the profits from her business. Emphasize that in this example Andrea is not choosing the price of her programs; she is choosing the best quantity to produce. (Advanced students may recognize that this example reflects a situation of perfect competition: Andrea can sell all she wants to at the going price, and price is equal to marginal revenue.)

4. Tell each student to choose a partner (or assign two students to a team). Each pair of students will act as a consulting team to help Andrea find the profit-maximizing quantity of software programs to produce.

5. Refer the students to Activity 2. (You may wish also to display the transparency of Activity 2 and work through a couple of rows on the chart to make sure everybody understands the computations.) Student teams should then work together to complete the chart and answer the questions that follow. They should make sure that both members of the team understand the answers. While the students are working, circulate around the room. When a team has filled in the chart and answered the questions correctly, announce that that team will now serve as a consulting team for other teams that may need help. Continue in this manner, allowing teams that finish to circulate and help other teams. When all the teams have finished, ask the students to return to their seats to discuss the activity.

6. Using the transparency of Activity 2, review the cost, revenue, and profit concepts and how they were derived. The discussion should bring out the following point:

   - Profit maximization occurs when Andrea produces and sells eight software programs for a total profit of $63. If she doesn't produce and sell eight programs, she is not making the most profit possible. If she produces only seven programs, her profit is only $62. She will increase her profit by producing the eighth program because the marginal revenue ($56) is greater than the marginal cost ($55). If she produces nine programs, her profit falls to $54 because the marginal revenue ($56) is less than the marginal cost ($65).

*Answers to Activity 2*

Total Fixed Costs: *$60 for each quantity.*

Total Costs: *$60, $105, $145, $180, $210, $245, $285, $330, $385, $450, $525.*

Marginal Costs: *$45, $40, $35, $30, $35, $40, $45, $55, $65, $75.*

Price: *$56 for each quantity.*

Total Revenue: *$0, $56, $112, $168, $224, $280, $336, $392, $448, $504, $560.*

Marginal Revenue: *$56 for each additional unit sold.*

Profit or Loss: *$60 loss, $49 loss, $33 loss, $12 loss, $14 profit, $35 profit, $51 profit, $62 profit, $63 profit, $54 profit, $35 profit.*

A. *Andrea should sell eight programs. Her profit would be $63. Marginal revenue for the eighth program is $56; marginal cost for the eighth program is $55. Producing this eighth program adds to her profit.*

B. *If Andrea sold nine programs, her profit would fall to $54. Marginal revenue for the ninth program is $56; marginal cost is $65. Producing this ninth program would decrease her profit.*

## CLOSURE

Review the **Rules for Economic Decision Making** on Activity 1 with the students. Emphasize the importance of using marginal analysis to make decisions. Have the students analyze the marginal benefits and marginal costs in decision-making examples from their own lives — for example, deciding whether or not to spend one more hour studying economics.

You may wish to point out that economists often state the profit-maximization rule by saying that firms should produce the quantity where "marginal revenue *equals* marginal cost." Of course, if marginal revenue were exactly equal to marginal cost, the firm would make neither profit nor losses on the last unit produced. The point of saying "marginal revenue equals marginal cost" is to emphasize that firms should produce up to this point and no further. If marginal revenue is greater than marginal cost, produce it. If marginal cost is greater than marginal revenue, don't produce it.

# Unit 4 | Teacher's Guide

## MULTIPLE-CHOICE QUESTIONS

(CORRECT ANSWERS SHOWN IN BOLD)

1. If a restaurant owner estimates that the marginal cost of staying open one hour later each evening is greater than the marginal benefit, the restaurant should:

    A. Stay open one hour later each evening.

    **B. Not stay open one hour later each evening.**

    C. Hire more waitresses.

    D. Serve more desserts.

2. Profit is defined as:

    A. Total cost minus total revenue.

    B. Total revenue plus total cost.

    C. Total cost times total revenue.

    **D. Total revenue minus total cost.**

## ESSAY QUESTION

A group of students is meeting to discuss the student store. The students buy goods from a local wholesaler and then sell them at higher prices in the store to earn profit. One student says, "We sold goods worth $250 in the past week, and that means we earned $250 in profit." Another student says, "Our profit wasn't $250! You're forgetting something!" Which student is correct? Explain your answer.

*(The second student is correct because profit is defined as total revenue minus total cost. The first student mistook the store's revenues for its profits. To find the week's profits, students would have to determine their total costs and subtract them from the revenues of $250.)*

UNIT 5

# THE VISIBLE HAND: THE ROLE OF GOVERNMENT IN A MARKET ECONOMY

Lesson 24   Government and the Environment

Lesson 25   The Economics of the U.S. Constitution

Lesson 26   Public versus Private Goods

Lesson 27   The Economics of Special Interest Groups

Lesson 28   The Economics of Voting

Lesson 29   Can Taxes Be Incentives?

Lesson 30   Poverty and Income Inequality

# Unit 5 | Teacher's Guide

## Unit 5 Lesson 24

## Government and the Environment

### INTRODUCTION

**Economics**   This lesson uses economic concepts to analyze some aspects of environmental issues. First, the lesson explains why markets may fail and how government can intervene to correct market failures. Because of positive and negative externalities, government intervention is necessary if we are to have a clean environment. Government should act to raise the price and lower the output of goods and services that cause negative externalities such as pollution. Government achieves this goal by forcing businesses and consumers to pay more of the costs of production. Government should also subsidize the production of goods and services, such as education, that cause positive externalities.

Second, this lesson uses economic concepts to analyze government failure. Students analyze why government intervention may fall short of its intended goals. Governments often rely on command-and-control policies to correct environmental problems. Such policies, no matter how well intended, often create new problems in which the costs outweigh the benefits. The Endangered Species Act is an example.

**Reasoning**   This lesson stresses three principles of economic reasoning. First, all choices involve costs. Government must consider the costs of pollution as well as the costs and benefits of pollution control if we are to effectively and efficiently clean up our environment. Second, people respond to incentives in predictable ways. Incentives explain why pollution exists and offer insights on how to clean it up. Ownership, for example, can provide incentives to protect the environment. Finally, economic systems influence individual choices and incentives. By changing the rules of the system, government can restructure incentives and improve our record on pollution control.

### CONCEPTS

- Choice
- Economic system
- Externalities
- Future consequences
- Government failure
- Incentives
- Market failure
- Opportunity cost
- Voluntary trade

### OBJECTIVES

*Students will:*

1. Define and give examples of negative and positive externalities.

2. Explain how private market activities can cause negative and positive externalities.

3. Explain why government intervention is necessary to reduce pollution.

4. Analyze the effectiveness of government policies designed to correct the negative externalities associated with environmental damage.

5. Analyze the Endangered Species Act.

### CONTENT STANDARDS

- Productive resources are limited. Therefore, people cannot have all the goods and services they want; as a result, they must choose some things and give up others. (NCEE Content Standard 1)

- Effective decision making requires comparing the additional costs with the additional benefits. Most choices involve doing a little more or a little less of something; few choices are all-or-nothing decisions. (NCEE Content Standard 2)

- Different methods can be used to allocate goods and services. People, acting individually or collectively through government, must choose which methods to use to allocate different kinds of goods and services. (NCEE Content Standard 3)

- People respond predictably to positive and negative incentives. (NCEE Content Standard 4)

- Voluntary exchange occurs only when all participating parties expect to gain. This is true for trade among individuals or organizations within a nation, and among individuals or organizations in different nations. (NCEE Content Standard 5)

- There is an economic role for government to play in a market economy whenever the benefits of a government policy outweigh its costs. Governments can provide for national defense, address environmental concerns, define and protect property rights, and attempt to make markets more competitive. Most government policies also redistribute income. (NCEE Content Standard 16)

- Costs of government policies sometimes exceed benefits. This may occur because of incentives facing voters, government officials, and government employees, because of actions by special interest groups that can impose costs on the general public, or because social goals other than economic efficiency are being pursued. (NCEE Content Standard 17)

# Government and the Environment

## Lesson Description

Students examine and discuss visuals to identify an economic mystery regarding the failure of the Endangered Species Act. They are introduced to the concepts of market failure and government failure. Using the **Guide to Economic Reasoning**, they focus on positive and negative externalities in analyzing the Endangered Species Act as an example of government failure.

*Time Required: 45 minutes*

## Materials

- A transparency of Visuals 1, 2, 3, and 4
- Activities 1 and 2

## Procedure

1. Tell the class that many Americans are concerned about the environment. They worry about air, water, and land pollution as well as threats to endangered species. Display Visual 1. Ask:

    - What action has the government taken to try to protect endangered species?

        *(Passed the 1973 Endangered Species Act.)*

    - What is the mystery?

        *(Why has the Endangered Species Act failed to protect more critters?)*

2. Display Visual 2. Ask the students to speculate about whether each statement is true or false.

    A. The government officials who enforce the Endangered Species Act are lazy. *(False)*

    B. Government polices sometimes have unintended consequences. *(True)*

    C. The Endangered Species Act offers incentives that encourage landowners not to cooperate in protecting endangered species. *(True)*

3. Before solving the Vanishing Wildlife Mystery, explain to the students that there is a role for government to protect the environment. This is the case when all the costs and benefits associated with producing a good or service are reflected in the price. Display Visual 3. Explain briefly the definitions of *externalities* and *market failure*.

4. Refer the students to Activity 1 and ask them to read it. Then ask:

    A. What are externalities?

        *(Externalities are economic side-effects. They are costs and benefits that arise from a given economic activity and affect people who are not parties to that economic activity. Externalities may be positive or negative. A negative externality imposes costs on third parties — as in the case of clean-up costs incurred by residents who live near a smoke-belching factory. A positive externality benefits third parties — as in the case of bees kept by Farmer Jones that pollinate plants belonging to Farmer Higgins. These external costs and benefits are not typically taken into account by the people deciding whether or not to go ahead with the economic activity in question and are therefore not fully reflected in prices charged by producers.)*

    B. Name at least two activities that involve negative externalities.

        *(Barking dogs, babies crying on airplanes, second-hand smoke, neighbors running lawn mowers at 5:00 a.m., factory emissions, auto exhaust, stench from a feedlot, and so forth.)*

    C. Name at least two activities that involve positive externalities.

        *(Painting the exterior of a home, maintaining a beautifully landscaped front yard, flu vaccinations, education, scientific research, and so forth.)*

    D. Why might governments choose to take action when markets produce negative and positive externalities?

        *(Governments may take action because not all the costs and benefits are considered by producers in the transactions in question. Government may take action to raise prices and lower the production of goods and services with negative externalities. Government may take action to lower the prices and increase the production of goods and services with positive externalities.)*

    E. Many citizens believe that education has positive externalities. Explain why this is so.

        *(Education helps people become more productive. Educated people are more likely to get a job, commit fewer crimes, vote, and have lower medical expenses.)*

5. Display Visual 4. Discuss ways in which government can help reduce negative externalities related to the environment.

    *(Defining property rights is an alternative preferred by many economists because property rights tend to reduce environmental problems efficiently. Most problems involving externalities are caused by a failure to assign ownership rights. They are "common pool problems." No one owns the oceans, rivers, air, or endangered species, so no one has an owner's incentive to take care of them. Finding creative ways to develop ownership is a powerful but underused approach to improving the environment. Here are some examples:*

    - *Individual Tradable Quotas (ITQs): A powerful way to preserve fisheries is establishing ITQs. Government establishes a quota for the quantity of fish that may be taken, setting the quota at a level that will sustain the fishery. Individual quotas are established at that level and are sold to fishers. Fishers can use the quota or sell it to others. Each fisher, in a sense, "owns" part of the fishery.*

    - *Trading Pollution Permits: Establishing air-pollution permits is similar to establishing fishing quotas. First, the government sets a standard for air quality. Businesses are granted flexibility in meeting the standard. If a business exceeds the standard (i.e., emits less pollution than the standard's permissible maximum), it can sell some portion of its remaining pollution permits to another business — one that will find it more expensive to meet the standard.*

    - *Owning Whales: Ownership rights could be assigned to whales by applying genetic tagging and using satellite technology. Conservation groups as well as "whale farmers" could purchase whale pods. Both would have incentives to preserve currently endangered whales.*

    - *Land Ownership: Ownership rights are now widespread which allow private conservation groups to bid on and own valuable habitat.*

    *Direct controls have been the government's main tool for improving environmental problems. Government often passes legislation demanding that businesses or individuals act in certain ways or face fines or imprisonment. Examples include pollution charges and emission standards. Command-and-control approaches are regarded as costly because no incentive is offered to firms to do better than the regulatory standards. In cases for which we are unable to devise market-oriented approaches, command-and-control approaches may be necessary.)*

6. Display Visual 1 and review the mystery. Refer the students to Activity 2; ask them to read it and answer the questions. Discuss their answers.

    A. What is the Endangered Species Act?

    *(A federal law intended to protect endangered animals and plants.)*

    B. What were the goals of the Act?

    *(The law allows government officials to deny landowners the use of their property if an endangered species is found to be present. The law makes it illegal to "harass, harm, pursue, hunt, shoot, wound, kill, trap, capture, or collect" or attempt any of these actions in regard to a plant or animal listed on the Endangered Species list.)*

    C. Why were the carrier pigeons destroyed?

    *(Carrier pigeons were hunted to extinction because they were not owned. There were incentives to kill them, but no incentives to protect them.)*

    D. Why does the Endangered Species Act appear to be a government failure?

    *(The Endangered Species Act creates incentives that encourage landowners to destroy habitat. By presenting perverse incentives to landowners, the ESA generates costs that appear to exceed the benefits gained in the protection of endangered species.)*

## Closure

Review the key points of the lesson. Ask:

- What are externalities?

    *(Externalities are economic side-effects. They occur when one person or group takes an action that imposes costs or confers benefits on other people who were not parties to the activity in question. The producer in such a case is unlikely to take account of the external costs and benefits arising from the action, and those costs and benefits are not therefore reflected in the prices the producer charges.)*

- Name a new example of a negative externality.

    *(Farmers using pesticides that run off into waterways.)*

- Name a new example of a positive externality.

    *(Government research into a cure for Alzheimer's disease.)*

- What are some policies government might make to reduce negative externalities?

    *(Individual tradable quotas, trading pollution permits, owning whales or other endangered animals, land ownership, direct controls.)*

# Government and the Environment

## Multiple-Choice Questions

(Correct answers shown in bold)

1. Which of the following is an example of a positive externality?

   A. **Vaccinations for pneumonia**

   B. Babies who cry on airplanes

   C. Auto emissions

   D. Bad breath

2. Government establishes a quota for the quantity of fish that may be taken, setting the quota at a level that will sustain a fishery. Individual quotas are established at that level and are sold to fishers. Fishers can use the quota or sell it to others. This policy is called:

   A. **Individual tradable quotas.**

   B. Trading pollution permits.

   C. Direct control.

   D. Charitable contributions.

3. The Endangered Species Act has had little success because of:

   A. Lax enforcement.

   B. **Perverse incentives to landowners to harm habitat.**

   C. Rewards to government officials to harass land owners.

   D. Lack of sense of mission for government workers.

## Essay Question

Pollution is an example of market failure. Because pollution is a negative externality, government should move to prevent it. One highly successful way of accomplishing this has been by providing polluters in some large cities with pollution permits. How could providing pollution permits reduce pollution efficiently?

*(Establishing tradable pollution permits improves the quality of the air but does it more efficiently than command-and-control policies. The government sets a standard for air quality. Then businesses are allowed flexibility in meeting the standard for their factory. What technology they use is up to them. If a business exceeds the standard [i.e., emits less pollution than the permissible maximum], it can sell portions of its remaining pollution permits to another business — one that would find it more expensive to meet the standard.)*

# Unit 5 | Teacher's Guide

**Unit 5, Lesson 24**
Visual 1

## THE VANISHING WILDLIFE MYSTERY

**MANY ACTIONS ARE TAKEN TO PROTECT ENDANGERED PLANTS AND ANIMALS.**

- Powerful laws such as the Endangered Species Act (ESA) have been in operation since 1973.

- The ESA allows government officials to deny landowners the use of their property if an endangered species is found to be present.

- Hundreds of plants and animals remain on the endangered list despite 30 years of legal efforts to help them.

- *Why has the Endangered Species Act failed to protect more critters?*

GOVERNMENT AND THE ENVIRONMENT

**Unit 5, Lesson 24**
Visual 2

## TRUE/FALSE CLUES

A. The government officials who enforce the Endangered Species Act are lazy.

True or False?

B. Government polices sometimes have unintended consequences.

True or False?

C. The Endangered Species Act offers incentives that encourage landowners not to cooperate in protecting endangered species.

True or False?

# Unit 5 | Teacher's Guide

**Unit 5, Lesson 24**
Visual 3

## EXTERNALITIES AND MARKET FAILURE

*Externality:* An economic side-effect that occurs when benefits or costs associated with the production or consumption of a good or service affect someone other than the direct producer or consumer of the good or service.

*Negative externalities:* Costs incurred by someone who was not associated with the production or consumption of the good or service.

- **Example:** Smedley operates a bustling auto body shop out of his garage in a quiet residential neighborhood; the clutter and traffic generated by Smedley's business detract from the value of his neighbors' property.

*Positive externalities:* Benefits provided to someone who was not associated with the production or consumption of the good or service.

- **Example:** Sigafoos paints her house and completes an attractive landscaping job on her lawn; these improvements increase the value of nearby homes.

*Market failure:* A market fails when:

- Too much of a good or service is produced, in part because the producer does not bear the costs of the negative externalities. Factories that pollute air are an example.

- Not enough of a good or service is produced, in part because the positive externalities are not adequately reflected in prices charged for that good or service. Education is an example.

GOVERNMENT AND THE ENVIRONMENT

**Unit 5, Lesson 24**
Visual 4

## WAYS OF CORRECTING NEGATIVE EXTERNALITIES THAT AFFECT THE ENVIRONMENT

**1. Assign Property Rights**

Most problems involving externalities are caused by a failure to assign ownership rights. No one owns the oceans, air, or endangered species, so no one has an owner's incentive to protect them.

Government can create several forms of ownership — e.g.:

- Individual tradable quotas
- Trading pollution permits
- Ownership of whales and other endangered animals
- Land ownership

**2. Impose Direct Controls**

Government can pass legislation demanding that businesses or individuals act in certain ways or face fines or imprisonment — e.g.:

- Pollution charges are taxes placed on polluters. For example, the government has placed a tax on chlorofluoro carbons (CFCs).
- Emission standards imposed on auto manufactures.
- Rules regarding curbside recycling.
- Requirements that factories use certain technology to reduce air emissions.

# Unit 5 | Teacher's Guide

## Unit 5 Lesson 25

## The Economics of the U.S. Constitution

### INTRODUCTION

**Economics** The U.S. Constitution is essentially a plan of government. Understanding how the plan functions and the values it promotes is important in becoming an informed citizen. That understanding should include understanding the economic institutions established by the Constitution. The U.S. Constitution provides a set of rules within which a market economy can flourish. The legal framework includes provisions for the protection of private property, the enforcement of contracts, and federal regulation of interstate commerce.

**Reasoning** Perhaps the greatest contribution of the writers of the Constitution is that, in a time of great uncertainty, they established institutions necessary for the efficient conduct of private economic activity. Those institutions have evolved to create a stable economic system that defined private property rights, reduced economic uncertainty, and protected individual economic freedoms. The Constitution thus created incentives that encouraged people to look to themselves rather than to government in their efforts to earn wealth.

### CONCEPT

- Market economy

### OBJECTIVES

*Students will:*

1. Recognize that the U.S. Constitution is an economic as well as a political document.
2. Identify the institutions of a market economy featured in the U.S. Constitution.

### CONTENT STANDARDS

- Institutions evolve in market economies to help individuals and groups accomplish their goals. Banks, labor unions, corporations, legal system, and not-for-profit organizations are examples of important institutions. A different sort of institution, clearly defined and well enforced property rights, is essential to a market economy. (NCEE Content Standard 10)
- There is an economic role for government to play in a market economy whenever the benefits of a government policy outweigh its costs. Governments often provide for national defense, address environmental concerns, define and protect property rights, and attempt to make markets more competitive. Most government policies also redistribute income. (NCEE Content Standard 16)

### LESSON DESCRIPTION

Students discuss why the American economy grew in the period following the American Revolution. After reading an essay by Douglass North and examining the U.S. Constitution, they identify the economic features of the Constitution.

*Time Required: 60 minutes*

### MATERIALS

- A transparency of Visual 1
- Activities 1 and 2
- A copy of the U.S. Constitution for each student

### PROCEDURE

1. Display Visual 1. Explain that after the American Revolution, it was not at all clear how the new nation would deal with the economic issues it faced.

   - Debt: The United States owed money to the French, to many of its citizens, and often others who had purchased war bonds.

   - Power to tax: The federal government could levy a tax only if the tax revenue was returned to the states on the basis of population. In other words, the federal government really had no way to collect revenue to pay for its own expenses.

   - Currencies: Congress issued currency and coins, but so did several states. In fact, foreign currencies were seen by many as more valuable than currency produced by the government under the Articles of Confederation.

   - Tariff wars: There were signs that tariff wars would erupt between the states. New York imposed a fee on vessels traveling to and from Connecticut and New Jersey. Not to be outdone, New Jersey imposed its own tax on a New York-owned lighthouse on New Jersey soil. New Jersey, lying between New York and Philadelphia, found its exports heavily taxed.

2. Ask: Why did the U.S. economy grow and prosper in the period following the American Revolution? Why didn't the United States collapse into squabbles over about taxes and trade as so often happened in Europe? *(Accept a variety of answers.)*

# The Economics of the U.S. Constitution

3. Explain that the economic "ground rules" established by U.S. Constitution have frequently been debated. Refer the students to Activity 1 and ask them to read it. (The author, Douglass C. North, is an internationally known economic historian; he received a Nobel Prize in Economics in 1993.) After the students have read the essay, ask:

   A. How did Adam Smith, through his book *The Wealth of Nations*, influence the writers of the Constitution?

   *(Smith had argued against mercantilism, a system involving government subsidies, bounties, and monopolies. Instead, Smith argued in support of specialization, division of labor, and free markets.)*

   B. In North's view, was the Constitution a document written to protect the interests of the founders?

   *(North acknowledges that certain features of the Constitution may have been in the long-term interests of the writers, but he finds this to be an uninteresting point. North argues that the real genius of the founders is shown in the provisions they wrote that made it difficult for legislators to redistribute income from rich to poor or poor to rich. In an environment in which wealth could not easily be taken from others by political means, people would seek to earn wealth through success in the private sector.)*

   C. Why is it difficult under the U.S. Constitution for factions or interest groups to redistribute income from rich to poor or poor to rich?

   *(The constitutionally required system of checks and balances among the legislative, executive, and judicial branches makes it difficult for one interest group or faction to gain control of the political process and redistribute wealth.)*

   D. What specific economic powers does the Constitution confer on the federal government?

   *(The Constitution provides that the federal government can levy taxes, coin money, and regulate its value. It gives the federal government authority over the conduct of foreign affairs, including the negotiation of tariffs and treaties. It gives the federal government sole authority to regulate interstate commerce. By specifying that contracts must be enforced and that private property may not be taken without compensation, it establishes the basis for a system of well-defined property rights, which are essential for a market system.)*

   E. Why might Adam Smith have approved of the U.S. Constitution?

   *(The Constitution permitted the development of free markets in the new nation. In Smith's view, this was essential to developing a productive economy.)*

   F. Ask the students to take a closer look at the economic features of the U.S. Constitution. Provide them with a copy of the U.S. Constitution, perhaps from a civics or U.S. history textbook. Refer the students to Activity 2. By reference to the U.S. Constitution, answer the first two questions together. When the students have completed the remaining questions, discuss the answers with the class.

*Answers to Activity 2*

### Question 1

How does the Constitution make it difficult for interest groups or factions to redistribute wealth?

**Answer:**

*The U.S Constitution established three branches of government that form a system of checks and balances, making it difficult for one interest group or faction to dominate.*

### Where is it in the Constitution?

*Article 1, Section 1*
*Article 2, Section 1*
*Article 3, Section 1*

### Question 2

In what body must bills for raising revenue originate?

**Answer:**

*House of Representatives*

### Where is it in the Constitution?

*Article 1, Section 7*

### Question 3

The writers insisted that taxes should be levied with the consent of the governed. Who has the power to levy and collect taxes and duties?

**Answer:**

*Congress*

### Where is it in the Constitution?

*Article 1, Section 8*

# Unit 5 | Teacher's Guide

**Question 4**

Who has the power to coin money?

**Answer:**

*Congress*

**Where is it in the Constitution?**

*Article 1, Section 8*

**Question 5**

What branch of government regulates business?

**Answer:**

*Congress*

**Where is it in the Constitution?**

*Article 1, Section 8*

**Question 6**

Some governments allow scientists to "own" their ideas for a period of time, to create an incentive for research. May writers and inventors be granted copyrights to protect their ideas? Explain.

**Answer:**

*Yes. Authors and inventors may have exclusive rights to their ideas for a period of time set by Congress.*

**Where is it in the Constitution?**

*Article 1, Section 8*

**Question 7**

The United States created an internal "free trade zone" among the states. May states levy taxes on exports or imports? Explain.

**Answer:**

*No. Taxes can not be applied to any good leaving one state for another.*

**Where is it in the Constitution?**

*Article 1, Section 9*

**Question 8**

Contracts are an important means of protection for private property. They require that people hold to their financial commitments. Courts enforce contracts. Does the federal government have the authority to abolish contracts? Explain.

**Answer:**

*No. Congress may not impair the obligations of contracts.*

**Where is it in the Constitution?**

*Article 1, Section 10*

**Question 9**

What branch of government has the power to make and ratify treaties?

**Answer:**

*The President has the power to negotiate treaties, with the advice and consent of the Senate.*

**Where is it in the Constitution?**

*Article 2, Section 2*

**Question 10**

Does "due process of law" (the government must follow certain steps or procedures specified by the law) apply to private ownership of property? Explain.

**Answer:**

*Yes. The Constitution states that people may not be deprived of their property without due process of law. Even then, people must be compensated for any loss.*

**Where is it in the Constitution?**

*Amendment 5*

**Question 11**

Can people be forced to work for others without compensation? Explain.

**Answer:**

*No. The United States Constitution makes slavery illegal.*

**Where is it in the Constitution?**

*Amendment 13*

# The Economics of the U.S. Constitution

## Closure

Review the key points of the lesson. Ask:

- Did the ideas of Adam Smith influence the writers of the Constitution? Explain.

  (*Yes. Smith's most famous book,* The Wealth of Nations, *was well known to the founders. In this book, Smith argues against mercantilism in favor of specialization, division of labor, and free markets.*)

- The message of the writers of the Constitution was that people should earn wealth on their own and not look to government to provide it for them. How did the Constitution make it difficult to redistribute wealth?

  (*The required system of checks and balances among the legislative, executive, and judicial branches made it unlikely that one interest group or faction could gain control of the political process and redistribute wealth.*)

- What specific economic powers does the Constitution confer on the federal government?

  (*The Constitution provides that the federal government can levy taxes, coin money, negotiate treaties, and regulate interstate commerce. By specifying that contracts be enforced, it creates the basis of a system of well-defined property rights, which are essential to a market system.*)

## Multiple-Choice Questions

(Correct answers shown in bold)

1. A key clause in the Constitution that helped create a system of well-defined property rights is the

   A. Statement establishing the Electoral College.

   **B. Contract clause.**

   C. Statement delegating powers to the executive branch.

   D. Copyright clause.

2. The Constitution discourages redistribution of wealth primarily by relying on a system of:

   **A. Checks and balances among the branches of government.**

   B. Spending originating in the House of Representatives.

   C. Regulated interstate commerce.

   D. Treaty negotiation and approval.

## Essay Question

The American colonies had been established during a period of mercantilism. This is an economic system that stresses providing special favors from government to people in business. For example, the government of Great Britain granted trade monopolies to certain groups and provided subsidies to encourage the production of certain goods. The colonies often benefited from these mercantilistic practices. What influenced the writers of the Constitution to resist mercantilism?

(*Adam Smith's book* The Wealth of Nations *had a large impact on the founders. The Declaration of Independence and the publication of* The Wealth of Nations *occurred in the same year, 1776. Smith argued against government subsidies, bounties, and monopolies. Instead, Smith argued in support of specialization, division of labor, and free markets.*)

# Unit 5 | Teacher's Guide

**Unit 5, Lesson 25**
Visual 1

## PROBLEMS FOR THE NEW NATION UNDER THE U.S. ARTICLES OF CONFEDERATION

- Debt

- Power to tax

- Currencies

- Tariff wars

# Unit 5 | Teacher's Guide

## Unit 5 Lesson 26

## Public versus Private Goods

### INTRODUCTION

**Economics** Private goods and services are ones that can be consumed only by one individual at a time. Public goods and services are ones that can be consumed jointly at no additional cost. Two concepts that explain which goods and services are best provided by government are *non-exclusion* and *shared consumption*. Non-exclusion means that it is difficult to exclude non-payers from receiving the benefit of a good or service. Shared consumption means that the consumption of a good or service by one consumer does not reduce the benefit to other consumers.

**Reasoning** When people can obtain a good or service whether they pay for it or not, they have less incentive to pay. If consumers have no incentive to pay the costs, producers will have little incentive to provide the benefits. Under these circumstances, goods and services will not be produced even if everyone wants them. However, government can provide goods and services when it is difficult to exclude non-payers and when the product or service involves shared consumption. Through taxation, government can require all citizens to pay for their share so that no one gets a "free" good or service. For example, everyone wants police protection. However, because it is difficult to exclude people from the benefits of police protection, government supplies the service to everyone, and everyone pays for it through taxation.

### CONCEPTS

- Free rider
- Non-exclusion
- Public good
- Private good
- Shared consumption

### OBJECTIVES

*Students will:*

1. Recognize that private parties will not produce goods and services unless producers have sufficient incentive to produce and consumers have sufficient incentive to pay.

2. Classify goods and services as examples of private or public, based on the criteria of non-exclusion and shared consumption.

### CONTENT STANDARDS

- There is an economic role for government to play in a market economy whenever the benefits of a government policy outweigh its costs. Governments often provide for national defense, address environmental concerns, define and protect property rights, and attempt to make markets more competitive. Most government policies also redistribute income. (NCEE Content Standard 16)

### LESSON DESCRIPTION

Students discuss the role of government in the economy. They complete an activity in which they classify goods and services as public or private.

*Time Required: 45 minutes*

### MATERIALS

- Activity 1

### PROCEDURE

1. Explain that the purpose of this lesson is to show why government plays an important role in producing particular goods and services.

2. Explain that the vast majority of the things we consume in our country are produced by the private sector — private business. Clothing, houses, books, apartments, cars, tools, office buildings, airplanes, toothpaste, medicines — nearly everything is produced by the private sector. But the government produces some goods and services. Examples include police and fire protection, highways, the criminal justice system, the public schools, and national defense. Ask: Why does the government produce some things and not other things?

   *(Accept a variety of answers.)*

3. Refer the students to Activity 1. Ask the students to read Part 1 and respond to the Questions for Discussion:

   A. What is the public sector?

   *(All the production and consumption activities of government.)*

   B. What is the private sector?

   *(Private producers in markets.)*

   C. What makes a private good unique?

   *(It conveys its benefits only to the purchaser.)*

   D. What makes a public good or service different from a private good or service?

   *(A public good or service conveys benefits to payers and non-payers.)*

# Public versus Private Goods

E. What is a "free rider"?

*(A person who consumes a good or service but does not pay for it.)*

F. What does non-exclusion mean?

*(A condition in which it is difficult to exclude non-payers from receiving a good or service.)*

G. What is shared consumption?

*(One person's consumption of the good or service does not reduce its usefulness to others.)*

4. Divide the class into small groups. Ask them to classify the examples in Part 2 of Activity 1. The following are possible answers.

| Good or Service | Public? Private? Both? | Why? Can non-payers be excluded? Does consumption by one person reduce usefulness for another? |
|---|---|---|
| Police | Public | When police squads patrol a neighborhood, for example, everyone benefits. It is difficult to exclude non-payers. Consumption by one does not diminish usefulness for another. |
| Flood control | Public | It is difficult to exclude non-payers from benefiting from flood control. Consumption by one does not diminish usefulness for another. |
| Gourmet coffee shops | Private | It is easy to exclude non-payers. If consumers could consume whether they pay or not, businesses would have no incentive to produce gourmet coffee shops. |
| High school education | Both | Consumers (students) can easily be excluded. However, there is an element of shared consumption. For example, the addition of 1 more student to a class of 20 probably will not do much to diminish the education of the original 20. Because of the overall benefits to society of education and because the private sector may not produce enough of it, we have chosen not to exclude people from receiving an education at public schools. |
| Movie tickets | Private | It is easy to exclude non-payers. If consumers could consume whether they pay or not, businesses would have no incentive to produce movies. |
| Severe weather warning system | Public | It is difficult to exclude non-payers from benefiting from hearing a siren. Consumption by one does not diminish usefulness for another. |
| Laptop computer | Private | It is easy to exclude non-payers. If consumers could consume whether they pay or not, businesses would have no incentive to produce laptop computers. |

## Closure

Review the key points of the lesson. Ask:

- What is the public sector?

  *(All the production and consumption activities of government.)*

- What is the private sector?

  *(Private producers in markets.)*

- What makes a private good unique?

  *(It conveys its benefits only to the purchaser.)*

- What makes a public good or service different from a private good or service?

  *(A public good or service conveys benefits to payers and non-payers)*

- What is a "free rider"?

  *(A person who consumes a good or service but does not pay for it.)*

- Give an example of a good or service considered to be a public good.

  *(Accept all plausible answers.)*

## Multiple-Choice Questions

(CORRECT ANSWERS SHOWN IN BOLD)

1. A public good is characterized by:

   A. Conveying benefits only to the purchaser.

   **B. Non-exclusion and shared consumption.**

   C. Conveying benefits to government officials.

   D. Efficiency and ability to pay.

2. Flood control is an example of a public good because it is:

   A. Attractive "pork barrel" legislation for elected officials.

   **B. Difficult to exclude non-payers from the benefits it provides.**

   C. A "free good."

   D. A "dead weight."

## Essay Question

In the United States, the deregulation of airlines and the attacks of September 11, 2001, created many problems for the airline industry. Some people have called for a greater role for government in regulating the airline industry. An extreme position would be that the federal government should run the airlines. Using the concepts of shared consumption and non-exclusion, explain whether the airline industry is best thought of as a private service, public service, or both?

*(Most economists would argue that the airline industry should be a private service because non-payers can be excluded from the benefits, and shared consumption is not likely — two consumers cannot share the same airplane seat.)*

# Unit 5 | Teacher's Guide

**Unit 5 Lesson 27**

# The Economics of Special Interest Groups

## Introduction

**Economics** Special interest groups have a substantial impact on the political system. Such groups can provide valuable services to individuals and elected officials by providing information and access. They also can generate substantial advantages or benefits for a small minority while imposing costs that seem small — because they are spread out over a large group — on other people. Voters may not notice the small increase in cost per individual taxpayer imposed by such programs and therefore may not take time to study the programs or call their elected officials to account for supporting them.

**Reasoning** The prospect of getting reelected acts as an important incentive for government leaders. Reelection depends on earning votes, a scarce "good" in the world of electoral politics. Elected officials compete with one another for votes and other resources. In these efforts, the support of special interest groups can be very helpful. Public officials may accordingly find it advantageous to work on behalf of programs favored by those special interest groups that seem likely to provide votes or other means of support in the next election, even if the programs in question are economically inefficient.

## Concepts

- Competition
- Incentives
- Interest group

## Objectives

*Students will:*

1. Identify a range of interest groups associated with various causes.
2. Identify the services special interest groups provide to individuals and to government leaders.
3. Analyze interest-group activity to determine how incentives might influence the behavior of public officials.

## Content Standards

- The costs of government policies sometimes exceed the benefits. This may occur because of incentives facing voters, government officials, and government employees, because of actions by special interest groups that can impose costs on the general public, or because social goals rather than economic efficiency are being pursued. (NCEE Content Standard 17)

## Lesson Description

Students learn about the diverse nature of special interest groups and read examples that show how incentives influence the actions of elected officials.

*Time Required: 45 minutes*

## Materials

- A transparency of Visuals 1, 2, and 3
- Activity 1

## Procedure

1. Display Visual 1. Explain that the U.S. Congress initiated farm subsidy programs in the 1930s in an effort to save small farmers from bankruptcy. Today, however, most government farm subsidies go to large farmers concentrated in a few states. Ask the students to speculate on why this shift might have occurred. Record their responses on the chalkboard.

2. In a discussion of the responses to the question about farm subsidy benefits, ask the students if they have ever wondered why politicians do not limit themselves to passing laws only when the laws are likely to benefit the nation as a whole. Why do our senators and representatives sometimes pass programs that impose costs on everyone but benefit only a few? Explain that the purpose of this lesson is to consider why special interest groups are able to receive special favors from government leaders.

3. Tell the class that many individuals belong to special interest groups. Display Visual 2 to illustrate the point. Explain that this list includes only a few of the thousands of interest groups in the United States. There are more than 20,000 people registered as lobbyists in Washington, D.C., and interest groups spend well over $1 billion annually on lobbying and related activities.

4. Address the point that special interest groups often have a bad reputation. If possible, provide current examples of newspaper editorials criticizing politicians for "caving in" to special interest groups. But if special interest groups are harmful, why do so many people join them, and why do elected officials so often support their causes? Pose this hypothesis: Special interest groups offer important benefits or advantages to the citizens who join them and to the elected officials who support their causes. To explore the hypothesis, ask the following questions:

# THE ECONOMICS OF SPECIAL INTEREST GROUPS

- What potential benefits or advantages do interest groups offer to the citizens who join them?

    *(Accept a variety of responses.)*

- What potential benefits or advantages do interest groups offer to elected officials?

    *(Accept a variety of responses.)*

5. In discussing responses to the questions above, display Visual 3. Elaborate on its contents to extend the discussion.

    *Potential advantages to elected officials:*

    - *Information:* In every session of Congress, thousands of pieces of legislation are introduced. The subjects vary widely: national defense, energy, the environment, health, welfare, jobs, education, and many others. Special interest groups provide officials with valuable information on complex issues associated with proposed legislation.

    - *Ideas:* Special interest groups usually understand how proposed legislation will affect their members and others. They can often alert politicians to alternative solutions to complex problems.

    *Potential advantages to citizens:*

    - *Diverse Interests:* In their backgrounds and interests, Americans are a highly diverse people. They speak various languages, practice more than 85 different religions, and trace their families to many different ethnic sources. They vary widely in the work they do, the income they earn, and the vision they have of a good life. Acting as individuals, some would find it difficult to pursue their interests effectively. By establishing or joining an organization of like-minded people, however, individuals enhance their capacity to represent their particular interests to the broader society.

    - *Effects of Government Policies:* As the role of government has expanded, many Americans have found that government policy affects them directly. Veterans and farmers are affected by benefits the government provides; business people in competition with foreign companies are affected by tariffs, quotas, and trade policy generally; people at risk of racial discrimination or discrimination based on disabilities are affected by civil rights legislation and judicial decisions. Many other examples could be given. In this environment of far-reaching government policy, the incentive to participate in interest-group activity is especially strong.

6. Explain that there are times when the political process tends to work in favor of special interest groups, even when their programs are inefficient or work against the public interest. Refer the students to Activity 1; introduce its content in relation to this point.

7. Ask the students to read Activity 1, Part 1. It describes a problem looming large for the people of Twin Lakes. To analyze the problem, the students should answer the questions at the end of the reading. Use the following preliminary questions to orient them to the problem:

    - What is the problem facing the citizens of Twin Lakes?

        *(Danger of the Muskies moving.)*

    - What plan have the local and state leaders in government, business, and labor decided upon?

        *(To build a new stadium instead of a proposed industrial park.)*

    - Why did the local and state leaders want help from the federal government?

        *(They needed an additional $50 million to build the new stadium.)*

8. Then assign the students to answer the questions posed at the end of Part 1; review their answers as follows:

    A. Who will benefit from the construction of the new stadium?

        *(People in local and state business, labor, and government all will benefit. The members of Congress from the state will benefit if their constituents know they helped to deliver the stadium.)*

    B. Will people in other states and communities derive much benefit from the construction of the new stadium? Why or why not?

        *(No — not unless they visit Twin Lakes or watch the Muskies on TV.)*

    C. If you knew that your taxes would increase by a few cents so the people in Twin Lakes could have a new stadium, would you protest the action to your members of Congress? Why or why not?

        *(No. The protest probably would not seem to be worth your effort.)*

    D. What do you predict will happen in this case?

        *(Twin Lakes might well get the federal money. The cost will be spread out over a large population, and the cost per individual taxpayer will therefore seem small. On the other hand, the concentrated benefits*

*will be great for people in and around Twin Lakes. The large number of state and local voters involved provides a strong incentive for the state's congressional delegation to work hard to deliver the federal funds.)*

9. Refer next to Activity 1, Part 2. Ask the students to read the examples in Part 2 and identify the incentives involved in the case of the proposed projects for Houston and Townsend. Discuss their responses as follows:

   - The Houston Subway

     A. Who will benefit from construction of the new subway?

     *(Interest groups in Houston, including labor, business, and government.)*

     B. Will people in other states and communities derive much benefit?

     *(No — not unless they visit Houston and use the subway.)*

     C. What do you predict will happen?

     *(There are many voters represented by interest groups in the Houston area. They would benefit a great deal, and the cost of the subway program would be spread widely among a much larger group of people. All this suggests that Houston's congressional delegation would work hard to obtain the necessary federal dollars.)*

   - The Townsend Dam and Reservoir

     A. Who will benefit from construction of the new dam and reservoir?

     *(Business and labor interests in Townsend.)*

     B. Will people in other states and communities derive much benefit?

     *(No — not unless they vacation in Townsend.)*

     C. What do you predict will happen?

     *(The effort probably will fail. Even though this project is of intense interest to groups in Townsend, and even though its costs would be spread widely among a larger group of people, the number of voters in Townsend is so small that members of Congress would have little reason to work hard to deliver the federal funding.)*

## Closure

Conclude the lesson by reminding the students that incentives influence behavior. People form interest groups because group organization offers potential benefits or advantages — to individual citizens and to people in government. At times, however, interest groups create an incentive structure that results in the passage of policies that are economically inefficient. Particular examples are always hotly contested, of course. Many people would agree that farm subsidy programs in the United States show how interest groups succeed in obtaining an advantage by means of the attractive incentives they present to government officials, regardless of the merit of their cause as judged by a public interest standard. Subsidy benefits, according to this view, are concentrated among a few farmers in a few states, while the costs are spread out over millions of taxpayers. The opposing view is that the farm subsidies benefit consumers broadly by ensuring an adequate supply of agricultural products at stable prices. These issues are amenable to economic analysis, as illustrated in this lesson.

## Multiple Choice Questions

(CORRECT ANSWERS SHOWN IN BOLD)

1. Interest groups, representing people who seek concentrated benefits, often influence the passage of inefficient government programs because:

   A. The prospect of reelection acts as a strong incentive to elected officials.

   B. The costs of government programs are often spread out over many taxpayers.

   C. Politicians are corrupt.

   **D. Both A and B.**

2. Elected officials often listen to interest groups because such groups provide:

   **A. Information about how government programs affect them.**

   B. Tax deductions to politicians.

   C. Illegal campaign contributions.

   D. Frequent flyer miles.

## Essay Question

In 1996 the U.S. Congress passed the Freedom to Farm Act. It was meant to phase out subsidies to farmers over a few years. But more recent legislation has strengthened farm subsidy programs. Some argue that the shift in favor of continued subsidies was brought about by a combination of factors including worldwide recession, natural disasters, and low crop prices. Based on what you know about incentives and interest groups, provide another explanation.

*(Farmers' interest groups have a concentrated interest in maintaining benefits to their members. These groups work*

# The Economics of Special Interest Groups

*hard to hold the attention of influential politicians. They seek to educate them about farm problems, and they propose means by which Congress might help their members. Elected officials compete for votes to gain reelection. They seek support and contributions from interest groups and their members. They know that most voters are not likely to notice the small cost per individual taxpayer that yields, nonetheless, a huge sum to be spent on behalf of a relatively small, concentrated group. Perhaps, for this reason, the Freedom to Farm Act was destined to fail.)*

# Unit 5 | Teacher's Guide

**Unit 5, Lesson 27**
Visual 1

## THE FARM SUBSIDIES MYSTERY

- American farmers collected $71 billion in subsidy payments from 1996 to 2000.

- While many taxpayers imagine that these funds are used to support small family farms, only 36 percent of all farms receive subsidies.

- According to the U.S. Department of Agriculture, 47 percent of subsidy payments go to large, wealthy, commercial operations farms.

- Almost half of the benefits go to farmers in six states.

- *Why would the United States government send payments to owners of large, prosperous farms when the farm subsidy was intended originally to help owners of small, family farms?*

**Unit 5, Lesson 27**
Visual 2

## TYPES OF INTEREST GROUPS

There are thousands of special interest groups in the United States — and more around the world. Here is a brief sampling:

1. Business and Corporate Groups
    - General Electric
    - McDonald's
    - National Football League

2. Labor Unions
    - AFL-CIO
    - National Education Association
    - United Mine Workers

3. Trade Associations
    - American Gas Association
    - American Farm Bureau Federation
    - U.S. Chamber of Commerce

4. Professional Organizations
    - American Medical Association
    - National Council for the Social Studies
    - Society for Human Resource Management

5. Political Organizations
    - National Organization for Women
    - National Association for the Advancement of Colored People
    - National Rifle Association

# Unit 5, Lesson 27
Visual 3

## WHY DO WE HAVE SPECIAL INTEREST GROUPS?

### POTENTIAL ADVANTAGES TO ELECTED OFFICIALS

- Information
- Ideas

### POTENTIAL ADVANTAGES TO CITIZENS

- Diverse Interests
- Effects of Government Policies

# Unit 5 | Teacher's Guide

## Unit 5 Lesson 28

## The Economics of Voting

### INTRODUCTION

**Economics**  Why do so many voters stay away from the polls on election day? This is a puzzle to many people interested in the well-being of our democratic system. Economists are among those who try to explain this outcome. They suggest that non-voters may be acting rationally: the costs associated with voting (taking time to register, rearranging work schedules, getting to the polls, gathering information on the candidates, and so on) may seem to outweigh the benefits (influencing the outcome of an election or gaining the satisfaction of being a good citizen).

**Reasoning**  In explaining human behavior, economists stress the incentives that influence behavior. In the case of voting, some incentives discourage voting. The cost in time and effort of obtaining detailed information about issues and candidates (e.g., by attending meetings, following debates, reading position papers) is so high, according to this view, that many voters settle for rational ignorance, relying on inexpensive forms of information about candidates obtained from media ads and conversations with friends. The cost of getting to the polls, similarly, encourages non-voting. If we favor encouraging higher rates of voter participation and improved voter knowledge about issues and candidates, we need to examine how to restructure the incentives at work in the voting process.

### CONCEPTS

- Choice
- Incentives
- Rational ignorance

### OBJECTIVES

*Students will:*

1. Analyze voting behavior by reference to the assumption that rules can influence people's choices and incentives.
2. Examine information about recent voter turnout in the United States.
3. Identify the costs and benefits associated with voting.
4. Suggest how incentives to vote might be reformulated to encourage broader voter participation.

### CONTENT STANDARDS

- People respond predictably to positive and negative incentives. (NCEE Content Standard 4)
- Costs of government policies sometimes exceed benefits. This may occur because of incentives facing voters, government officials, and government employees, because of actions by special interest groups that can impose costs on the general public, or because social goals other than efficiency are being pursued. (NCEE Content Standard 17)

### LESSON DESCRIPTION

Students examine a visual to identify patterns of voter turnout in U.S. presidential elections. They analyze the costs and benefits of voting and discuss how people's voting behavior is influenced by incentives.

*Time Required: 45 minutes*

### MATERIALS

- A transparency of Visuals 1, 2, 3, and 4

### PROCEDURE

1. Explain that the purpose of this lesson is to help students see how economic reasoning can be applied in the analysis of a wide range of human behavior. Specifically, this lesson allows students to extend their understanding of incentives by analyzing the economics of voting.

2. Explain that the level of voter turnout is often worrisome to people interested in preserving our democratic traditions. Display Visual 1. Ask: What seems to be the pattern of voter turnout in U.S. presidential elections?

   *(The pattern shows a low level of voter turnout ranging from a high of 63 percent in 1960 to a low of 49 percent in 1996. Point out that in non-presidential elections, the results are even lower, ranging from 47 percent to 36 percent.)*

3. Display Visual 2. Ask: Which groups of people tend to vote less? Why might this be the case?

   *(People who seem not to have much "stake" in society, such as the young or the less educated, tend to vote less than others.)*

4. Ask: What do you think might be the costs and benefits of voting? List plausible student responses on the board.

   *(Accept a variety of responses.)*

# The Economics of Voting

5. Display Visual 3. Explain the costs and benefits of voter participation presented there.

6. Explain that many voters who do go to the polls are not very well informed about the issues or candidates. Ask: What are the costs associated with obtaining information on the candidates? (Stress that most of these costs involve the time spent in gathering information. List students' ideas on the board. The following are a few possibilities.)

   *(Reading candidates' position papers. Attending meetings at which candidates appear. Reading newspapers. Reading news magazines. Watching special TV news programs about elections and the issues.)*

7. Tell the students that the concept of rational ignorance is used to explain voter reluctance to gather much political information. Display Visual 4 and discuss the definition of the concept with the class.

8. Invite the students to apply what they have learned about incentives for voting. Explain that an important goal of our political system is to encourage voter participation. Perhaps we can attain that goal by changing the rules to reduce the costs or increase the benefits. Ask: What might be some ways to reduce the costs of voting or increase the benefits?

   *(Ways of reducing the costs of voting might include:*

   A. *Allowing voter registration at the polls on election day.*

   B. *Developing electronic voting systems allowing people to vote from their homes.*

   C. *Allowing voter registration by mail.*

   D. *Reducing residency requirements for voters.*

   E. *Holding elections on holidays or weekend days.*

   *(Ways of increasing benefits of voting might include:*

   A. *Encouraging more attractive candidates to run for elected office, such as people known for their strength of character, bravery, or heroism.*

   B. *Nominating candidates with sharp differences on the issues.*

   C. *Encouraging more competition between candidates.)*

## Closure

Review the key points of the lesson. Ask:

- What is the pattern of voter turnout in the United States?

  *(The pattern shows a low voter turn out from 1960 until 2000.)*

- What are some of the costs associated with voting?

  *(Some costs involve registration, taking time off from work, time and effort spent getting to polls. Another cost is time preparing to vote; gathering information about the candidates takes time.)*

- What are some of the benefits associated with voting?

  *(The chance that your vote will make a difference and the satisfaction of doing your duty as a citizen.)*

- What is rational ignorance?

  *(In the case of voting behavior, it involves a decision not to obtain information about political issues or candidates because the costs of doing so outweigh the benefits.)*

- What are some ways to change the incentives associated with voting?

  *(Some suggestions include encouraging higher levels of formal education, allowing voter registration at the polls on election day, developing electronic voting systems, encouraging more civic groups to offer rides to the polls, and so forth.)*

## Multiple Choice Questions

### (Correct answers shown in bold)

1. Recent evidence suggests that American voter turnout is low — even in presidential elections. Using economic reasoning, how would you explain this?

   A. American voters are lazy.

   **B. American voters have decided that the costs of voting may not be worth the benefits.**

   C. Studies show that few Americans know how to cast a ballot.

   D. Reform is long overdue in the financing of presidential campaigns.

2. The age group with the lowest voter turnout is:

   **A. 18-20 years.**

   B. 21-24 years.

   C. 25-44 years.

   D. 45-64 years.

# Unit 5 | Teacher's Guide

## Essay Question

Penny threw up her hands in frustration when she saw the sample ballot published in the local newspaper the day before election day. She had been looking forward to voting for the first time. But she was shocked when she saw that the ballot had 15 races on it. She knew about the race for Congress and the Senate, but she had not heard of any of the candidates running for other offices. "Who are these people?" she wondered. The ballot also contained one referendum proposing a change in the state constitution and a second referendum proposing selling government bonds to build a new library. Penny knew nothing about these other issues. She decided not to vote. How would economists describe Penny's behavior?

*(Voters like Penny apparently decide that the costs of casting an informed vote are not worth the benefits. Voters are expected to cast ballots in many elections during the year. Often, each ballot addresses many races including local, state, and national campaigns. Voters are often asked to decide on referendums. The cost of becoming informed on each decision can be high; it would involve spending a great deal of time following local, state, and national events. Rational ignorance is the term used to describe situations like Penny's — when the costs of gathering information to cast an informed vote are thought to be too high.)*

# THE ECONOMICS OF VOTING

**Unit 5, Lesson 28**
Visual 1

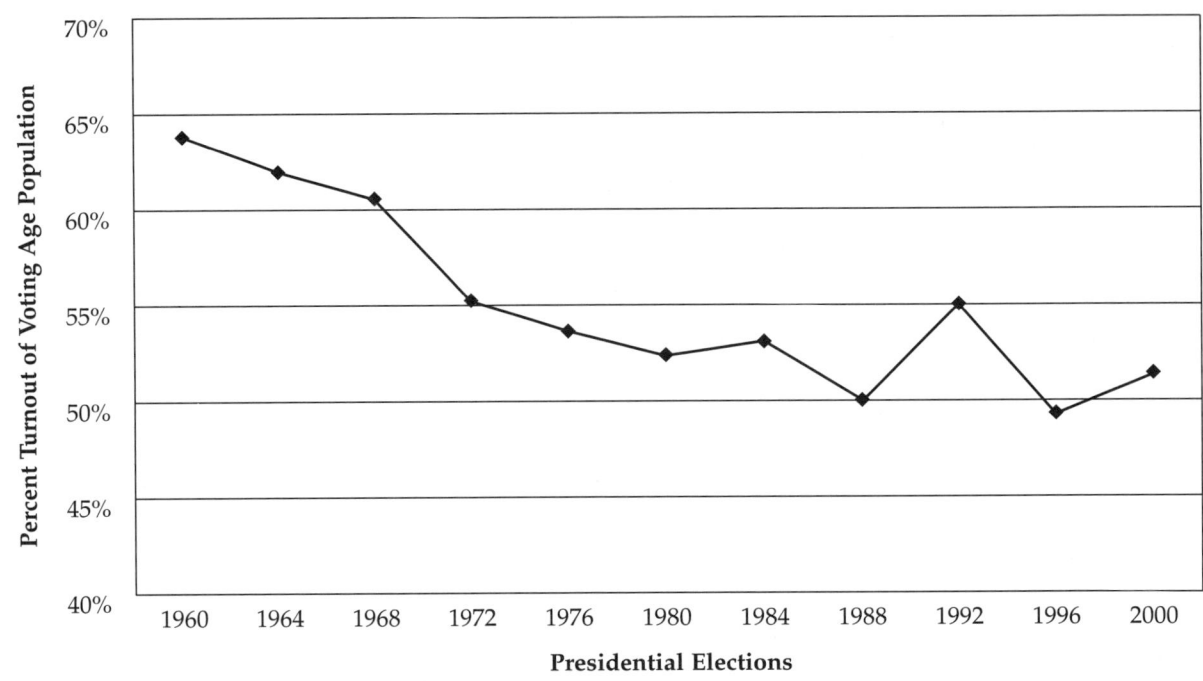

### NATIONAL VOTER TURNOUT IN PRESIDENTIAL ELECTIONS: 1960-2000

# Unit 5 | Teacher's Guide

**Unit 5, Lesson 28**
Visual 2

## WHO VOTES LESS?

1. People aged 18-20 had a voter turnout of 13.5 percent in 1998. Historically, young voters have the lowest voter turnout of all age groups.

2. Nonwhite citizens vote less than whites.

3. People with a college education are twice as likely to vote as are high school dropouts.

4. Unemployed people vote less than employed people.

5. Females are more likely to vote than males.

6. People living in the Midwest are more likely to vote than people living in the Northeast, West, or South.

**Unit 5, Lesson 28**
Visual 3

## COSTS AND BENEFITS OF VOTING

### COSTS

1. Voter registration: Many states require voters to register 30 days in advance of elections.

2. Time off from work: Elections are held on weekdays, so many people need to rearrange work schedules in order to vote.

3. Time preparing to vote: Voters may vote in primaries, local elections, special elections, and so forth. Ballots may include candidates for many local, state, and national elections. Gathering information about the candidates in all these races takes time.

4. Getting to the polls: Polls may be located in places that are not convenient for some people to get to.

5. Time in line: There is often a line of people waiting to vote at the poll.

### BENEFITS

1. There is a chance that your vote will make a difference in the outcome of the elections.

2. You will gain satisfaction from performing your duty as a citizen.

### Unit 5, Lesson 28
Visual 4

# RATIONAL IGNORANCE

A decision not to obtain information about political issues or candidates because the costs of doing so outweigh the benefits.

# Unit 5 | Teacher's Guide

## Unit 5 Lesson 29

## Can Taxes Be Incentives?

### INTRODUCTION

**Economics**   Different levels of government impose several different types of taxes and fees. The purpose of imposing these taxes is to generate revenue to pay for goods and services provided by government. Federal, state, and local governments depend on different types of taxes and provide different types of government services. The different types of taxes have different advantages and disadvantages. Economists have attempted to identify criteria for a fair tax. Four criteria commonly noted are the ability to pay, efficiency, simplicity, and benefits derived.

**Reasoning**   Governments depend on taxes for revenue. While most people agree that government is essential, most do not like to pay taxes. Two reasons are frequently cited. First, government has the authority to set the rules of the economic system. Within our system of laws, government is authorized to use coercion to enforce the rules. Since the exchange of taxes for government services is not voluntary, it may not be of equal benefit to all taxpayers. Second, the nature of taxation diminishes the link between payment and consumption. In some cases, individuals pay their taxes but do not see much direct benefit for their payment. In other words, the cost is obvious but the benefit is not.

Taxes are a cost. As such, they influence people's behavior in predictable ways. Changing the types of taxes or the tax level will encourage certain types of behavior and discourage others. For example, increasing or decreasing taxes influences people's behavior by encouraging or discouraging the use of substitutes for goods and services which are taxed.

### CONCEPTS

- Incentives
- Substitutes
- Taxes

### OBJECTIVES

*Students will:*

1. Recognize that governments impose many different types of taxes and fees in order to collect revenue.

2. Identify reasons why people might dislike paying taxes, including government coercion and the diminished link between payments and consumption.

3. Identify and apply criteria for judging what constitutes a fair tax, including ability to pay, efficiency, simplicity, and benefits received.

4. Recognize that taxes are incentives or disincentives that influence people's behavior.

5. Predict how people will respond when the incentive structure is changed by tax changes.

### CONTENT STANDARDS

- People respond predictably to positive and negative incentives. (NCEE Content Standard 4)

- There is an economic role for government to play in a market economy whenever the benefits of a government policy outweigh its costs. Governments often provide for national defense, address environmental concerns, define and protect property rights, and attempt to make markets more competitive. Most government policies also redistribute income. (NCEE Content Standard 16)

### LESSON DESCRIPTION

Students examine different types of taxes and criteria for determining a fair tax. Students work in pairs to predict how changes in taxes will change people's behavior.

*Time Required: 60 minutes*

### MATERIALS

- A transparency of Visuals 1, 2, 3, and 4
- Activities 1 and 2

### PROCEDURE

1. Explain that the purpose of this lesson is to analyze the effects of taxes on individual behavior.

2. Remind the students that public goods are paid for by taxes. Display Visual 1 and Visual 2 to illustrate the categories of taxes and spending (federal, state, and local).

3. Ask: Why do you think that people often dislike paying taxes? List the students' ideas on the board. Accept any plausible answers.

4. Display Visual 3. Explain the two reasons why people might dislike paying taxes.

5. Refer the students to Activity 1. Ask them to read Part 1 and identify criteria for assessing a fair tax. Display Visual 4. Use it to review the criteria of ability to pay, efficiency, simplicity, and benefits received.

# CAN TAXES BE INCENTIVES?

6. Direct the student's attention to Part 2 of Activity 1. Make sure that they understand the directions. Do the driver's license example together. Then divide the class into small groups and ask them to complete Part 2. After the groups have completed their work, discuss the results.

*Possible Answers to Activity 1, Part 2*

| Tax/Fee | Ability to Pay | Efficiency | Simplicity | Benefits Received |
|---|---|---|---|---|
| 1. Driver's license fee (a fixed amount for each driver) | - | + | + | + |
| 2. Personal income tax (a percentage of wages and salaries up to a limit) | + | + | - | - |
| 3. Social Security tax (a percentage of wages and salaries up to a limit) | - | + | + | + |
| 4. Sales tax (a percentage of the pre-tax retail price of covered goods or services) | - | + | + | - |
| 5. Property tax (a percentage of the property's value) | + | - | - | + |

7. Explain that governments have created many ways to raise revenue. The most common are taxes on sales, income, and property; fees and licenses also are important. Whenever government imposes a new tax or changes an old one, people may change their behavior.

8. Refer the students to Activity 2. Read the introductory paragraphs to the students. Emphasize that taxes act as incentives and that changes in taxes may encourage people to substitute one action for another.

9. Ask the students to predict how individuals might respond to Situation 1. Some possible responses appear below.

    **Situation 1:** Congress increases the federal income tax by 25 percent for all income groups. How might individuals respond?

    *(People would be discouraged from earning income. They might begin to substitute more leisure time for work time. People would be encouraged to cheat on paying their taxes.)*

10. Ask the students to work in pairs and write predictions for each of the remaining four situations. The following are some sample predictions:

    **Situation 2:** Your state raises the fee for a driver's license to $500 per person. How might individuals respond?

    *(People would be discouraged from driving. They might begin to substitute the use of mass transit or car pools. They might also substitute the use of other vehicles that do not require a car driver's license. In some states, for example, there are special licenses for operating motorcycles. People would be encouraged to drive without a license. Young people would be discouraged from getting driver's licenses.)*

    **Situation 3:** Complaints are increasing every year about tourists overcrowding the U.S. National Parks. The federal government increases the National Parks' camping fee to $50. How might individuals respond?

    *(People would be encouraged to substitute visits to private, state, or county parks for visits to National Parks. People would be encouraged to substitute overnight stays in motels for stays in National Parks. People would be encouraged to enter parks without permits and substitute the risk of being caught for paying the increased fee.)*

    **Situation 4:** Freeways are very busy and travel is slow during morning and evening rush hours. The state government decides to make the freeways tollways during the peak hours (from 7:00 a.m. until 8:30 a.m. and from 4:00 p.m. until 5:30 p.m.) by imposing a $5.00 fee per car at each entrance ramp along the most-traveled 10-mile stretch of freeway. How might individuals respond?

    *(People would be encouraged to rearrange work schedules so they could travel during non-peak hours. People would be encouraged to substitute mass transit and car pools for the increased fee. People would be encouraged to enter the freeway outside the 10-mile toll zone.)*

    **Situation 5:** Congress changes federal law so that homeowners are no longer permitted to deduct home mortgage interest from their taxable income. How might individuals respond?

    *(People would be discouraged from keeping or purchasing homes. People would be encouraged to seek other ways to "shelter" their taxable income. People would be encouraged to seek rented apartments as substitutes for owned homes.)*

11. Discuss the students' predictions in the whole group.

# Unit 5 | Teacher's Guide

## Closure

- Why do people often dislike paying taxes?

  *(Government coercion; diminished link between payment and consumption: the cost is obvious but the benefit is not.)*

- What taxes does the federal government charge?

  *(Individual income taxes, social insurance taxes, corporate income taxes, excise taxes, estate and gift taxes, customs duties.)*

- What sorts of taxes do state and local governments charge?

  *(Sales taxes, property taxes, individual income taxes, corporate income taxes.)*

- What do you think is the most important criterion for deciding what is a fair tax?

  *(Encourage the students to present reasons for any of the following: ability to pay, efficiency, simplicity, benefits received.)*

- Remind the class that taxes are valuable sources of government revenue and that they also create incentives that influence behavior. Ask them to imagine that the student parking lot is overcrowded. The student council and the principal decide that a $25 fee should be charged each semester to all students who want to park a car in the lot. How might some individuals respond?

  *(Some students might substitute riding the school bus or walking to school for the convenience of using a car. Some students might substitute car pools, rides with parents, bicycles, motorcycles, or the use of mass transit. Students who place a high value on the convenience of parking in the school lot, perhaps because of an after-school job, would probably pay the fee.)*

## Multiple-Choice Questions
### (Correct answers shown in bold)

1. A fee charged to campers for the use of state parks does not fulfill the principle of:

   **A. Ability to pay.**

   B. Benefits received.

   C. Simplicity.

   D. Efficiency.

2. The first internal tax levied by the federal government was a tax on distilled spirits produced in the United States. This tax was justified not only as a source of revenue but also as a way to discourage the use of alcohol. This is a case of using a tax as:

   **A. An incentive.**

   B. A device based on ability to pay.

   C. A device based on simplicity.

   D. A voluntary exchange.

3. A good or service that can be used in place of another good or service is a(n):

   A. Inferior good.

   B. Complement.

   **C. Substitute.**

   D. Economic want.

## Essay Question

Officials in your school no longer want students to bring backpacks to school. Rather than impose a ban on backpacks, they have decided to impose a $5.00 tax on each backpack students bring to school. What do you predict will happen?

*(Students would be encouraged to leave books or notebooks in lockers or at home. They would be encouraged to substitute briefcases for backpacks.)*

CAN TAXES BE INCENTIVES?

**Unit 5, Lesson 29**
Visual 1

## CATEGORIES OF FEDERAL TAXES AND SPENDING

### FEDERAL TAXES

- Individual income taxes
- Social insurance taxes
- Corporate income taxes
- Excise taxes
- Estate and gift taxes
- Customs duties

### FEDERAL SPENDING

- Social Security
- National defense
- Medicare
- Interest on the debt
- Health and human services
- Transportation
- Agriculture
- Education and training

**Unit 5, Lesson 29**
Visual 2

## CATEGORIES OF STATE AND LOCAL TAXES AND SPENDING

### STATE AND LOCAL TAXES

- Sales taxes
- Property taxes
- Individual income taxes
- Corporate income taxes

### STATE AND LOCAL SPENDING

- Education
- Health and welfare
- Transportation
- Civilian safety

**Unit 5, Lesson 29**
Visual 3

## WHY DO PEOPLE DISLIKE PAYING TAXES?

1. Government can coerce people.

   - Most economic transactions depend on voluntary exchange.

   - Government has the exclusive right to coerce individuals to pay taxes.

2. Costs are obvious; benefits are not.

   - Government spending of tax dollars diminishes the link between payment and individual consumption.

   - Usually, when consumers make a purchase, they see a direct benefit from the goods or services they receive.

   - When people pay taxes, the benefits (from national defense or cancer research, for example) are often delayed, indirect, or spread out so thinly that people may see little benefit from their payments.

**Unit 5, Lesson 29**
Visual 4

## CRITERIA FOR A FAIR TAX

1. Ability to pay
   - Proportional (flat tax)
   - Progressive tax
   - Regressive tax
2. Efficiency
3. Simplicity
4. Benefits received

# Unit 5 | Teacher's Guide

## Unit 5 Lesson 30

## Poverty and Income Inequality

### INTRODUCTION

**Economics**  Poverty amidst plenty is a persistent and perplexing problem in the United States, and one of interest to high school students. Income inequality can be measured by comparing the percentage of total income received by different quintiles of the population. The causes of poverty and income inequality are varied, and many studies have addressed their relative importance.

**Reasoning**  The **Guide to Economic Reasoning** tells us that people make choices, and that their choices have costs and consequences. In discussing why some people are wealthy and others are poor, it is important to point out that some causes of income inequality are the result of choices, whereas others are not. For example, most people can choose whether or not to obtain more education and training, thereby reducing the chances that they will be poor. Also, most people can choose to work harder or longer hours, making themselves more valuable workers and more likely to receive higher incomes. Middle-aged people — people with more work experience and skills — tend to have higher incomes than younger people. On the other hand, a few people are wealthy simply because they were born with talents that helped them to become great athletes. A few more are wealthy because they were just plain lucky and won the lottery. Others are poorer because they have experienced discrimination based on race, gender, or other factors unrelated to choice. Students should realize, nonetheless, that they would be unwise to overlook the importance of making good choices. The probability of attaining a high income by luck or good fortune is very low.

### CONCEPTS

- Causes of income inequality
- Income inequality
- Poverty

### OBJECTIVES

*Students will:*

1. Describe measures of poverty used by the U.S. Census Bureau.
2. Analyze issues related to income inequality in the United States.
3. Explain why equal distribution of income is not a goal of a market economy.
4. Analyze possible causes of and solutions for problems of poverty and income inequality.

### CONTENT STANDARD

- Income for most people is determined by the market value of the productive resources they sell. What workers earn depends, primarily, on the market value of what they produce and how productive they are. (NCEE content standard 13.)

### LESSON DESCRIPTION

Students take part in an activity that simulates the unequal distribution of income in the United States, based on U.S. Census data. They discuss how equal distribution of income would affect incentives to work hard, especially for high-income earners. They discuss measures of poverty, who is most likely to be poor in the United States, and causes of income inequality and poverty.

*Time Required: 60 minutes*

### MATERIALS

- 100 small items such as paper clips or candy kisses, divided into five small plastic bags as follows: First bag: 1 paper clip; second bag: 7 paper clips; third bag: 14 paper clips; fourth bag: 23 paper clips; fifth bag: 55 paper clips.

  *(Note: The paper clips or candy represent income, and the number represents the percentage of income received. You may use fewer than 100 items, but be sure to divide them into the percents shown above.)*

- Transparencies of Visuals 1A, 1B, and 2

### PROCEDURE

(Before class begins, compute the total number of points your students received on a recent test or quiz, divided by the number of students who took it. For example, if you have 20 students and five earned 95 percent, five earned 80 percent, five earned 70 percent, and five earned 50 percent, the total is 1,480 points. That point total divided by 20 yields an average of 74 percent.)

1. Divide the class into five equal groups of students. (If the number of students does not divide evenly by five, make the groups as close in size as possible.) Have the groups sit or stand apart from one another, but placed so that they can see the other groups. (Arranging the groups in a circle works well.) Tell the students that each group represents one fifth (a quintile) of families in the U.S. population.

# Poverty and Income Inequality

2. Announce that you are going to distribute items (paper clips or candy) to each group. The number of items will represent the amount of income earned by the groups in the United States in 1999, in percents. The income represents money earned from wages and salaries, as well as from dividends, interest, and employer-provided health insurance. It is income before any income taxes or payroll taxes are paid, and before any transfers are made to the poor for things such as social security, welfare assistance, housing subsidies, and food stamps.

   - Walk up to the first group and tell the students that they represent the poorest 20 percent of Americans. Announce that they will receive a bag with one candy, representing one percent of total U.S. income in 1999.

   - Tell the students in the second group that they represent the second-poorest 20 percent of the population; give them a bag with 7 candies, representing 7 percent of U.S. income.

   - Tell the students in the third group that they represent the middle fifth, which earned 14 percent of total income in the United States in 1999. Give the students in this group a bag with 14 candies.

   - Tell the students in the fourth group that they represent the second-highest income group, which earned 23 percent of total income in the United States in 2000. Give them the bag with 23 candies.

   - Tell the students in the last group that they represent the wealthiest 20 percent of Americans, who earned more than 55 percent of the total U.S. income. Give them the bag with 55 candies.

   - Make sure that the students in all groups know what the students in other groups received, and that there were 100 candies in total.

3. Write this information on the board*:

   **U.S. Family Income Shares (1999) Before Taxes and Transfers: Lowest fifth: 1 percent / Second fifth: 7 percent / Middle fifth: 14 percent / Second-highest fifth: 23 percent / Highest fifth: 55 percent.**

   *These figures and those in Procedure 4 are from the U.S. Census Bureau, www.census.gov, as reported in Microeconomics, by Campbell R. McConnell and Stanley L. Brue, Fifteenth Edition, 2002: McGraw Hill Higher Education, pp. 411-412. The figures are rounded to equal 100 percent.

   Refer to the numbers on the board and ask how the students in the different quintiles feel about their income shares.

   *(Answers will vary, but some students will probably comment that the poorest group or groups need more income, and that the distribution is unfair.)*

4. Write the following information on the board next to the first figures:

   **U.S. Family Income Shares (1999) After Taxes and Transfers: Lowest fifth: 5 percent / Second fifth: 10 percent / Middle fifth: 16 percent / Second-highest fifth: 23 percent / Highest fifth: 46 percent.**

   - Tell the students that the government redistributes income by collecting taxes and providing transfer payments. These new figures represent the distribution of income among quintiles (fifths) of U.S. families after taxes and transfer payments have been taken into account. If necessary, define "transfer payments" as payments given to people for which no goods or services are produced in return. Examples of government cash transfer payments are social security payments and unemployment insurance payments. Examples of non-cash transfer payments are Medicare and food stamps.

   - Tell the students that you will now redistribute income among the groups to reflect income redistribution due to taxes and transfer payments. Collect 9 candies from the wealthiest group and give 4 to the poorest group, 3 to the second poorest group, and 2 to the middle group. When it is clear that students are aware of the effects of the redistribution, ask them to return to their seats.

   *(Students may ask why the second-highest group doesn't contribute anything. In fact they do, but it is less than half a percent, so it doesn't show up in the rounded figures.)*

5. Ask how the students in the different quintiles feel about their income shares after the redistribution reflecting taxes and transfers.

   *(Answers will vary. Some students may say that the poorer groups are still too poor; others may say that the wealthier groups should be able to keep what they earn.)*

6. Ask what distribution of income they believe would be fair. Remind students that "fairness" is a matter of opinion. Record the students' suggestions on the board.

   - When a student suggests that income should be distributed equally (as someone most likely will), discuss the implications of this.

   *(If the paper clips or candy were distributed equally, each group would receive 20 pieces. Almost all of the redistributed candy would come from the wealthiest group.)*

7. Tell the students that you have been thinking that equality would also be a good basis for distributing points on their last test or quiz. Write the scores earned on a recent test or quiz on the board (the number of A's, B's, etc.); also write down the total number of points earned. Now divide the total by the number of students, computing an average of, for example, 74 points. Announce that whereas some students had earned grades of A or B while others had earned grades of D or F, everyone now will receive (for example) 74 percent, or a grade of C. Ask the students if they think that this case of equal distribution is fair, and why or why not.

   *(Answers will vary. Students who earned the higher grades will most likely complain, while students who earned the lower grades will most likely be happy. Those who earned the higher grades may say that they deserved them because they worked harder and learned more. There may also have been an element of luck involved.)*

8. Ask the students how your system of equally distributing grade points would affect their incentives to study.

   *(Probably all students, and especially the top students, would believe that they had less incentive to study, and overall grades would decrease.)*

9. Relate the example of equally distributing grade points back to the suggestion of equally distributing income. Why do some people earn higher incomes than others? How would equal distribution affect peoples' incentive to work?

   *(Answers will vary as students note, for example, that some people have more education, are more productive, work longer and harder, have new ideas, have job experience, live close to many businesses, experience a high demand (or a low supply) for what they do, are lucky, and so forth. Probably people would not work as hard — especially those who are most productive — if they knew they would not benefit as much from their work. In discussing these remarks, emphasize that absolute income equality is not a goal of market systems, since the rules needed to ensure such equality would affect people's incentive to work and also people's property rights. You may choose at this point to relate the discussion to problems of low productivity and shoddy goods in the former Soviet Union, where wages were determined by government rules rather than market forces.)*

10. Tell the students that, in measuring income inequality, economists use the same measures used with the paper clip or candy distribution activity: They look at the percentages of income going to different quintiles of the population.

11. Display Visual 1A and Visual 1B and discuss the content with the students. Discussion may include the following points:

    - *The definition of poverty is problematic. For example, it is much more expensive to live in San Francisco than in rural Kansas, yet the income levels used to define poverty are the same for both places.*

    - *Most of the poor in the United States (14.6 million out of 31.1 million) are White; however, higher percentages of Blacks, Asians and Pacific Islanders, and Hispanics are poor.*

    - *Blacks and Hispanics are about twice as likely to be poor as members of other racial groups.*

    - *Over a third (31,139 divided by 11,633) of the poor in the United States are children under age 18.*

    - *Families headed by a female without a husband present are more than five times as likely to be poor as families headed by married couples.*

    - *The higher the education level of the head of the household, the less likely it is that the household will be poor.*

12. Ask the students to speculate about why some people are poor. Write their suggestions on the board. Display Visual 2; compare the list shown there to the students' suggestions. Discuss each of the factors listed as a possible cause of income inequality and poverty. The discussion may include ideas such as these:

    - *In general, a lack of education and training result in a lack of skills and in low-paying jobs.*

    - *Those with more skills and more experience and those who work harder are more valuable to employers and are thus more likely to receive higher wages and salaries.*

    - *People who are middle-aged earn more income than people who are young or old.*

    - *Some people are luckier than others. Some are born with special talents for sports or singing or mathematics; others are not. Some people inherit money or (a very few) win the lottery.*

    - *Many studies of the effects of discrimination conclude that discrimination accounts for some of the differences in pay between men and women, and between whites and minorities. However, the differences also derive in part from factors other than discrimination, such as more work experience or more education.*

    - *Some people — members of labor unions, for example — may receive higher wages because they enjoy strong bargaining power. Or some people may be good bargainers on their own.*

# POVERTY AND INCOME INEQUALITY

## CLOSURE

Summarize the main points of the lesson. Ask:

- According to the U.S. Census Bureau, and accounting for taxes and transfer payments, how is income divided in the United States?

    *(Lowest fifth, 5 percent; second-lowest fifth: 10 percent, middle fifth: 16 percent, second-highest fifth, 23.0 percent; highest fifth, 46 percent.)*

- How is poverty defined?

    *(Money income levels are set. If a family's income is below these levels, the family is considered to be in poverty.)*

- What explains income inequality?

    *(Factors about which people can often make choices, including educational attainment and work-related skills; also factors about which people cannot choose, including talent, luck, and race- or gender-based discrimination.)*

## MULTIPLE CHOICE QUESTIONS

### (CORRECT ANSWERS SHOWN IN BOLD)

1. According to the U.S. Census Bureau's definition of poverty, about _____ percent of the overall U.S. population is poor.

    A. 1 percent

    **B. 11 percent**

    C. 23 percent

    D. 48 percent

2. According to U.S. Census Bureau figures, which of the following statements is true, after taxes and transfer payments are considered?

    A. The lowest 20 percent of U.S. households receive about 25 percent of total income in the United States.

    **B. The wealthiest 20 percent of U.S. households receive almost half of total income in the United States.**

    C. The wealthiest 5 percent of households receive almost 70 percent of the income.

    D. The lowest 20 percent of households receive 20 percent of the total income.

## ESSAY QUESTION

Many factors determine why some people are poor and others are not. In a short essay, list at least five of these factors, and state which you think is most important. Explain the reasons for your choice.

*(As noted on Visual 2, possible factors include education and training, work hours and work effort, work experience, discrimination, inherited wealth, and luck. Answers for which is most important will vary, and will depend on student opinions.)*

**Unit 5, Lesson 30**
Visual 1A

## POVERTY IN THE UNITED STATES*

### HOW IS POVERTY DEFINED?

The U.S. Census Bureau uses a set of money income levels that vary by family size to decide who is poor. (The amounts do not vary geographically.) If a family's income is less than these levels, everyone in the family is considered to be poor.

Here are some examples:

- Family of two with one child under 18:     $11,869

- Family of four with two children under 18:   $17,463

- Family of six with four children under 18:   $23,009

*Source: U.S. Census Bureau, Current Population Reports: *Poverty in the United States: 2000* (www.census.gov.).

POVERTY AND INCOME INEQUALITY

**Unit 5, Lesson 30**
Visual 1B

## POVERTY IN THE UNITED STATES*

### HOW MANY PEOPLE ARE POOR, AND WHO ARE THEY?

|  | Poverty Rate (% of poor, by group) | Number of Poor (rounded to nearest 1,000) |
|---|---|---|
| **OVERALL U.S. POPULATION** | 11.3 | 31,139,000 |
| **RACE:** | | |
| White, Non-Hispanic | 7.5 | 14,572,000 |
| Black | 22.1 | 7,901,000 |
| Asian, Pacific Islander | 10.8 | 1,226,000 |
| Hispanic** | 21.2 | 7,155,000 |
| **AGE:** | | |
| Under 18 years | 16.2 | 11,633,000 |
| 18 - 64 years | 9.4 | 16,146,000 |
| 65 and over | 10.2 | 3,360,000 |
| **TYPE OF FAMILY:** | | |
| Married couple | 4.7 | 2,638,000 |
| Female head of family, no husband present | 24.7 | 3,099,000 |
| **EDUCATION of HEAD OF HOUSEHOLD (all races):** | | |
| No high school diploma | 21.7 | 2,247,000 |
| High school diploma | 9.1 | 1,980,000 |
| Some college | 5.9 | 1,078,000 |
| College graduate or more | 2.1 | 391,000 |

*Source: U.S. Census Bureau, Current Population Reports: *Poverty in the United States: 2000* (www.census.gov.). Education statistics are from *Statistical Abstract of the United States 2001*, p. 445.

** Hispanics may be of any race.

# Unit 5 | Teacher's Guide

**Unit 5, Lesson 30**
Visual 2

## CAUSES OF INCOME INEQUALITY

- Education and Training
- Work Hours and Work Effort
- Work Experience
- Age
- Discrimination
- Inherited Wealth
- Bargaining Power
- Inherited Mental and Physical Talents
- Luck

# Unit 6

# The Macroeconomy

Lesson 31  Measuring Unemployment: A Labor Market Mystery
Lesson 32  The Effects of Inflation
Lesson 33  Gross Domestic Product (GDP) and How to Measure It
Lesson 34  Money and Monetary Policy
Lesson 35  Fiscal Policy: A Two-Act Play
Lesson 36  Should We Worry about the National Debt?
Lesson 37  Can Government Manage the National Economy?
Lesson 38  Aggregate Demand and Aggregate Supply

# Unit 6 | Teacher's Guide

## Unit 6 Lesson 31

## Measuring Unemployment: A Labor Market Mystery

### INTRODUCTION

**Economics** The rate of unemployment is one of the indicators or signals we examine to decide how well the economy is performing. Measuring unemployment is done by the Bureau of Labor Statistics (BLS), the principal fact-finding agency in the United States for labor statistics. The BLS conducts a monthly survey called the Current Population Survey (CPS) to measure the extent of unemployment in the country. The CPS has been conducted in the United States every month since 1940 when it began as a Work Projects Administration project. The basic concepts involved in identifying the employed and unemployed are quite simple: People with jobs are classified as employed. People who are jobless, looking for jobs, and available for work are classified as unemployed. People who are neither employed nor unemployed are classified as not in the labor force.

**Reasoning** Workers and employers make choices regarding employment. These choices are influenced by incentives. These choices ultimately influence changes in labor markets. For example, employers make choices about hiring workers. If employers think their businesses will expand, they may be interested in hiring more workers. If they think their businesses will contract, they decide to let workers go. When workers think their job prospects are good, they might choose to enter the job market and look for a job. If workers think that their job prospects are poor, they might choose to leave the labor market entirely. The results of these choices can sometimes produce unexpected measurement outcomes. For example, the number of people classified as unemployed can increase at the same time that the number of people classified as employed increases.

### CONCEPTS

- Choice
- Employment rate
- Incentives
- Labor force
- Unemployment rate

### OBJECTIVES

*Students will:*

1. Identify measures of employment and unemployment.
2. Explain how labor market conditions change in light of choices made by employers and workers.

### CONTENT STANDARD

- A nation's overall levels of income, employment, and prices are determined by the interaction of spending and production decisions made by all households, firms, government agencies, and others in the economy. (NCEE Content Standard 18)

### LESSON DESCRIPTION

Students examine an economic mystery regarding employment and unemployment statistics. They learn how the Bureau of Labor Statistics measures employment and unemployment. They use the **Guide to Economic Reasoning** and some arithmetic to solve the mystery of how employment and unemployment can increase at the same time.

*Time Required: 45 minutes*

### MATERIALS

- A transparency of Visuals 1, 2, 3, and 4
- Activity 1

### PROCEDURE

1. Tell the class that jobs are a concern to many Americans. Most people rely on a job to earn an income. The loss of a job is often a devastating event for an individual or a family. Display Visual 1 and discuss recent changes in the unemployment rate.

2. Display Visual 2. Discuss the information reported by the Bureau of Labor Statistics. Ask: How can the unemployment rate increase at the same time that more people are getting jobs?

   *(Accept a variety of answers.)*

3. Display Visual 3. Ask the students to speculate about whether each statement is true or false.

   A. Employed people are people with jobs. *(True)*

   B. Unemployed people are people without jobs. *(False)*

   C. The civilian labor force is the number of people aged 16 years and older who are not in the armed forces. *(False)*

4. Display Visual 4. Explain briefly the definitions of *employment, civilian labor force*, and *unemployment rate*.

5. Refer the students to Activity 1 and ask them to read it. Then ask:

   A. What agency measures the unemployment rate?

   *(The Bureau of Labor Statistics.)*

CAPSTONE: EXEMPLARY LESSONS FOR HIGH SCHOOL ECONOMICS @ NATIONAL COUNCIL ON ECONOMIC EDUCATION, NEW YORK, NY

# Measuring Unemployment: A Labor Market Mystery

B. Who gets classified as employed?

*(The Bureau of Labor Statistics classifies people with jobs as employed. People are considered employed if they did any work at all for pay during the week in which the Current Population Survey was conducted.)*

C. Who gets classified as being in the labor force?

*(To be counted as in the labor force, individuals must be aged 16 years and over. They must also have a job or be actively looking for a job.)*

D. How is the unemployment rate calculated?

*(The unemployment rate equals the total number of unemployed persons divided by the total number of people in the labor force.)*

E. How can the unemployment rate increase at the same time that employment is increasing?

*(If the total number of individuals entering the civilian labor force increases more rapidly than the number of people obtaining jobs, both the unemployment rate and the number of people with jobs can increase.)*

## Closure

Review the key points of the lesson. Ask:

- What agency measures and reports the employment and unemployment statistics?

  *(The Bureau of Labor Statistics.)*

- Who gets classified as being in the labor force?

  *(To be counted as in the labor force, individuals must be aged 16 years and over. They must also have a job or be actively looking for a job.)*

- If I am sick on the day that the people from the BLS call, am in the labor force?

  *(Yes. People who are ill and miss work are still counted as being in the labor force.)*

- If I am in jail, am I in the labor force?

  *(No. People in the labor force are not in institutions like prisons.)*

- If I am a stay-at-home parent, am I in the labor force?

  *(No.)*

- If I have just graduated from high school and have begun looking for a job, without success, am I in the labor force?

  *(Yes.)*

- How is the unemployment rate calculated?

  *(The unemployment rate equals the total number of unemployed persons divided by the total number of people in the labor force.)*

## Multiple-Choice Questions

### (Correct answers shown in bold)

1. The government agency that measures unemployment is the:

   A. Government Accounting Office.

   B. Census Bureau.

   **C. Bureau of Labor Statistics.**

   D. Unemployment Bureau.

2. Individuals are classified as unemployed if they:

   **A. Do not have a job, have actively looked for work in the prior four weeks, and are currently available for work.**

   B. Do not have a job and are actively looking.

   C. Have a part-time job.

   D. Were ill the day that survey was taken.

3. The unemployment rate equals the:

   **A. Total number of unemployed persons divided by the total number of people in the labor force.**

   B. Total number of people in the labor force divided by the number of unemployed.

   C. Total people employed minus total unemployed.

   D. Total people unemployed minus total employed.

## Essay Question

The civilian labor force is the number of people aged 16 years and older who are not in the armed forces. They must also have a job or be actively looking for a job. Can a person who is retired be counted in the labor force? Can a full-time student be counted in the labor force?

*(Retired people and students are typically not counted as in the labor force. However, if retired people accept jobs, they are counted in the labor force. Similarly, if students accept jobs, they also would be counted in the labor force.)*

# Unit 6 | Teacher's Guide

**Unit 6, Lesson 31**
Visual 1

## Annual Unemployment Rates

| Year | Annual Unemployment Rate |
|------|--------------------------|
| 1990 | 5.6 |
| 1991 | 6.8 |
| 1992 | 7.5 |
| 1993 | 6.9 |
| 1994 | 6.1 |
| 1995 | 5.6 |
| 1996 | 5.4 |
| 1997 | 4.9 |
| 1998 | 4.5 |
| 1999 | 4.2 |
| 2000 | 4.0 |
| 2001 | 4.8 |
| 2002 | 5.8 |

Source: U.S. Department of Labor, Bureau of Labor Statistics

**Unit 6, Lesson 31**
Visual 2

## MEASURING UNEMPLOYMENT: A LABOR MARKET MYSTERY, JANUARY 2001

### THE BUREAU OF LABOR STATISTICS REPORTED TODAY THAT:

- Unemployment increased in January.

- The number of unemployed rose by about 300,000 to nearly 6.0 million, pushing the unemployment rate from 4.0 to 4.2 percent.

- Payroll employment rose by 268,000 jobs.

- Construction employment alone increased by 145,000.

- *How can the unemployment rate increase when more people are getting jobs?*

# Unit 6 | Teacher's Guide

**Unit 6, Lesson 31**
Visual 3

## True/False Clues

A. Employed people are people with jobs.

> True or False?

B. Unemployed people are people without jobs.

> True or False?

C. The civilian labor force is the number of people aged 16 years and older who are not in the armed forces.

> True or False?

**Unit 6, Lesson 31**
Visual 4

## Employment Definitions

- The Bureau of Labor Statistics is the government agency that tracks the number of people who are employed and unemployed.

- The civilian labor force is the number of people aged 16 years and older who are not in the armed forces and who are employed or are seeking employment.

- Employed people are people with jobs.

- The unemployment rate is the percentage of the civilian labor force that is unemployed.

# Unit 6 | Teacher's Guide

**Unit 6 Lesson 32**

## The Effects of Inflation

### Introduction

**Economics**  Inflation is defined as a sustained increase in the average price level of goods and services produced in an economy. The fundamental cause of inflation is that the rate of growth of the money supply is greater than the rate of growth of goods and services. In a period of inflation, money loses value as goods and services become more expensive. Unanticipated inflation can have serious negative consequences for individuals and for the countries experiencing it. People lose the value of their savings and cannot plan for the future. Since interest rates do not keep up with price increases, lenders lose and borrowers gain, causing wealth transfers and disrupting financial markets.

Most U.S. high school students in the early 21st century have not experienced significant inflation during their lifetimes. Between 1985 and 2001, U.S. inflation rates averaged around three percent, considered by economists to be low. By comparison, countries in the former Soviet Union and Eastern Bloc faced inflation rates ranging from more than 100 percent to more than 1,000 percent in the early 1990s. The stories of how people coped during this period of hyperinflation provide an important lesson about the effects of inflation on those who live through it.

**Reasoning**  Economic reasoning tells us that people respond to incentives in predictable ways, and that the consequences of actions lie in the future. How people react to inflation provides classic examples of these principles. Faced with hyperinflation, people have incentives to hold their wealth in forms other than money. This "buy now" philosophy increases demand and leads to inflationary spirals. People have disincentives to save their money in banks, and they look to other, non-productive methods of saving — such as hoarding goods and services to avoid future price increases. Therefore bank deposits fall, leading eventually to decreases in investment and decreases in long-run economic growth.

### Concepts

- Effects of inflation
- Hyperinflation
- Inflation

### Objectives

*Students will:*

1. Read descriptions of the effects of high inflation in 10 countries in the former Soviet Union and Eastern Bloc in the 1990s.
2. Participate in a group activity and discussion to identify the effects of high inflation.
3. In a class discussion, demonstrate understanding of why high inflation is a problem.

### Content Standard

- Unexpected inflation imposes costs on many people and benefits some others because it arbitrarily redistributes purchasing power. Inflation can reduce the rate of growth of national living standards, because individuals and organizations use resources to protect themselves against the uncertainty of future prices. (NCEE Content Standard 13)

### Lesson Description

Students examine recent inflation rates in the United States and discuss the interpretation of inflation rates. They read about the inflation-related experiences of teachers in the former Soviet Union and Eastern Europe and use these experiences as a basis for identifying the effects of high rates of inflation.

*Time Required: 60 minutes*

### Materials

- One copy of Activity 1 for each group of four students
- One blank transparency and one transparency marker for each group of four students

### Procedure

1. Explain that the purpose of this lesson is to study inflation and how to interpret inflation rates. (Before beginning the lesson, you may wish to cover the basic causes of inflation with students, and provide background on the breakup of the Soviet Union and the ensuing problems facing transition economies.) Explain that inflation is caused when the money supply grows faster than the supply of goods and services in an economy, thus pulling up prices. Under the communist regimes of the former Soviet Union, prices were held artificially low and government-owned industries were notoriously inefficient. When the Soviet Union fell apart in the early 1990s, the new governments were faced with problems of moving from planned to market economies. During the transition period, while industries were being privatized, governments printed vast quantities of money to pay workers. Predictably, this led to hyperinflation.

## The Effects of Inflation

2. Explain recent inflation rates in the United States, and how to interpret these rates.

   *(According to the 2001 Economic Report of the President, annual U.S. inflation rates as measured by the Consumer Price Index from 1995 to 1999 were: 1995: 2.5 percent, 1996: 3.3 percent, 1997: 1.7 percent, 1998: 1.6 percent, and 1999: 2.7 percent. An annual inflation rate of 3 percent means that what you could have bought for $100 last year now costs $103.00.)*

3. Define *hyperinflation*, and discuss recent hyperinflation rates in the former Soviet Union.

   *(Hyperinflation is defined as an exceptionally high rate of inflation. If the rate of inflation is 100 percent, prices double, meaning that what you could have bought for $100 a year ago would cost $200 today. Therefore, if the rate of inflation is 89 percent as it was in Estonia in 1993, Estonians would need $189 [or 189 kron] in 1993 to buy what $100 [or 100 kron] would have bought in 1992. If the inflation rate is 4,735 percent as it was in Ukraine in 1993, Ukrainians would need $4,835 [or 4,835 gryvnia] to buy what $100 [or 100 gryvnia] would have bought in 1992.)*

4. Ask the students how they think people would cope during periods of hyperinflation. Discuss responses briefly.

5. Tell the students that they will now have an opportunity to read true accounts of how people were affected by periods of hyperinflation after the fall of communism in the early 1990s in the former Soviet Union and Eastern Europe. Activity 1 gives testimonials from 10 economics teachers who lived in periods of hyperinflation in their formerly communist countries. The accounts were written in 1998. Inflation rates are given for 1993, although the examples may reflect other years during the years 1990-1998.

6. Divide the students into groups of four. Give each group one copy of Activity 1, a blank transparency, and a marker. Each group member should read one page of Activity 1, which contains accounts from two or three teachers whose countries experienced hyperinflation. Each student should report to the group on the effects of inflation from the accounts she or he read. Groups should choose a recorder and group spokesperson. The recorder should list the effects of inflation identified by group members on the transparency.

7. When groups have finished reading and discussing Activity 1 and listing effects of inflation on their transparencies, call a spokesperson from one of the groups to come to the front of the room. He or she should display the group's transparency and discuss the effects of inflation that the group recorded. Other groups should follow, reporting any effects of inflation that they recorded that were not reported by prior groups.

   *(Group reports will vary. Some of the effects of inflation reported in Activity 1, with brief explanations, are as follows:*

   - *Money loses value during inflation (because it takes more money to buy goods and services).*
   - *When prices grow faster than wages, people's real (inflation-adjusted) wages fall.*
   - *Many people don't have money to save, and, when they do, they don't want to save it in banks.)*
   - *Money in savings accounts loses value, so people who keep money in banks lose. Interest rates may be high, but they are generally not as high as the rate of inflation. This can hurt future economic growth because people do not have incentives to keep their money in banks, so there is less money available for businesses to borrow for investment purposes.*
   - *People have incentives to buy goods and hoard them — to avoid paying higher prices in the future. They try to buy goods that they think will increase in value, such as real estate or jewelry, to keep up with inflation. Or they may buy goods to resell to others in the future to try to make a profit.*
   - *Borrowers can gain from unanticipated inflation (since the money they pay back is not worth as much as the money they borrowed). Also, borrowers may use the money to buy goods and services that increase in value.*
   - *In countries with high inflation, people try to convert money into more stable currencies, such as U.S. dollars.*
   - *People on fixed incomes, such as retirees, are hurt when their pensions do not keep up with inflation. Retirees may look for work to try to earn money for survival.*
   - *Governments may try to keep ahead of inflation by printing money to pay government workers. (But this may lead to increases in the money supply and more inflation in the future.)*
   - *People may avoid using money and resort to barter and in-kind payments.*
   - *People may grow their own food to avoid having to buy it.*
   - *Governments may index wages to help people keep up with inflation, or to partially keep up.*
   - *People have incentives to spend their money right after receiving it to avoid higher prices in the future.*

# Unit 6 | Teacher's Guide

- *Desperate people may resort to very risky investments such as the Albanian pyramid schemes to try to keep up with inflation.*
- *People may try to buy goods from other countries that do not have high inflation.)*

## Closure

Using the information from Procedure 5 and from student group reports, make a list summarizing effects of high inflation on a transparency or on the board. Review the list with the students, making sure that they understand why high inflation is a problem for people in the countries that experience it.

## Multiple-Choice Questions
### (Correct answers shown in bold)

1  A very high rate of inflation is called:

   A. Disinflation.

   B. Stagflation.

   **C. Hyperinflation.**

   D. Monoinflation.

2. During periods of high inflation:

   **A. Money loses value.**

   B. Money gains value.

   C. People want to hold on to money.

   D. The government has printed too little money.

## Essay Question

After the fall of communism in the early 1990s, many former communist countries experienced periods of very high inflation. Describe some of the effects of inflation on people's lives.

*(Information provided by testimonials from 10 countries suggests several effects: money loses value, real wages fall, people have disincentives to save their money in banks, people on fixed incomes are hurt, people hoard goods, borrowers can gain and lenders can lose, and so on.)*

# Unit 6 | Teacher's Guide

## Unit 6 Lesson 33

## Gross Domestic Product (GDP) And How to Measure It

### INTRODUCTION

**Economics**  *Gross Domestic Product (GDP)* is defined as the total market value of all final goods and services produced in a country in a year. Economists generally measure GDP using one of two equivalent methods: the expenditure approach or the income approach. This lesson focuses on the expenditure approach, which calls for computing GDP by totaling household spending on consumption, business investment spending, government spending on goods and services, and spending on net exports (exports minus imports). Understanding GDP is important in part because it relates to several other macroeconomic concepts. Fluctuations in GDP over time reflect periods of economic growth and decline (recessions). Economic forecasting frequently involves trying to predict GDP fluctuations and turnarounds.

**Reasoning**  When one person spends money, it becomes someone else's income. This idea is often represented by the "circular flow" diagrams commonly found in high school economics textbooks. This idea also leads to the two major ways in which government accountants compute GDP: by measuring total spending (as in this lesson) or by measuring national income.

The definition of GDP could in itself lead to several lessons in economics. What is meant by market value? What are final goods? What is the difference between GDP and GNP? What is the difference between nominal and real GDP? What is excluded from GDP calculations, and why? These and other related topics could be addressed following this introductory lesson, in which students apply reasoning skills to classify different economic events and determine their likely effects on GDP.

### CONCEPTS

- Consumption
- Exports
- Gross domestic product (GDP)
- Government spending on goods and services
- Imports
- Investment
- Net exports

### OBJECTIVES

*Students will:*

1. Discuss GDP and how economists measure it.

2. Classify economic events by reference to four macroeconomic categories, and predict the effects the events will have on GDP.

### CONTENT STANDARD

- A nation's overall levels of income, employment, and prices are determined by the interaction of spending and production decisions made by all households, firms, government agencies, and others in the economy. (NCEE Content Standard 18)

### LESSON DESCRIPTION

Students examine GDP. They distinguish between nominal and real GDP. They study how GDP is comprised of household spending on consumption goods and services (C), business investment spending (I), government spending on goods and services (G), and net exports (X-M). They participate in a simulation in which they classify economic events into the categories C, I, G, or (X-M), and predict whether the event will lead to an increase or decrease in GDP.

*Time Required: 60 minutes*

### MATERIALS

- A transparency of Visual 1. (You may also wish to copy it as a handout for students.)

- Six signs (on 8.5 by 11-inch paper — or larger, and brightly colored, if possible), each containing one of the following inscriptions printed in large letters: **GDP, =, C, I, G,** and **X=M**

- One copy (on brightly colored card stock, if possible) of Handout Material (see p. 218), cut apart and put into a paper bag or shoe box

### PROCEDURE

1. Explain that the purpose of this lesson is to introduce the definition of GDP and to show how various events may lead to changes in GDP.

2. Display Visual 1. Discuss the definition of GDP and its components.

3. Using Visual 1, make sure that students understand the following points:

    - When C, I, or G increase, GDP increases.

    - When C, I, or G decrease, GDP decreases.

    - When exports (X) go up, GDP goes up because it means more is produced in the United States.

    - When imports (M) go up, GDP goes down because it means people in the United States are buying what is produced in other countries.

# Gross Domestic Product (GDP) and How to Measure It

- When GDP increases, the economy experiences economic growth and unemployment goes down.
- When GDP decreases for two consecutive quarters, the economy is in a recession and unemployment goes up.
- In macroeconomics, the term investment is used to mean spending by business on capital goods, such as tools and machinery.

4. Announce that the students will now participate in an activity to test their understanding of some factors that cause GDP to increase or decrease. *(For this activity, assume that the overall price level in the economy is constant, so that changes in GDP are changes in real GDP.)* Ask for six volunteers to come to the front of the room. Give the volunteers the signs **GDP**, **=**, **C**, **I**, **G,** and **(X-M)**. Arrange the students facing the class so that the signs spell out the following equation: **GDP = C + I + G + (X-M)**. Make sure the students understand the abbreviations. Explain that the plus signs are implicit (or, if you wish, make three plus signs and have the students hold them also). Tell the students that the equation shows that GDP can be measured by adding consumption spending, investment spending, government spending, and net exports (**X** for exports, minus **M** for imports.) Remind them that an example of this equation for 2000 was given on Visual 1.

5. Show the students the cards from the Handout Material. Tell them that all the cards describe macroeconomic events that affect one of the components of GDP: consumption, investment, government spending, or net exports. Divide the class into two teams.

   - Choose a student from one of the teams to come to the front of the room and draw one of the cards from the bag *(for example, "Due to a tax cut, consumers decide to buy more new cars")*. Ask the students to identify (1) which of the parts of GDP is affected, and (2) whether this event would cause GDP to go up or down. (The rest of the class must be silent and not help with the answers.) When both answers have been given, the students holding the signs should raise or lower their signs as appropriate to show the proposed answer. *(For example, if the student says that consumption would increase and GDP would increase, the student holding the C sign would raise it up, and the student holding the GDP sign would raise it up.)*

   - To involve the rest of the students, ask whether they agree with both parts of the answer. If so, they should give a "thumbs up" sign. If they disagree, they should give a "thumbs down" sign. (These responses can lead to discussion.) If the student is correct, award his or her team one point. If the student is incorrect, choose one of the opposing team's students who gave a "thumbs down" and have him or her come up and suggest an answer. Have the students holding the signs raise them or lower them according to the suggested answer. Give the team that gets the correct answer to both parts of the question first a point.

   - To reinforce the concept, read the card again and the correct answer while the students holding the signs raise or lower them as indicated.

6. Follow the steps of Procedure 5 until all the cards have been drawn. Give a round of applause for the winning team and for the sign-holders. (Note: if you don't wish to divide the class into teams and play the game as a competition, you could conduct the activity in a different way. For example, the students could come up, draw a card and read it to the class, and then the class as a whole could suggest the answer. The students holding the signs could still demonstrate the effects by raising or lowering the signs.)

## Closure

Display Visual 1 again. Review the idea that GDP can be measured by adding spending by households (consumption), by business (investment), by the government on goods and services, and in the foreign sector (net exports, or exports minus imports). Emphasize the example at the bottom of the Visual 1.

## Multiple-Choice Questions

(Correct answers shown in bold)

1. Investment is a major component of GDP, along with consumption, government spending, and net exports. Which of the following best describes investment in this context?

   A. Members of the public buy shares of stock.

   **B. Businesses spend money on items such as machinery and factories.**

   C. Citizens deposit money into savings accounts in banks and credit unions.

   D. U.S. citizens and foreigners deposit savings into the Federal Reserve Bank.

2. Which of the following makes up the largest part of GDP?

   **A. Consumption spending**

   B. Investment spending

   C. Government spending

   D. Net exports

# Unit 6 | Teacher's Guide

ESSAY QUESTION

Give an example of each of the following spending categories that make up GDP: Consumption spending, investment spending, government spending, net exports.

*(Sample answer: An example of consumption spending is when households purchase food or clothing. An example of investment spending is when a business buys new computers. An example of government spending is when the government builds new freeways or buys new military equipment. An example of net exports is when the United States imports cars from Japan and exports computer chips to Mexico.)*

*Answers to the Handout Material:*

(Numbers correspond to the numbers on the bottom right corner on the cards. Note that the responses refer to immediate or short-run impacts of the events.)

1. *Consumption increases, GDP increases.*
2. *Government spending decreases, GDP decreases.*
3. *Imports to the U.S. increase (net exports decrease), GDP decreases.*
4. *Consumption decreases, GDP decreases.*
5. *U.S. exports increase (net exports increase), GDP increases.*
6. *U.S. exports decrease (net exports decrease), GDP decreases.*
7. *Investment increases, GDP increases.*
8. *Imports to the U.S. increase (net exports decrease), GDP decreases.*
9. *Consumption decreases, GDP decreases.*
10. *Investment decreases, GDP decreases.*
11. *Consumption increases, GDP increases.*
12. *Investment increases, GDP increases.*
13. *Government spending increases, GDP increases.*
14. *Investment increases, GDP increases.*
15. *Government spending increases, GDP increases.*

# Gross Domestic Product (GDP) and How to Measure It

## Unit 6, Lesson 33

### Handout Material

Events Affecting Spending on Consumption, Investment, Government Spending, or Net Exports

| | | |
|---|---|---|
| *Due to a tax cut, consumers decide to buy more new cars.* <br><br> 1 | *Worried about an increasing budget deficit, the government decides to buy fewer military planes.* <br><br> 2 | *Increasing prices in the U.S. encourage Americans to buy more foreign goods.* <br><br> 3 |
| *Due to a tax increase, consumers decrease purchases on vacation travel.* <br><br> 4 | *Due to increased incomes, Europeans buy more U.S. goods and services.* <br><br> 5 | *A foreign government imposes a tariff that discourages its citizens from buying goods from the U.S.* <br><br> 6 |
| *Businesses are optimistic about the future and increase construction of new factories.* <br><br> 7 | *Many more Americans decide to buy Japanese cars rather than American cars.* <br><br> 8 | *Households worry about future unemployment and decide to spend less income.* <br><br> 9 |
| *Because interest rates increased, businesses cut back on spending for new machinery.* <br><br> 10 | *Consumers feel good about the future and take out loans to buy more durable goods such as washing machines.* <br><br> 11 | *Decreases in interest rates encourage businesses to take out loans to construct more buildings.* <br><br> 12 |
| *To fight unemployment, the government decides to hire more people to work in national parks.* <br><br> 13 | *Tax cuts to businesses give businesses incentives to buy more computers.* <br><br> 14 | *To stimulate the economy and provide jobs, the government builds more bridges in California.* <br><br> 15 |

# Unit 6 | Teacher's Guide

**Unit 6, Lesson 33**
Visual 1

## GROSS DOMESTIC PRODUCT (GDP):

- The market value of all final goods and services produced in a country in a year.

- Final goods and services have been purchased for final use. They are not for resale or further manufacture.

- Economists often measure GDP by totaling the money spent on four major categories of goods and services:

    **Consumption (C):** Spending by households on goods and services. Includes spending on things such as cars, food, and visits to the dentist. Makes up two-thirds of GDP spending.

    **Investment (I):** Spending by businesses on machinery, factories, equipment, tools, and construction of new buildings.

    **Government (G):** Spending by all levels of government on goods and services. Includes spending on the military, schools, and highways.

    **Net Exports (X - M):** Spending by people abroad on U.S. goods and services (exports, or X) minus spending by people in the U.S. on foreign goods and services (imports, or M).

EXAMPLE:

In 2000, in trillions of U.S. dollars, third-quarter GDP estimates were:

GDP    =   C    +   I    +   G    +  ( X   -   M )
$10.04 = $6.81 + $1.87 + $1.75 + ($1.13 - $1.52)*

\* Source: *Economic Report of the President, 2001, page 274.*

# Unit 6 | Teacher's Guide

## Unit 6 Lesson 34

## Money and Monetary Policy

### INTRODUCTION

**Economics**  The supply of money in the economy (narrowly defined as currency plus balances in checking-type accounts) is a very important macroeconomic variable. Too much money in the economy relative to the supply of goods and services can cause inflation. Too little money in the economy relative to the supply of goods and services can cause deflation, declining GDP, and unemployment.

The Federal Reserve (the Fed), the nation's central bank, is responsible for controlling the money supply through monetary policy. The three major tools of monetary policy are open market operations, whereby the Fed buys and sells government securities on the open market, directly affecting bank reserves; changes in the discount rate, which encourage or discourage bank lending; and changes in the reserve requirement, which affect the amount of money banks have to lend.

Expansionary monetary policy encourages banks to make loans. This process is usually described in high school and college economics textbooks as the banks' ability to "create money." Through contractionary monetary policy, banks are discouraged from lending and may "destroy money" or, as is more likely, decrease the rate of growth of the money supply. When banks make more loans, the money supply increases. When banks make fewer loans, the money supply, or the rate of growth of the money supply, decreases.

**Reasoning**  The Guide to Economic Reasoning tells us that people respond to incentives in predictable ways. This is true for banks also. Banks earn profits in part by making loans and charging interest on loans. The Fed, through monetary policy, provides incentives for banks to make more loans or fewer loans, and either result affects the money supply.

Changes in the money supply do not take effect immediately, and most economists agree that the time lags are unpredictable. Therefore the Fed must exercise caution in using monetary policy, taking care not to implement too large a change in the money supply — one that could have adverse effects down the road.

### CONCEPTS

- Federal Reserve
- Fractional reserve banking system
- Money
- Monetary policy
- Money supply

### OBJECTIVES

*Students will:*

1. Explain the functions of money and why the money supply is important in the economy.

2. Participate in an activity demonstrating how banks create money.

3. Apply concepts from the activity in analyzing monetary policy.

### CONTENT STANDARDS

- Institutions evolve in market economies to help individuals and groups accomplish their goals. Banks, labor unions, corporations, legal systems, and not-for-profits organizations are examples of important institutions. A different kind of institution, clearly defined and well enforced property rights, is essential to a market economy. (NCEE Content Standard 10)

- Federal government budgetary policy and the Federal Reserve System's monetary policy influence the overall levels of employment, output, and prices. (NCEE Content Standard 20)

### LESSON DESCRIPTION

The concept of *money creation* by banks is often not intuitive for students, but it is important to their understanding of the role of the Federal Reserve. In this lesson, students first discuss money, its functions, and why the money supply is important in the economy. Then they take part in a short activity to learn how banks create money and affect the money supply. They then apply the concepts from the activity to an analysis of monetary policy.

*Time Required: 60 minutes*

### MATERIALS

- A transparency of Visuals 1, 2, 3, and 4

- 50 dried beans (such as white beans, red kidney beans, etc.), or similar items. (If beans are not used, the "receipts" in Activity 1 should be revised.)

- One or more copies of the Handout Material (see p. 224), cut up. You may wish to use brightly colored paper.

### PROCEDURE

1. Explain that the purpose of this lesson is to introduce relationships among money, the money supply, and banking. Display Visual 1 and review the concepts with the class. Discuss why money and the money supply are important in the economy.

# Money and Monetary Policy

2. Tell the students that they will participate in an activity focused on how bank lending enables banks to create money and increase the money supply. After the simulation, they will discuss how the Federal Reserve exerts control over the amount of money banks can create.

3. Quickly distribute the 50 beans to the class. The beans should not be equally distributed: some students may have several beans, several students should have no beans, and so forth. Tell the students that in your classroom economy, beans (and only beans) are considered to be money at this time. Ask the students what the money supply is at that point. *(50 beans.)* Display Visual 2, showing only the information for Round 1 (cover the information for Rounds 2 and 3 with paper). Read the information for Round 1 on Visual 2 with the class.

4. Tell the students that you are opening a bank where they will be able to deposit their beans. Ask: Why might people deposit money in a bank?

   *(Students might mention keeping the beans safe or avoiding the awkwardness of having to carry beans around. If any students mention that they want to earn interest, tell them that this is a good reason for depositing beans, but that checking-type accounts pay very low interest, and you aren't paying any in the activity. Assure the students that you are a very trustworthy person and your bank is very safe. For every bean deposited, you will issue a receipt that can be exchanged for a bean at any time. Show the students the Bank Deposit Receipts.)*

5. **100 percent Reserve Banking System:** Ask who would like to deposit money in your bank. Walk around the room and accept 10 beans for deposit; put the beans into your pocket (the bank). When students give you beans, give them one receipt for each bean deposited. This is an example of a banking system with a 100 percent reserve requirement.

6. Explain the role of the Bank Deposit Receipts, and point out that it is logical for them to circulate as money as well as the beans themselves. The Bank Deposit Receipts are worth one bean each, since each one can be exchanged for one bean at the bank. Anyone who has the receipt could turn it in to the bank for money. If someone has a Bank Deposit Receipt and wants to buy something worth one bean, she or he could pay with the receipt and avoid having to go to the bank and withdrawing a bean. The seller would accept the receipt because sellers trust the bank. They know they can exchange the receipt at the bank for a bean or use the receipt to buy something. Demonstrate that the receipts can circulate as money by having a student with a receipt "buy" a pencil from another student — exchanging the receipt for the pencil.

7. Ask the students what the money supply is now, given that Bank Deposit Receipts are also accepted as money. *(The money supply is still equal to 50 beans: the 40 beans in circulation and the 10 bank receipts backed up by the 10 beans in the bank. The beans deposited in the bank do not count since they are not in circulation.)* Uncover the information for Round 2 on Visual 2, and read the information with the class. Tell the students that this demonstrates a "100 percent reserve banking system." All bank receipts (100 percent) are backed up by a bean on reserve in the bank.

8. **Fractional Reserve Banking System:** Tell the students that your bank has decided to go into the lending business. Ask who would like to borrow money. Suggest that students who don't have beans or receipts probably want some money to buy lunch or school supplies. Emphasize that since the receipts are circulating as money and people trust your bank, it is unlikely that everyone will want to turn in their receipts for beans at the same time. Therefore you feel secure in lending out some of the beans you have in reserve. Agree to lend out five beans, and write the names of the borrowers on the board. This is an example of a fractional reserve banking system.

9. Reach into your pocket to give students beans for the loans — then stop. Point out that you may as well give Bank Deposit Receipts instead of the actual beans, since the receipts are accepted as money also. Give the borrowers a total of five Bank Deposit Receipts.

10. Ask the students what the money supply is now. *(The money supply is equal to 55 beans: the 40 beans in circulation and the 15 Bank Deposit Receipts in circulation.)* Point out that now there is a "fractional reserve banking system." The 15 Bank Deposit Receipts are backed by 10 beans, or only a fraction (2/3) of a bean on deposit in the bank. Uncover the information for Round 3 on Visual 2, and read the information with the class.

11. Discuss how the money supply increased, and emphasize the following points:

    - Since the Bank Deposit Receipts are accepted as money, the bank, by making loans, has increased the money supply from 50 beans to the amount equal to 55 beans.

    - The bank could increase the money supply further by making more loans, as long as people do not withdraw all the beans at one time (equivalent to a banking panic — in which case there would not be enough beans).

    - The ability of banks to create money by making loans is based on the fractional reserve system of banking. People must trust banks for this system to work successfully.

# Unit 6 | Teacher's Guide

12. Relate the activity to real life by asking the students what the beans represent *(currency — i.e., coins and paper money)* and what the Bank Deposit Receipts represent *(checks, backed by bank deposits)*. Point out that the United States does have a fractional reserve banking system, and banks can create money by making loans. The Federal Reserve, through monetary policy, regulates the amount of money banks can create through loans.

13. Display Visual 3. Describe some of the institutional features of the Federal Reserve System.

14. Display Visual 4 and discuss the tools of monetary policy. Relate the concepts to the bean activity, emphasizing that the Federal Reserve controls the money supply through its control of bank lending.

15. **Closure** Review the lesson. Ask:

    - What is money?

      *(Anything that is generally accepted as final payment for goods and services.)*

    - What are the three purposes of money?

      *(Medium of exchange, unit of account, store of value.)*

    - How do banks increase the money supply?

      *(Banks create money by making loans based on fractional reserve requirements.)*

    - Why is the supply of money important?

      *(Too much money can cause inflation; too little can lead to falling prices and falling production.)*

    - What is the Fed?

      *(The U.S. central banking system.)*

    - The Fed uses open market operations to control the money supply. When would the Fed want to buy securities?

      *(When it wishes to increase the money supply.)*

    - When would the Fed sell securities?

      *(When it wishes to decrease the money supply.)*

## Multiple-Choice Questions

### (Correct answers shown in bold)

1. If the amount of money in the economy grows much faster than the amount of goods and services, the result will be:

   **A. Inflation.**

   B. Unemployment.

   C. Improvements in education.

   D. Price decreases.

2. In the United States, local banks create money by:

   **A. Making loans in the form of checking accounts.**

   B. Printing money on their printing presses.

   C. Making profits by charging high interest rates on loans.

   D. None of the above; it is illegal for banks to create money.

## Essay Question

What is monetary policy? Who (or what agency) is in charge of monetary policy in the United States?

*(Monetary policy is defined as changes in the money supply intended to maintain stable prices, full employment, and economic growth. Monetary policy is controlled by the Federal Reserve, the central banking system in the United States. The money supply is important because too much money can lead to inflation and too little money can lead to falling production and unemployment. The three major tools of monetary policy are open market operations, changes in the discount rate, and changes in the reserve requirement.)*

# Money and Monetary Policy

## Unit 6, Lesson 34

### Handout Material

**Bank Deposit Receipts**

| | | |
|---|---|---|
| **Bank Deposit Receipt**<br><br>*Good for one bean* | **Bank Deposit Receipt**<br><br>*Good for one bean* | **Bank Deposit Receipt**<br><br>*Good for one bean* |
| **Bank Deposit Receipt**<br><br>*Good for one bean* | **Bank Deposit Receipt**<br><br>*Good for one bean* | **Bank Deposit Receipt**<br><br>*Good for one bean* |
| **Bank Deposit Receipt**<br><br>*Good for one bean* | **Bank Deposit Receipt**<br><br>*Good for one bean* | **Bank Deposit Receipt**<br><br>*Good for one bean* |
| **Bank Deposit Receipt**<br><br>*Good for one bean* | **Bank Deposit Receipt**<br><br>*Good for one bean* | **Bank Deposit Receipt**<br><br>*Good for one bean* |
| **Bank Deposit Receipt**<br><br>*Good for one bean* | **Bank Deposit Receipt**<br><br>*Good for one bean* | **Bank Deposit Receipt**<br><br>*Good for one bean* |
| **Bank Deposit Receipt**<br><br>*Good for one bean* | **Bank Deposit Receipt**<br><br>*Good for one bean* | **Bank Deposit Receipt**<br><br>*Good for one bean* |

# Unit 6 | Teacher's Guide

**Unit 6, Lesson 34**
Visual 1

## MONEY AND THE MONEY SUPPLY

**Money:** Anything that is generally accepted as final payment for goods and services.

### MONEY SERVES THESE PURPOSES:

- *Medium of exchange:* It can be used to purchase goods and services.

- *Unit of account:* It can be used to compare the value of different goods and services.

- *Store of value:* It can be held to buy something in the future.

## MONEY SUPPLY:

- Narrowly defined by economists as currency (coins and paper money) in the hands of the public, plus checking-type accounts. Currency makes up about 48 percent of the total, and checking-type accounts about 52 percent.

- The supply of money in the economy is important for price stability and economic growth.

- ***Too much money in the economy can cause inflation.*** An extreme example of this occurred in Germany after World War I, when the German government printed so much money that prices increased 5,470 percent in 1923.

- ***Too little money in the economy can lead to falling prices and falling production.*** An example of this occurred in the U.S. between 1929 and 1933. The money supply fell by 30 percent, and most economists agree that this was a major cause of the Great Depression.

- The Federal Reserve controls the money supply through monetary policy. Monetary policy works through encouraging or discouraging banks from making loans.

MONEY AND MONETARY POLICY

**Unit 6, Lesson 34**
Visual 2

# HOW BANKS CREATE MONEY

### ROUND 1. MONEY SUPPLY = 50 BEANS

*50 beans are circulating as money in the economy.*

### ROUND 2. MONEY SUPPLY = 50 BEANS

*40 beans plus 10 Bank Deposit Receipts are in circulation. Both Bank Deposit Receipts and beans are accepted as money.*

(Students deposited 10 beans in the bank and received 10 Bank Deposit Receipts. Each Bank Deposit Receipt is backed by a bean in the bank.)

### ROUND 3. MONEY SUPPLY = 55 BEANS

*40 beans plus 15 Bank Deposit Receipts are in circulation. Both Bank Deposit Receipts and beans are accepted as money.*

(Students borrowed 5 beans from the bank and received 5 Bank Deposit Receipts. The bank created money by making these loans. The 15 Bank Deposit Receipts are backed by 10 beans in the bank.)

**Unit 6, Lesson 34**
Visual 3

## THE FEDERAL RESERVE SYSTEM

- The Fed was created in 1914 after a series of bank failures.

- The Fed Board of Governors:
  - 7 members appointed by the President, with confirmation by the Senate.
  - Board members serve 14-year terms.
  - President appoints the chairperson to a 4-year term.

- 12 Regional Federal Reserve Banks:
  - Regional banks are located in major cities around the country.
  - Each bank has a president chosen by the bank's board of directors.
  - The board of directors is typically drawn from the local business and banking community.

**Unit 6, Lesson 34**
Visual 4

## THE FEDERAL RESERVE AND MONETARY POLICY

**FEDERAL RESERVE (THE FED):**

The U.S. central banking system. One of the functions of the Fed is to control the money supply through monetary policy.

**MONETARY POLICY:**

Changes in the money supply, intended to maintain stable prices, full employment, and economic growth.

If the Fed is fighting unemployment and declining GDP, it wants to increase the money supply.

If the Fed is fighting inflation, it wants to decrease the money supply.

**TOOLS OF MONETARY POLICY**

- **Open Market Operations:**

  When the Fed buys or sells U.S. government securities to influence the money supply.

  When the Fed buys securities, bank deposits increase, banks have more money to lend, and the money supply increases.

  When the Fed sells securities, bank deposits decrease, banks have less money to lend, and the money supply decreases.

- **Changes in the Discount Rate:**

  The discount rate is the interest rate that the Fed charges on loans to banks.

  When the Fed lowers the discount rate, banks are encouraged to make more loans and the money supply increases.

  When the Fed raises the discount rate, banks are discouraged from making loans and the money supply decreases.

- **Changes in the Reserve Requirement:**

  The reserve requirement is the minimum percentage of deposits that banks must keep on reserve to back up checking-type accounts.

  When the Fed lowers the reserve requirement, banks have more money to lend and the money supply increases.

  When the Fed raises the reserve requirement, banks have less money to lend and the money supply decreases.

# Unit 6 | Teacher's Guide

## Unit 6 Lesson 35

## Fiscal Policy: A Two-Act Play

### Introduction

**Economics**  The U.S. government is often blamed during times of unemployment, decreasing GDP, or inflation. Many economists believe that the federal government can (and should) help to alleviate these problems by traditional, discretionary fiscal policy. Traditional (demand-side) fiscal policy advocates that in times of recession and above-normal unemployment, the government should deliberately increase spending on goods and services and/or reduce taxes to increase aggregate demand. In theory, this spending has multiplier effects and stimulates other spending, resulting in increased production and more jobs. In times of inflation, traditional fiscal policy calls for reduced government spending and/or increases in taxes to decrease aggregate demand. Reductions in demand should then lead to decreased inflation.

Traditional fiscal policy has its critics, for several reasons. Economists do not know with certainty how large the multiplier effects are or how long it takes for fiscal policy to work. Therefore, by the time an expansionary fiscal policy takes effect, the economy may no longer be in a recession and the policy may actually lead to inflation. Also, events in other countries can greatly affect the outcome of U.S. fiscal policy measures. Most economists recognize the possibility of crowding out, which occurs if government borrowing (for example, to finance expansionary fiscal policy) causes interest rates to rise and private investment spending to decrease.

Some economists emphasize possible supply-side effects of fiscal policy, particularly with respect to tax cuts. In this scenario, because people and businesses have more after-tax income to spend as they choose, business tax cuts would lead to increased production and investment in capital goods. These outcomes should in turn lead to a direct increase in aggregate supply and to lower unemployment and lower inflation.

**Reasoning**  Whether fiscal policy is effective or not depends in part on how people respond to incentives. For example, if you are given a tax cut, will you spend the extra money or save it? If you spend it, it becomes someone else's income, and if they spend their income (and their tax cut), this has a stimulative effect on the economy. However, if everyone saves the tax cuts, which may also be rational, the desired effect of the fiscal policy may be much smaller or nonexistent. Issues like these make the effects of fiscal policy difficult to predict.

### Concepts

- Contractionary fiscal policy
- Crowding out (optional)
- Expansionary fiscal policy
- Fiscal policy
- Multiplier effects
- Supply-side fiscal policy

### Objectives

*Students will:*

1. Describe the effects of expansionary/contractionary fiscal policies.

2. (Optional) Analyze current arguments related to the effectiveness of fiscal policy.

### Content Standard

- Federal government budgetary policy and the Federal Reserve System's monetary policy influence the overall levels of employment, output, and prices. (NCEE Content Standard 20)

### Lesson Description

Groups of students are given outlines for one of two acts in a play describing either expansionary or contractionary fiscal policy. After choosing parts and preparing lines for their roles, two groups are chosen to perform the play. Events in the play are discussed by reference to concepts of fiscal policy. More advanced classes may then discuss current debates about the effectiveness of fiscal policy.

*Time Required: 60 to 75 minutes*

### Materials

- A transparency of Visual 1
- A transparency of Visual 2 (optional)
- Activity 1

### Procedure

1. Tell the class that the purpose of this lesson is to introduce fiscal policy. In learning about fiscal policy, the students participate in a two-act play (see Activity 1). This play is a little different from others, in that actors and actresses have to write their own lines. Divide the students into groups of eight. Assign responsibility for Act 1 to half the groups; assign responsibility for Act 2 to the other half. If there are fewer than eight students in a group, some students may play more than one part, or the last part before the narrator may be eliminated. The students may also add parts if necessary, once they get the idea.

# Fiscal Policy: A Two-Act Play

2. Read through the directions on Activity 1 with the students. Announce that they will have about 15 minutes to prepare their act. After the groups have finished, you will choose one group to perform each act for the class. Encourage the students to be creative, but to stick to the ideas in the script. Emphasize that performances of Act 1 and Act 2 should each be about 10 minutes or less; thus each character should plan to say only a few sentences. (If you do not impose this time limit, some students may get carried away with their roles!) Circulate among the groups to answer questions while the students are preparing the play. You may want to give examples to help some groups get started. When most groups are close to finishing, announce that there are three minutes remaining before the curtain rises.

3. Select one group to come to the front of the room to perform Act 1. When they have finished, give the group a round of applause and tell them that you will discuss the economic events after Act 2. Select a group to perform Act 2, and give them a round of applause when they have finished. Ask all the students to return to their seats. (You may wish to explain that Act 2 does not necessarily follow from Act 1. That is, demand-pull inflation is not always an immediate result of expansionary fiscal policy, although it may occur in the long run. The play was written with the same characters in each act to show multiplier effects taking place on the same people in different directions.)

4. Display Visual 1 on an overhead projector. Discuss the play as it relates to the terms. Encourage the students to take notes from the transparency as you discuss the concepts.

    (Discussion ideas: Both acts of the play show examples of fiscal policy. Act 1 shows a tax decrease, an example of expansionary fiscal policy intended to help fight the recessionary problems of decreasing GDP and unemployment. Because the house-husband decided to spend his tax cut, this became income to the car salesperson, whose spending became income to the computer salesperson, and so on. This is an example of the fiscal policy multiplier effect leading to higher GDP and more jobs. Act 2 shows a decrease in government spending, an example of contractionary fiscal policy intended to help fight inflation. Here the multiplier effect worked in reverse, as the engineer's lower income led to lower demand and lower prices. Supply-side fiscal policy is displayed in Act 1 when the restaurant owner uses the tax cut to expand the business, thus creating jobs for people who build the new restaurants, thereby increasing GDP.)

5. (Optional) Tell the students that fiscal policy is controversial, and has its critics. Economists do not agree about how it works. For example, what if people in Act 1 decided to save the money from their tax cuts instead of spending it? *(This would have limited or eliminated the expansionary effect of the tax cut.)* Display Visual 2. Use the transparency to discuss the issues surrounding the effectiveness of fiscal policy. *(Although these issues are covered in most high school textbooks, they are somewhat complex and you may wish to reserve this discussion for more advanced classes.)*

## Closure

To test student understanding of the desired effects of expansionary and contractionary fiscal policy, assign the students to write another act for the Fiscal Policy Play. The additional act could be "Expansionary Fiscal Policy: The Increase in Government Spending" or "Contractionary Fiscal Policy: The Tax Increase." Choose the best acts turned in, and give groups extra credit for performing them for the class.

## Multiple-Choice Questions

(Correct answers shown in bold)

1. Which of the following is an example of fiscal policy?

    A. The Federal Reserve System tries to prevent inflation.

    B. The International Monetary Fund makes a loan to a developing country.

    **C. The government decreases taxes to fight unemployment.**

    D. The principal says seniors no longer need to take physical education.

2. Contractionary fiscal policy is used in:

    **A  Periods of inflation.**

    B. Periods of unemployment.

    C. Periods of war.

    D. Periods of recession.

## Essay Question

Say that the government, in an effort to fight unemployment, decides to increase its spending by hiring people to repair roads. Explain how hiring one person to repair a road could result in several people having more income to spend (the multiplier effect).

*(One possible answer: The person hired to repair the road uses his or her income to buy a car. The car salesperson [or auto producer, etc.] would then use his or her extra income to buy clothes, and so on.)*

# Unit 6 | Teacher's Guide

**Unit 6, Lesson 35**
Visual 1

## Fiscal Policy Terms

- ***Fiscal Policy:***
  Changes in federal government spending or tax revenues designed to promote full employment, price stability, and reasonable rates of economic growth.

- ***Expansionary Fiscal Policy:***
  An increase in government spending and/or a decrease in taxes designed to increase aggregate demand in the economy. The intent is to increase GDP and decrease unemployment.

- ***Contractionary Fiscal Policy:***
  A decrease in government spending and/or an increase in taxes designed to decrease aggregate demand in the economy. The intent is to control inflation.

- ***Multiplier Effects:***
  Based on the idea that increased spending by consumers, businesses, or government becomes income for someone else. When this person spends the income, it becomes income for someone else, and so on, leading to increased production in an economy. Multiplier effects can also work in reverse when spending decreases.

- ***Supply-Side Fiscal Policy:***
  The idea that fiscal policy may directly affect aggregate supply and not only aggregate demand. For example, a tax cut may give businesses incentives to expand or invest in capital goods, since they have more after-tax income to spend as they choose.

# FISCAL POLICY: A TWO-ACT PLAY

**Unit 6, Lesson 35**
Visual 2

## DEBATES ABOUT FISCAL POLICY

Fiscal policy is controversial. Economists cite several possible problems relating to how effective fiscal policy is in stabilizing the economy. Here are some of the controversies:

**1. How large are the multiplier effects?**

It is important to know this in order to decide, for example, how large a change in taxes or government spending is necessary to fight recession or inflation. Too large a change could cause more problems, and too small a change would not solve anything. However, economists do not know precisely how large multiplier effects are.

**2. How fast does fiscal policy work?**

There are time lags that frequently occur with fiscal policy:

- The time it takes to realize that there is a problem in the economy.
- The time it takes to get a change in taxes or spending passed by Congress.
- The time it takes for the fiscal policy to help the recession or inflation.

Economists cannot predict how long these lags will be, and therefore cannot predict how long it will take fiscal policy to help the economy.

**3. How is fiscal policy affected by international events?**

The U.S. economy is part of the world economy, and is greatly affected by world events that it does not control. Actions in other countries may affect how or whether U.S. fiscal policy achieves its goals. For example, the U.S. government may try to fight a recession by increasing aggregate demand. But people in other countries may offset this if they decide to buy fewer U.S. exports, thereby decreasing aggregate demand for U.S. goods and services.

**4. How does fiscal policy affect the national debt and interest rates?**

Since expansionary fiscal policy means that government spending goes up or tax revenues go down, this will most likely increase the current national deficit or reduce the current surplus. This may lead to increased interest rates in the economy. When interest rates increase, private businesses may borrow less and decrease their investment in capital goods. This "crowding out" of private investment may offset the expansionary effects of fiscal policy.

# Unit 6 | Teacher's Guide

## Unit 6 Lesson 36

## Should We Worry About the National Debt?

### INTRODUCTION

**Economics** The U.S. national (or public) debt is one of the most discussed and least understood issues in macroeconomics. People frequently fail to distinguish the national debt from an annual budget deficit, and, when there is a budget surplus, they think there is no longer a national debt. The national debt represents the sum of the annual budget deficits, minus annual surpluses, incurred since the Revolutionary War. Whether or not it should be paid off and how it affects the economy are topics that are both interesting and controversial among economists.

**Reasoning** The **Guide to Economic Reasoning** tells us that the consequences of actions lie in the future. This point seems to raise questions about the national debt: does today's deficit, or failure to pay off the debt today, impose costs on future generations? With respect to the debt held by foreigners, the answer is probably yes. Economic reasoning also tells us that it is important to weigh the costs and benefits of actions in making decisions. In analyzing the costs and benefits of incurring a budget deficit or what to do with a surplus, government decision makers are employing the economic way of thinking.

### CONCEPTS

- Bonds
- Budget deficit
- Budget surplus
- National (public) debt

### OBJECTIVES

*Students will:*

1. Explain the difference between the national debt and an annual deficit.

2. Identify and explain causes of the national debt, and how it is financed.

3. Analyze issues concerning the problem of the national debt.

### CONTENT STANDARDS

- Costs of government policies sometimes exceed benefits. This may occur because of incentives facing voters, government officials, and government employees, because of actions by special interest groups that can impose costs on the general public, or because social goals other than economic efficiency are being pursued. (NCEE Content Standard 17)

- Federal government budgetary policy and the Federal Reserve System's monetary policy influence the overall levels of employment, output, and prices. (NCEE Content Standard 20)

### LESSON DESCRIPTION

Students discuss the size of the current national debt and what this means. A class discussion covers the causes of the debt, how it is financed, definitions of a budget deficit and budget surplus, and the difference between a budget deficit and a trade deficit. Students then participate in an activity presenting different perspectives on whether the national debt is a problem of major concern.

*Time Required: 60 minutes*

### MATERIALS

- A transparency of Visual 1
- Handouts 1 and 2 (see pp. 236, 237)

### PROCEDURE

1. Explain that this lesson will focus on the national debt and issues related to it. The level of the national debt is often expressed in trillions. Ask the students to describe how big a trillion is.

   *(Answers will vary. A trillion is a one followed by 12 zeros, or a thousand billion. In terms of time, it takes over 30 years for a billion seconds to pass, so it takes over 30,000 years for a trillion seconds to pass.)*

2. Tell the students that the national debt, also called the public debt, was almost $6 trillion in February 2002. (Note: You can easily find out the current size of the national debt to the penny, and other information about the national debt, by going to www.publicdebt.treas.gov.)

3. Display Visual 1. Discuss the answers to the questions.

   A. What is the national debt?

   *(The government gets revenues from taxes, and it spends on goods and services. If spending in any one year is equal to revenues, the government's budget is balanced. If spending is greater than revenues in any one year, there is an annual budget deficit. If revenues are greater than spending in any one year, there is an annual budget surplus. The national debt, also called the public debt, is the total owed by the*

# Should We Worry About the National Debt?

*federal government to those from whom it has borrowed. The national debt is the total of all the annual deficits accumulated since 1776, minus all the annual surpluses.)*

B. What caused the national debt?

*(Most of the U.S. national debt can be attributed to three things: paying for wars, increased government spending during recessions, and tax decreases not accompanied by decreases in government spending.)*

C. Where does the government get the money when it wants to spend more than it takes in?

*(The government borrows money. It does this by selling government securities, such as bonds. A bond is essentially an I.O.U. — that is, those who buy government bonds are loaning money to the government. When bonds come due, bondholders are paid back the money that they paid for the bond initially. Meanwhile, bondholders are paid interest on their bonds. The government also has the power to print money, and some governments finance their deficits in this way. The U.S. government generally does not do this.)*

D. What is a budget deficit?

*(A budget deficit occurs in any year in which federal government spending is greater than federal revenues, and is measured as the difference between the two. For example, in 1993 there was an annual deficit of about $255 billion.)*

E. What is a budget surplus?

*(A budget surplus occurs in any year in which federal government revenues are greater than federal spending, and is measured as the difference between the two. For example, in 2000 there was an annual surplus of about $236 billion. It is important to realize that just because there is a surplus in any given year, this does not mean that there is no national debt.)*

F. Is a budget deficit the same as a trade deficit?

*(No. A budget deficit is the difference between government revenues and spending in any year for which spending is greater than revenues. A trade deficit occurs when the value of goods and services imported is greater than the value of goods and services exported in a country.)*

4. Tell the students that they will now read a one-page handout addressing the issue of whether or not the national debt is a big problem. Divide your class in half. Give each student in half the class a copy of Handout 1; give each student in the other half a copy of Handout 2. (Handout 1 presents the view that the national debt is not a big problem; Handout 2 presents the opposite view.) Provide time for the students to read the handouts.

5. Discuss the handouts. Do not reveal to the students that there were two different versions of the handout until they figure this out from the discussion. The discussion should bring out some of the very real controversies about the national debt. The information presented on both Activities is true, and it represents opinions held by some economists.

Suggested discussion questions, and possible answers:

- Will the national debt cause the United States to go bankrupt?

  *(Handout 1: Not as long as people are willing to purchase U.S. bonds, so the debt can be refinanced.)*

- Are the interest payments on the debt important?

  *(Handout 2: Yes. They represent 14 percent of total government spending. This money could be used for other things.)*

- What about paying off the national debt by increasing taxes?

  *(Handout 1: This could be done.)*

  *(Handout 2: If taxes are increased, the increase affects people's incentives to work and invest. This could hurt economic growth.)*

- Does running deficits today, and adding to the national debt, put a burden on future generations?

  *(Handout 1: This isn't a big problem because people in the future also inherit the bonds, and today's spending may benefit future generations.)*

  *(Handout 2: The portion of the debt held by foreigners, about 22 percent, is a problem for future generations because the money paid back to bondholders will go out of the country.)*

- Is "crowding out" a problem resulting from the national debt?

  *(Handout 1: Not necessarily, provided the government uses the money borrowed for investment, and provided that government investment is viewed as being as good as private investment.)*

  *(Handout 2: Among other things, crowding out results in the government growing larger and the private sector growing smaller. Most Americans don't want big government.)*

- Would a law or a Constitutional amendment requiring a balanced budget be a good idea?

# Unit 6 | Teacher's Guide

*(Handout 1: No, because it would limit the government's ability to conduct discretionary fiscal policy, and that could make problems of recession and inflation worse.)*

*(Handout 2: This could be a good idea, because the government doesn't appear to be able to control its spending in other ways.)*

- How does the U.S. national debt compare to that of other countries?

   *(Handout 1: In terms of percentage of GDP, it is lower than that of many industrialized nations.)*

   *(Handout 2: The U.S. national debt is the largest in the world.)*

- Does the national debt hurt poor people more than wealthier people?

   *(Handout 2: The people who buy the bonds tend to be wealthier, while all taxpayers pay interest, including poorer Americans. Therefore, wealthier people may benefit at the expense of the poor.)*

## Closure

Assign the students who read Handout 1 to read Handout 2; assign those who read Handout 2 to read Handout 1. For homework, assign the students to write a one-page essay assessing both sides of the question, "Should We Worry about the National Debt?"

## Multiple-Choice Questions

(CORRECT ANSWERS SHOWN IN BOLD)

1. The U.S. national debt:

    A. Is zero. The United States is not in debt to anyone.

    **B. Is owed to people who have bought U.S. government bonds.**

    C. Is owed mostly to people in foreign countries who export goods to the United States.

    D. Is less than $1 trillion.

2. A government budget deficit occurs when:

    **A. The government spends more than it collects in revenues.**

    B. The government collects more in revenues than it spends.

    C. The Federal Reserve lends more than it borrows.

    D. The Federal Reserve borrows more than it lends.

## Essay Question

Some people believe we should worry about the national debt; others believe that it is not a big problem. Select one side of this argument and defend your opinion.

*(Answers will vary. Those who say the debt is a problem can argue that the interest payments on the debt are significant; that the portion of the debt held by foreigners imposes a burden on future generations; that "crowding out" may occur; and that the U.S. national debt is the largest in the world. Those who say it is not a problem can argue that as long as people are willing to buy U.S. bonds, the debt can be rolled over; that the debt is not that large as a percentage of GDP; that the debt doesn't really burden future generations; and that crowding out is not a big problem.)*

# Should We Worry About the National Debt?

## Unit 6, Lesson 36

### Handout 1

**Should We Worry about the National Debt?**

In early 2002, the U.S. national debt was almost $6 trillion. This amounts to over $20,000 for every man, woman, and child in the United States. Is this a problem for our economy? Many economists argue that this is not as big a problem as it may appear. Let's look at the reasons for this point of view.

When individuals are seriously in debt, they may be in danger of going bankrupt because they can't get enough money to pay their bills. This is not true for the U.S. government. For one thing, the government can continue to refinance or "roll over" the national debt. When one person's bonds become due, it can sell bonds to someone else to pay off the first person. U.S. government bonds are a very safe investment paying competitive interest rates, so there is no shortage of people here and abroad willing to buy them. As long as people are willing to buy U.S. government bonds, the government will be able to refinance the debt. Also, the government has the ability to tax. If people wanted to pay off the debt with tax revenues, the government could do this.

Sometimes people say that if the government runs a deficit today, it will put a burden on future generations. They argue that your children and grandchildren will have to pay off today's debt and therefore won't be as well off. But this ignores the fact that people in the future will inherit bonds (an asset) as well as the debt (a liability). And spending today may benefit people in the future. Much of our debt today was used to pay for wars fought by our fathers and grandfathers. Do we feel burdened by this today?

"Crowding out" is frequently cited as a problem of the national debt. When the government borrows money for deficit spending, there is less money for private businesses to borrow, and interest rates increase. This "crowds out" private investment spending and could lead to lower economic growth in the future. But this argument ignores the fact that the government may be using the money it borrows today for investment — in capital goods or in human capital. It may use the money to build roads or bridges, to fund education, or for health care. Certainly these projects would help people today and in the future.

It is important to recognize the problems that would occur if laws were passed requiring the government to balance its budget annually. During times of recession, government tax revenues fall because incomes go down. If it were required to balance the budget, the government would have to reduce its spending to match the lower tax revenues, which would make the recession worse. The opposite is true in periods of inflation: tax revenues go up because people's incomes go up. If it were required to balance the budget, the government would have to increase its spending to equal the higher tax revenues, which would lead to more inflation. The important thing for the government to worry about is controlling unemployment and inflation. A law or Constitutional amendment requiring a balanced budget could take away this power.

It's certainly true that $6 trillion is a large number and a lot of dollars. But it is important to look at this as a percentage of GDP. U.S. GDP was about $10 trillion in 2001, making the national debt about 60 percent of GDP. This is a lower percentage than in many other industrialized countries including Japan, Canada, Italy, Spain, France, and Germany. Another thing to keep in mind is that much of the debt — about 78 percent of it — is owed to U.S. citizens, U.S. businesses and banks, and agencies of the U.S. government. It is Americans owing money to Americans. Viewed this way, paying it off wouldn't really accomplish much: American taxpayers would pay money to American bondholders, but overall national income would remain the same.

# Unit 6, Lesson 36

## Handout 2

### Should We Worry about the National Debt?

In early 2002, the U.S. national debt was almost $6 trillion. This amounts to over $20,000 for every man, woman, and child in the United States. Is this a problem for our economy? Many economists argue that it is a significant problem for both current and future generations of Americans. Let's look at the reasons for this point of view.

The United States has the world's largest national debt, although it is not the largest in terms of percent of GDP. People who hold U.S. government bonds must be paid interest on these bonds. Because the debt is so high, the amount paid in interest is also high: in 2000, interest payments on the debt represented 14 percent of total federal government spending. If interest rates go up in the future, there is a danger of larger and larger portions of government spending going merely to pay this interest. Money spent for interest payments means that less money can be spent on other items like education and health care.

Some people argue that we may never have to pay off the national debt because it can be "rolled over." That is, when some bonds come due, the government can sell more bonds to other people to pay off the first group. Furthermore, the argument goes, the interest paid on the bonds is just a transfer from one group of Americans (the taxpayers) to another (the bondholders), so overall income doesn't really change. But this ignores the issue of the distribution of income. It is generally the more wealthy Americans who are the bondholders — to whom the government debt is owed. But poorer Americans pay taxes too. Therefore the national debt may cause money to be paid to bondholders (richer people) by all taxpayers (including poorer people). Many would argue that this redistribution of income is not fair.

It is true that much of the national debt is owed to U.S. citizens and U.S. government agencies. But a major concern is that 22 percent of the debt is owed to foreigners — up from about 14 percent in 1990. When the bonds owed to foreigners become due in the future, our children and grandchildren will have to pay off these bonds out of their current income. This money will go to foreign countries, not to spending programs in the United States. This foreign held or "external" debt therefore places a burden on future generations of Americans. Our children and grandchildren will have to pay off the debts from our spending today. This is not fair to them.

Some people say we shouldn't worry about the debt because we could pay it off by increasing taxes. A problem with this argument is that raising taxes affects people's incentives to work, to invest, and to innovate. If tax rates go up to pay off the debt or to pay more interest on the debt, people may decide to work less rather than seeing more of their incomes go to taxes. This may hurt economic efficiency, future investment, and the prospects for economic growth in the economy.

"Crowding out" is frequently cited as a problem of the national debt, and it also relates to economic growth. When the government borrows money for deficit spending, there is less money for the private businesses to borrow, and interest rates increase. This "crowds out" private investment spending and could lead to lower economic growth in the future. Additionally, crowding out means that the government ends up controlling a larger share of the economy, and private businesses a smaller share. Most Americans are not in favor of bigger government, and would rather have more control in the hands of private businesses.

If we look at patterns of government spending in the last decades of the 20th century, we see evidence (up to 1998) of growing deficits and a lack of ability on the part of government officials to control their spending. If government bureaucrats can't control their spending, then the people are in a position to do something about it. A law or a Constitutional amendment could be passed to force the government to balance its budget annually.

# Should We Worry about the National Debt?

**Unit 6, Lesson 36**
Visual 1

## QUESTIONS ABOUT THE NATIONAL DEBT

A. What is the national debt?

B. What caused the national debt?

C. Where does the government get the money when it wants to spend more than it takes in?

D. What is a budget deficit?

E. What is a budget surplus?

F. Is a budget deficit the same as a trade deficit?

# Unit 6 | Teacher's Guide

## Unit 6 Lesson 37

## Can Government Manage The National Economy?

### INTRODUCTION

**Economics**  Macroeconomics is the branch of economics that focuses on economic growth, unemployment, and inflation. One major issue in economics concerns the effectiveness of government policies in managing the economy. Which policies work best? Is government even capable of managing the economy?

Before the 1930s, the prevailing economic theory was that a free-market economy is self-adjusting. According to the Classical economists, there may be temporary periods of inflation and unemployment, but in the long run the economy will stay on course. And then came the Great Depression.

In the 1930s, economist John Maynard Keynes said that in the long run we're all dead. More importantly, he theorized that controlling aggregate demand through monetary and fiscal policies could influence inflation, unemployment, and economic growth. By the 1970s, there was a Keynesian consensus that inflation and unemployment could be controlled by increasing or decreasing aggregate demand. There was, of course, a trade-off between unemployment and inflation.

And then came high inflation and high unemployment. The Keynesian consensus ended. New Classical economists built the case that the government's ability to manage the economy is limited at best. The economy is too complex and the secondary effects are too great to be managed by government.

What can we learn from these theories? Will a new consensus emerge?

**Reasoning**  Economic facts and relationships are too complicated to organize themselves. Theories simplify the world and provide a structure enabling us to analyze economic behavior and to predict future behavior. Theory is an important tool of analysis, and a high school economics course should emphasize analysis rather than easy answers to today's economic problems.

### CONCEPTS

- Aggregate demand
- Aggregate supply
- Assumptions
- Fiscal policy
- Keynesian theory
- Monetarist theory
- Monetary policy
- New Classical theory
- Rational Expectations theory

### OBJECTIVES

*Students will:*

1. Describe the role of theory in macroeconomic analysis.
2. Explain why economists sometimes disagree on policy recommendations.
3. Analyze the assumptions, values, theoretical support, and applicable time periods underlying recommendations concerning monetary and fiscal policies that are in conflict.
4. Explain the assumptions of the Keynesian and New Classical theories.
5. Describe, compare, and contrast the Keynesian and New Classical theories.
6. Evaluate how well the government can manage the economy.

### CONTENT STANDARD

- A nation's overall levels of income, employment, and prices are determined by the interaction of spending and production decisions made by all households, firms, government agencies, and others in the economy. (NCEE Content Standard 18)

### LESSON DESCRIPTION

Although economists agree much more often than they disagree, the opinions of prominent economists on economic policy often conflict. This lesson seeks to clarify why economists disagree. Understanding the reasons for disagreement among experts may help students to make their own judgments about economic policies. The lesson concludes by having students compare and contrast the major macroeconomic theories, which are Keynesian and New Classical. New Classical economics includes the Monetarist and Rational Expectations theories.

*Time Required: 90 minutes*

### MATERIALS

- Transparencies of Visuals 1 and 2
- Activities 1, 2, and 3

### PROCEDURE

1. Explain to the class that the purpose of this lesson is to show why economists sometimes disagree. Have the students read Activity 1; discuss reasons why economists disagree.
2. Have the students read Activity 2. Tell them to keep in mind that they will be asked to analyze each professor's arguments on the basis of differences in time periods, assumptions, economic theories, and values.

# CAN GOVERNMENT MANAGE THE NATIONAL ECONOMY?

3. In class discussion, analyze the arguments of Professor Cut. Elicit answers from the class on each major point and record them on the board. Try to reach consensus on each major point — time periods, assumptions, theoretical support, and values. At the end of the discussion, you may want to project a transparency of the analysis of Professor Cut's arguments. Don't show the analysis of the other professors' arguments. Be flexible in comparing student answers to those on the transparency. There are many correct ways to state these points.

4. Divide the class into groups of four students each. Tell one group it will analyze the arguments of Professor U.R. Nutts, another the arguments of Professor E.Z. Money, and another the arguments of Professor Fred Critic. If the class is large, have more than one group analyze each professor.

5. Allow each group about 15 minutes to analyze its professor's arguments, using Activities 1 and 2. Appoint a recorder for each group or have each group choose a recorder to enter the group's conclusions on the handout.

6. Solicit analysis from one group at a time. Have each group's recorder write the group's conclusions on the board. Have the rest of the class evaluate the conclusions. Compare the conclusions with those on the transparency. The answers are as follows:

*Name of professor: Professor Cut*

*Major point:* Tax cut will stimulate the economy.

*Time period:* Present and near future.

*Assumptions:* The administration's budget proposals are not inflationary.

*Theoretical support:* Tax cuts stimulate business investment as well as spending by all private sectors and may encourage greater work effort.

*Values:* Economic freedom and distrust of big government.

*Name of professor: Professor Nutts*

*Major point:* Higher interest rates will cause recovery to fail.

*Time period:* Next year.

*Assumptions:* Deficits are large and getting larger.

*Theoretical support:* Government borrowing is so large that it causes interest rates to rise and crowds out consumer and business borrowing.

*Values:* Tax cuts must be fair, and fairness means taxing wealthier people more than poorer people. Government must maintain economic security for Americans with low incomes.

*Name of professor: Professor Money*

*Major point:* Relatively free expansion of money will bring down interest rates and sustain recovery.

*Time period:* Near future.

*Assumptions:* Relatively free expansion of money supply by the Fed will sustain the recovery.

*Theoretical support:* Lower interest rates increase consumer spending and business investment. The primary effect of lower interest rates is on investment.

*Values:* A growing economy is desirable.

*Name of professor: Professor Critic*

*Major point:* There will be a period of inflation, then another recession.

*Time period:* One or two years from now.

*Assumptions:* The Fed will continue past policies — policies that have brought about periods of inflation and recession.

*Theoretical support:* Not enough money growth causes recession; too much money growth causes inflation.

*Values:* Steady economic growth without inflation or recession is desirable.

7. Ask the students which economist they agree with most and why.

8. This should be the end of the class period and the first half of the lesson.

9. Use Visual 1 to discuss the Keynesian theory.

10. Use Visual 2 to discuss the New Classical theory.

11. Divide the class into groups; have each group classify each idea in Activity 3 under Keynesian or New Classical theory.

12. Now put two headings on the board and allow plenty of space to write under each. The headings are **Keynesian** and **New Classical**. The answers are as follows:

*Keynesian Theory*

1. Recessions and depressions occur because of too little aggregate demand.
2. Government can and should play a positive role in managing the economy.
3. Monetary policy works through interest rates.
4. Fiscal policy is more effective than monetary policy.
5. Government may not be able to completely control the economy, but it can make it better.
6. Lowering taxes or increasing government spending affects aggregate demand.

7. There is a trade-off between unemployment and inflation.

*New Classical Theory*

1. Monetary and fiscal policies are generally ineffective in managing the economy.
2. Monetary and fiscal policies have some short-term effects but have little influence in the long run.
3. Fool me once, shame on you. Fool me twice, shame on me.
4. That government that governs least governs best.
5. Inflation is caused by the government increasing the money supply by more than 3 to 5 percent a year.
6. Taxes primarily affect people's incentives to save, work, and invest.
7. It is important that government economic policies be clear and consistent.

13. Have one student at a time classify an idea under one or more of the headings and write it on the board. Discuss each idea as it is classified. Is it classified correctly?

## CLOSURE

Ask the following questions.

- Does the evidence show that the government can or cannot manage the economy?

  *(The evidence is mixed. In the 1970s, the United States had high inflation and high unemployment. In the 1990s, the United States had low inflation and low unemployment, but unemployment increased early in the 2000s. Economists even differ as to why the good and bad effects occurred.)*

- Can something be good in theory but bad in practice?

  *(No. The test of a theory is its ability to predict. If the theory does not predict correctly, it is a bad theory and will lead to bad practice.)*

- Students are late to class. The teacher lectures them but does not penalize them. The next day the same students are late. How does this relate to the New Classical theory?

  *(Intelligent students have made decisions on the costs and benefits of government policy. This behavior supports the New Classical theory.)*

## MULTIPLE-CHOICE QUESTIONS

(CORRECT ANSWERS SHOWN IN BOLD)

1. According to which macroeconomic theory is decreasing taxes and increasing government spending a sound policy to recover from a recession?

   A. New Classical

   **B. Keynesian**

   C. Monetarist

   D. Rational Expectations

2. Which statement is most consistent with the New Classical theory?

   A. The velocity of money is unstable.

   B. The Federal Reserve should set interest rate targets.

   **C. Government fiscal and monetary policies cause more economic instability than stability.**

   D. Fiscal policy works better than monetary policy.

## ESSAY QUESTIONS

1. Tell whether you think the following statement is true, false, or uncertain, and explain your reasoning: "Economics is not a science because economists disagree too much."

   *(False. Economists agree much more than they disagree. However, they do disagree for several reasons: different time periods, different assumptions, different economic theories, different values.)*

2. Why do New Classical theorists believe that monetary and fiscal policies will be ineffective?

   *(The key point in the New Classical theory is that people behave rationally. They gather information, process that information, and make intelligent expectations about how events and decisions will affect them monetarily. In highly competitive markets, people will anticipate the effects of monetary and fiscal policy changes and act defensively to protect themselves from these changes. These acts can negate the effects of the policy changes. For example, the government might conduct an expansionary fiscal policy, and the Fed accommodates this with an expansionary monetary policy. The aim of the policies is to increase output and unemployment. However, businesses and consumers see the policies as inflationary and act to protect themselves from the coming inflation. Businesses borrow more, and workers push for higher wages. This causes wage-price inflation and higher interest rates. Rather than getting an increase in investment spending and real GDP, the government policies cause more inflation.)*

**Unit 6, Lesson 37**
Visual 1

## KEYNESIAN THEORY

- Recessions and depressions can occur because of too little aggregate demand for goods and services.

- Inflation can occur because of too much aggregate demand for goods and services.

- Government can influence macroeconomic activity by influencing aggregate demand through fiscal and monetary policies.

- Fiscal policy (changes in government spending and taxes) is more powerful than monetary policy (changes in the money supply and interest rates).

- Monetary policy affects investment spending through interest rates.

**Unit 6, Lesson 37**
Visual 2

## NEW CLASSICAL THEORY

- The government's power to influence the macro-economy is limited and often ineffective.

- Consumers, business leaders, and investors are intelligent decision makers and take the effects of government policies into account in deciding on their behavior.

- People's actions often offset the effects of government fiscal and monetary policies.

- Monetarists believe the government should increase the money supply 3 to 5 percent a year and do no more.

- Rational Expectations theorists emphasize the role of forward-looking expectations in affecting economic growth, inflation and unemployment.

- Monetary and fiscal policies affect expectations and have unanticipated secondary effects that make these policies ineffective.

# Unit 6 | Teacher's Guide

## Unit 6 Lesson 38

## Aggregate Demand and Aggregate Supply

### Introduction

**Economics**  During the past 20 years, one of the major pedagogical innovations in the college introductory course has been to use aggregate demand and supply curves to illustrate important macroeconomic concepts and policy issues. This analysis is now becoming more common in the high school course, although different texts treat it in slightly different ways. Because these curves look and operate much like microeconomic supply and demand curves, students view them as identical.

However, the conceptual underpinnings of aggregate supply and demand curves are quite different from the conceptual underpinnings of microeconomic supply and demand curves for an individual product or productive resource. Consequently, an important goal of this lesson is to make sure that students understand these differences. Once students understand what the aggregate supply and demand curves are, they can use them to explain or predict the effect of a macroeconomic event or policy on the overall price level and the level of national output. But it is also important for students to understand that microeconomic and macroeconomic (i.e., aggregate) supply and demand curves are very different things and have the similar shapes they are normally shown as having for very different reasons.

**Reasoning**  Aggregate demand and aggregate supply provide students with an analytical framework to understand the causes of macroeconomic problems and to predict the economic consequences of proposed government policies. This understanding helps future voters to make informed choices among alternative political candidates and policies. Macroeconomic policies will have a strong effect on students' future job opportunities and incomes and on the prices they will pay for goods and services. While the analysis is abstract, the consequences are concrete and real.

### Concepts

- Aggregate demand and shifting
- Aggregate supply and shifting
- Fiscal policy
- Macroeconomic equilibrium
- Monetary policy
- Price level
- Real gross domestic product

### Objectives

*Students will:*

1. Define *aggregate demand, aggregate supply,* and *macroeconomic equilibrium.*

2. Identify and describe the factors that can cause the aggregate demand or aggregate supply schedule to shift.

3. Use aggregate demand and aggregate supply analysis to predict the effects of macroeconomic events.

4. Use aggregate demand and aggregate supply analysis to predict the effects of different government economic policies.

### Content Standard

- A nation's overall levels of income, employment, and prices are determined by the interaction of spending and production decisions made by all households, firms, government agencies, and others in the economy. (NCEE Content Standard 18)

### Lesson Description

Students build their understanding of aggregate demand and aggregate supply. They use their new skills to analyze the effects of events and government monetary and fiscal policies on inflation, unemployment, and economic growth. In the first two Activities, students identify different components of AD and AS and the factors that shift AD and AS. In the last two Activities, students use AD and AS analysis to predict the effect of events and government monetary and fiscal policies on inflation, unemployment, and economic growth.

*Time Required: 150 minutes*

### Materials

- A transparency of Visuals 1, 2, 3, 4, 5, and 6
- Activities 1, 2, 3, and 4

### Procedure

1. Project Visual 1 and use it to explain the aggregate demand curve. Be sure to explain why the AD curve is downward-sloping and how it differs from a demand curve for a microeconomic good or resource. The rationale for the downward-sloping AD curve has these three factors: (1) the wealth effect, (2) the income effect, and (3) the foreign purchases effect.

2. Continue using Visual 1 to explain the determinants of aggregate demand. These are factors that cause the AD curve to shift and are changes in (1)

# Aggregate Demand and Aggregate Supply

consumer spending, (2) investment spending, (3) government spending, and (4) net export spending. Increases in aggregate demand increase real GDP and the price level. Decreases in aggregate demand decrease real GDP and the price level.

3. Have the students complete Activity 1. You might go over the first event with the class to make sure they have the idea.

4. Review the answers to Activity 1. Be sure to press the students to describe why they shifted the curve. For example, in situation 1, a tax cut increases consumer disposable income which increases consumer spending which increases aggregate demand. The key is to describe the process that causes AD to increase or decrease.

*Answers to Activity 1*

1. Congress cuts taxes.

    AD *increase*     Curve *D*

2. A survey shows business investment spending decreased last month.

    AD *decrease*    Curve *C*

3. Government spending will increase next fiscal year; the President promises no increase in taxes.

    AD *increase*     Curve *D*

4. A survey shows consumers are confident about the future economy.

    AD *increase*     Curve *E*

5. Business leaders feel the economy is headed for recession.

    AD *decrease*    Curve *D*

6. The stock market collapses — investors lose billions.

    AD *decrease*    Curve *C*

7. Productivity rises for the fourth straight year.

    AD *no change*   Curve *C*

    NOTE: *Increases in productivity increase aggregate supply, not aggregate demand.*

8. The President cuts defense spending by 20 percent; there is no increase in domestic spending.

    AD *decrease*    Curve *B*

5. Project Visual 2 and explain the short-run aggregate supply curve. Discuss the nature of aggregate supply. The AS curve has been simplified as an upward-sloping curve. Reality can be more complex. In fact, AS is more vertical as the economy moves toward full employment. Some texts depict the AS curve with three distinct stages. The important thing is for students to understand the overall nature of AS; they should not get caught up in the details.

6. Use Visual 2 to explain the determinants of aggregate supply. These are factors that cause the AS curve to shift and are changes in (1) the prices of inputs (land, labor, capital, and entrepreneurship); (2) productivity; (3) technology; and (4) government taxes, subsidies, and regulations. Increases in AS increase real GDP and lower the price level. Decreases in AS decrease real GDP and raise the price level.

7. Have the students complete Activity 2. You might go over the first event with the class.

8. Review the answers to Activity 2. Once again, press the students to explain the logic behind their answers. For example, in situation 1, higher wages increase the costs of production, which decreases aggregate supply.

*Answers to Activity 2*

1. Unions grow more aggressive; wage rates increase.

    AS *decrease*    Curve *B*

2. OPEC successfully increases oil prices.

    AS *decrease*    Curve *A*

3. Labor productivity increases dramatically.

    AS *increase*    Curve *B*

4. A giant natural gas discovery decreases energy prices.

    AS *increase*    Curve *C*

5. Computer technology brings new efficiency to industry.

    AS *increase*    Curve *D*

6. Government spending increases.

    AS *no change*   Curve *D*

    Note: *A government spending increase will increase AD and will not change AS.*

7. Cuts in tax rates increase incentives to work, save, and invest.

    AS *increase*    Curve *E*

8. The low birth rate will decrease the labor force in the future.

    AS *decrease*    Curve *D*

9. Research shows that improved schools have increased the skills of American workers and managers.

    AS *increase*    Curve *E*

9. Project Visual 3 and explain how shifts in aggregate demand affect the equilibrium level of real GDP and the price level. The actual effect depends on how close the economy is to full employment. In a recession, the effect is primarily on real GDP, while at full employment the effect is primarily on the price level.

10. Project Visual 4 and explain how shifts in aggregate supply affect the equilibrium level of real GDP and the price level.

11. Have the students complete Activity 3. Go over the first problem with the class.

12. Use Visual 5 to review the answers to Activity 3.

## Closure

- Use Activity 4 to summarize the effects of shifts in AD and AS. Have the students complete Activity 4 in groups. Have each group draw a graph on the board for one of the problems. Then use Visual 6 to go over the answers as a class.

- Have the students bring in headlines of current economic events and proposed government policies. Have them draw AD and AS curves to analyze the events and policies.

## Multiple-Choice Questions

(CORRECT ANSWERS SHOWN IN BOLD)

1. Aggregate supply is:
   A. The amount buyers plan to spend on output.
   B. Equal to the money income received by the owners of the factors of production.
   C. Always equal to aggregate demand.
   **D. A schedule indicating the level of real GDP that will be produced at each possible price level.**

2. Aggregate demand is:
   A. The amount consumers want to buy at each and every price level.
   **B. The total spending in the economy by consumers, businesses, governments, and foreigners at each price level.**
   C. Never equal to aggregate supply.
   D. Horizontal to real GDP at every price level.

3. Aggregate demand will increase or shift to the right if:
   A. Productivity increases.
   **B. Business investment increases.**
   C. Taxes increase.
   D. Energy prices decrease.

4. The aggregate supply curve will increase or shift to the right if:
   A. Energy prices increase.
   **B. Labor costs decrease.**
   C. Productivity levels decrease.
   D. Investment spending decreases.

5. Which of the following events would most likely increase both the price level and real GDP?
   A. An increase in labor productivity
   **B. An increase in consumer spending**
   C. An increase in taxes
   D. A decrease in energy prices

6. The government wants to increase real GDP without increasing the price level. Which of the following policies has the best chance to achieve this?
   **A. Decrease income and business taxes**
   B. Increase government regulations on businesses
   C. Increase the minimum wage
   D. Increase government spending

## Essay Questions

1. In 2000-2001, stock prices decreased by a large percentage. What effect did this have on aggregate demand, aggregate supply, the price level, and real GDP? Why?

   *(Aggregate demand decreased because consumers had less wealth and therefore decreased their spending. Aggregate supply was unchanged. There is a movement along the AS curve. Both the price level and real GDP decreased.)*

2. Indicate how each of the following events would increase or decrease aggregate demand and tell why.
   A. Businesses are confident of the future.
   
      *(Confident businesses increase investment spending, which increases AD.)*
   
   B. The nation fears a recession next year.
   
      *(Consumers who fear losing their jobs decrease spending, which decreases AD.)*

# Aggregate Demand and Aggregate Supply

C. The federal government increases income taxes.

*(Higher income taxes decrease disposable income, which decreases consumer spending and AD.)*

3. Indicate how each of the following situations would increase or decrease aggregate supply and tell why.

   A. New computer technology increases productivity.

   *(Higher productivity decreases costs and increases AS.)*

   B. Widespread strikes result in big pay raises.

   *(Higher wages increase costs and decrease AS.)*

   C. Terrorists destroy the World Trade Center.

   *(People are killed and their skills and productivity are lost to the economy. Capital is destroyed. This would decrease AS.)*

# Unit 6 | Teacher's Guide

**Unit 6, Lesson 38**
Visual 1

## SHIFTS IN AGGREGATE DEMAND

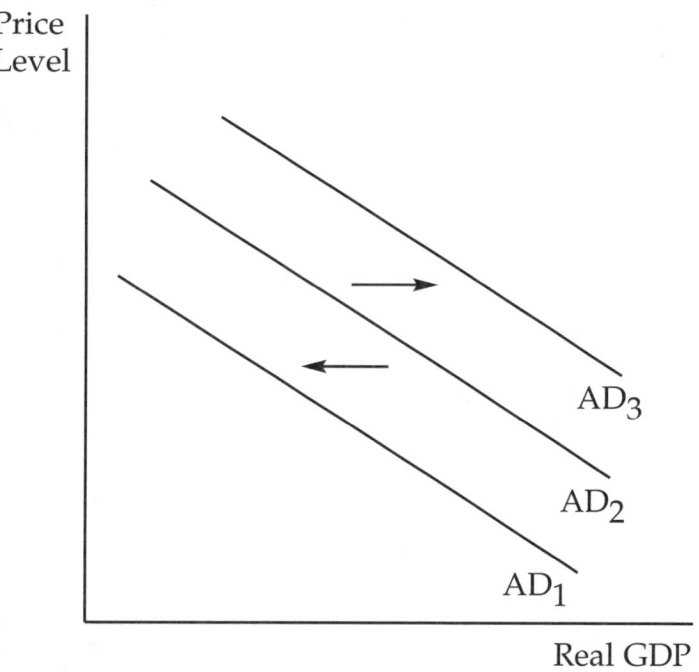

1. What factors can cause the aggregate demand curve to shift rightward, or increase?

2. What factors can cause the aggregate demand curve to shift leftward, or decrease?

# AGGREGATE DEMAND AND AGGREGATE SUPPLY

**Unit 6, Lesson 38**
Visual 2

## SHIFTS IN AGGREGATE SUPPLY

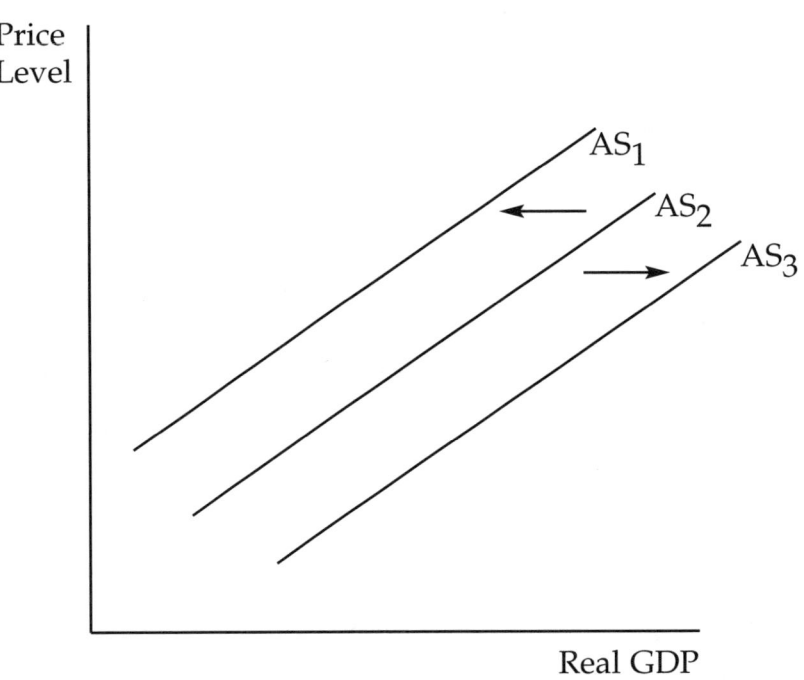

1. What factors can cause the aggregate supply curve to shift rightward, or increase?

2. What factors can cause the aggregate supply curve to shift leftward, or decrease?

**Unit 6, Lesson 38**
Visual 3

## THE EFFECTS OF SHIFTS IN AGGREGATE DEMAND

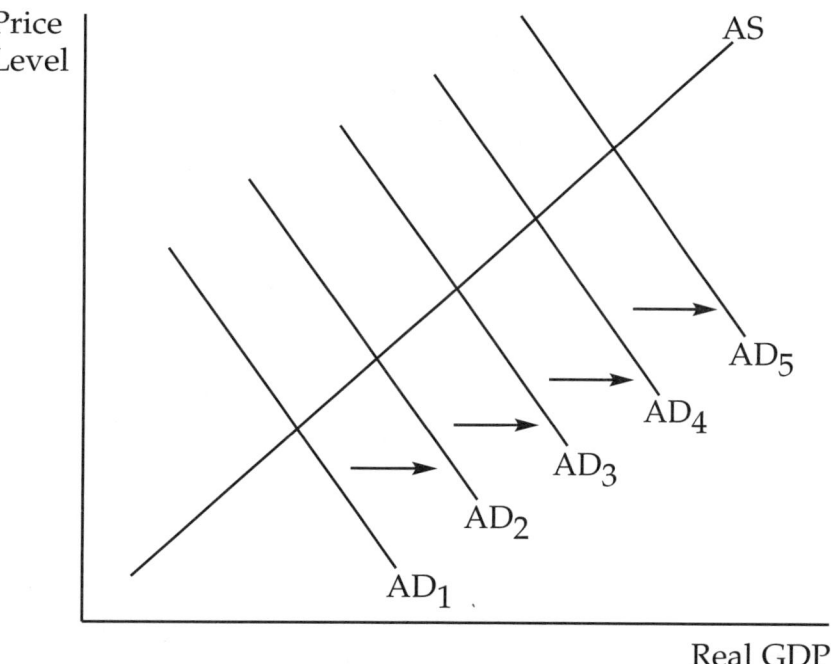

1. If AD increases, what will happen to the price level and real GDP?

2. If AD decreases, what will happen to the price level and real GDP?

3. What factor determines whether the price level or real GDP increases more?

AGGREGATE DEMAND AND AGGREGATE SUPPLY

**Unit 6, Lesson 38**
Visual 4

# THE EFFECTS OF SHIFTS IN AGGREGATE SUPPLY

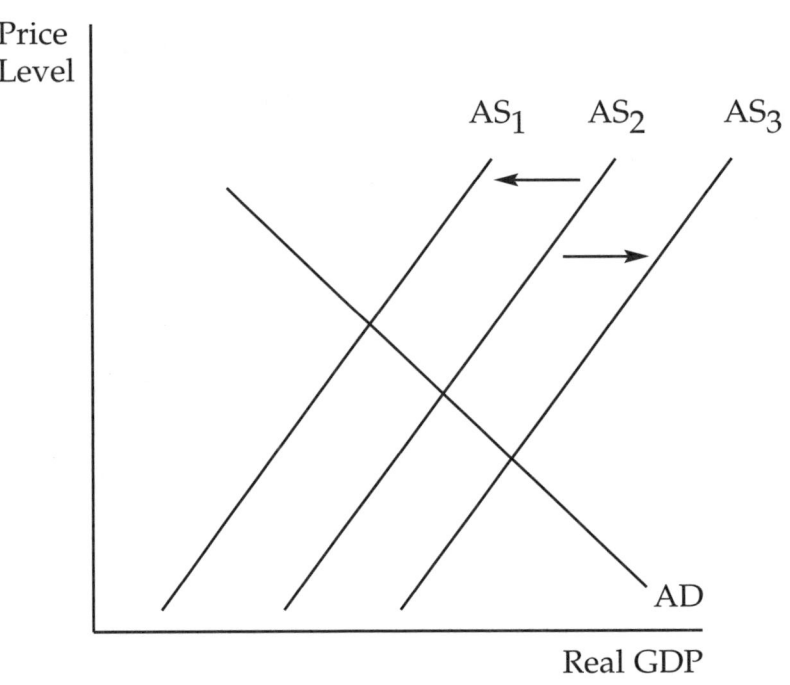

1. What effect does a decrease in aggregate supply have on the price level and real GDP?

2. What effect does an increase in aggregate supply have on the price level and real GDP?

# Unit 6 | Teacher's Guide

**Unit 6, Lesson 38**
Visual 5

## Answers to Activity 3

### Summarizing Aggregate Demand and Aggregate Supply Shifts

| | 1. Increase in labor productivity due to technological change | 2. Increase in the price of inputs used by many firms | 3. Boom in investment, assuming some unemployed resources are available* | 4. A major reduction in investment spending |
|---|---|---|---|---|
| | (PL/Real GDP graph: AS shifts right to AS₁; AD) | (PL/Real GDP graph: AS shifts left from AS₁ to AS; AD) | (PL/Real GDP graph: AS; AD shifts right to AD₁) | (PL/Real GDP graph: AS; AD shifts left to AD₁) |
| AD curve | A | A | S | S |
| AS curve | S | S | A* | A |
| Real GDP | + | − | + | − |
| Price level | − | + | + | − |
| Unemployment | − | + | − | + |

*In situation 3, AS could increase also because increased investment causes increased productivity. However, only AD increases with the original investment.

CAPSTONE: EXEMPLARY LESSONS FOR HIGH SCHOOL ECONOMICS @ NATIONAL COUNCIL ON ECONOMIC EDUCATION, NEW YORK, NY     253

# AGGREGATE DEMAND AND AGGREGATE SUPPLY

**Unit 6, Lesson 38**
Visual 6

## ANSWERS TO ACTIVITY 4
### SUMMARIZING CHANGES IN THE EQUILIBRIUM PRICE LEVEL AND REAL GDP

### 1. Increase in Government Spending

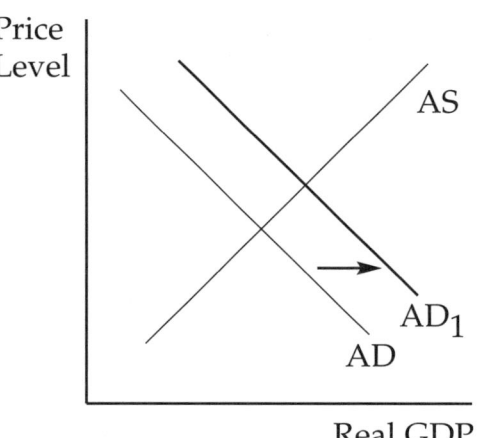

During a recession, the government increases spending on schools, highways, and other public works.

Price level  ⓐ↓ –

Real GDP  ⓐ↓ –

### 2. New Oil Discoveries

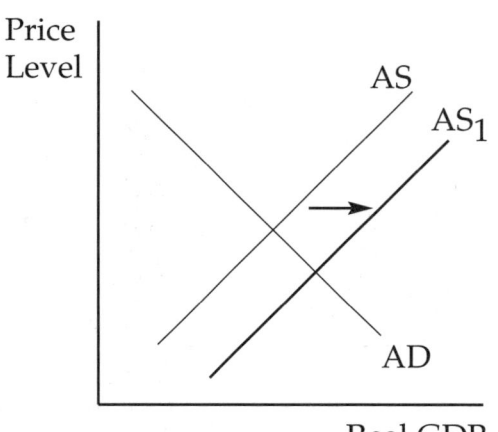

New oil discoveries cause large decreases in energy prices.

Price level  ↑ⓓ –

Real GDP  ⓐ↓ –

**Unit 6, Lesson 38**
Visual 6 cont.

### 3. Effects of New Technology and Better Education

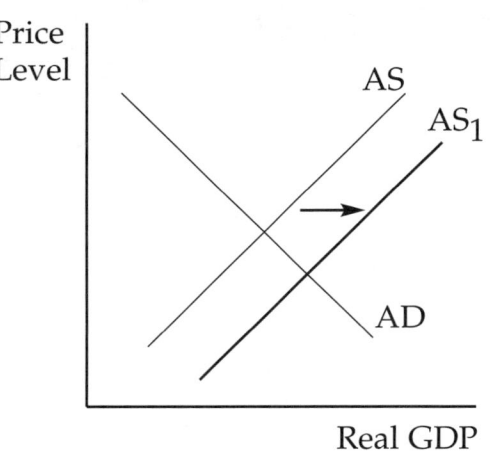

New technology and better education increase productivity.

Price level ↑ⓓ –

Real GDP ⓤ↓ –

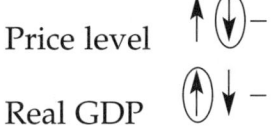

### 4. Increased Confidence for Future Economy

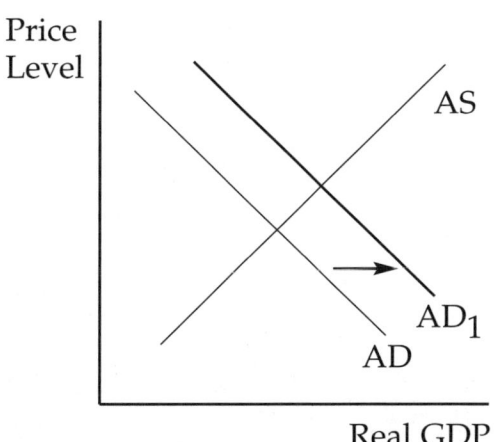

A new President makes consumers and businesses more confident about the future economy. *Note: Show the change in AD only.*

Price level ⓤ↓ –

Real GDP ⓤ↓ –

# Aggregate Demand and Aggregate Supply

**Unit 6, Lesson 38**
Visual 6 cont.

### 5. Income Tax Cut

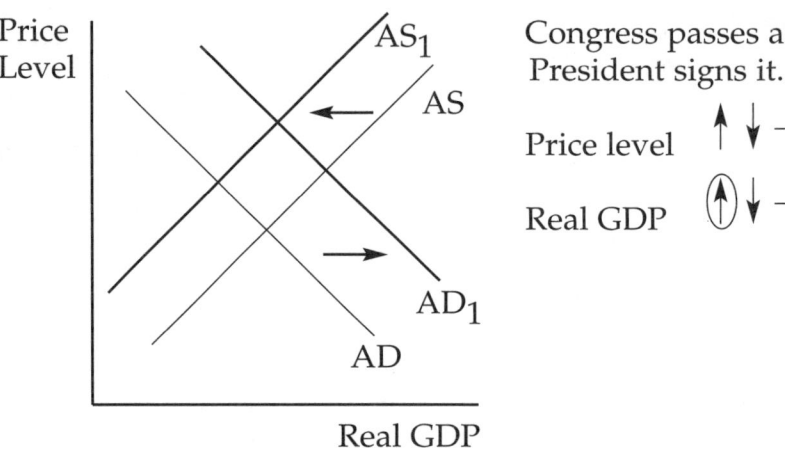

Congress passes a tax cut, and the President signs it.

Price level ↑ ↓ –

Real GDP ↑ ↓ –

*The price level depends on whether AD increased more or less than AS. A tax cut has demand-side and supply-side effects. Therefore, the changes in the price level cannot be predicted. Real GDP will rise.*

# CAPSTONE

## UNIT 7

# MARKETS WITHOUT BORDERS: THE GLOBAL ECONOMY

Lesson 39  Why Go Global?

Lesson 40  Why Do People Trade across National Borders?

Lesson 41  Why People Trade: Comparative Advantage

Lesson 42  Foreign Currencies and Foreign Exchange

Lesson 43  Why Are Some Nations Wealthy?

Lesson 44  World Environmental Issues: Is the Market at Fault?

Lesson 45  International Trade: How Do We Measure Trades across Political Borders?

# Unit 7 | Teacher's Guide

## Unit 7 Lesson 39

## Why Go Global?

### Introduction

**Economics** The U.S. economy is increasingly integrated into the world economy. One cause of this change has been a decrease in transaction costs such as those in telecommunications and transportation. The global economy offers several advantages to its participants. It offers businesses an expanded market for goods and services. It offers consumers goods and services from around the world.

Global trade also changes economic relationships. While these disruptions can increase costs to some, economists believe that the benefits outweigh those costs.

**Reasoning** The principles involved in international trade are essentially the same as those in any voluntary transaction. Trade allows each partner to produce and consume more than would otherwise be possible. Nations that are open to trade allow their consumers and their businesses to access world markets. The increased competition provides incentives to businesses to provide goods and services at the lowest possible cost. Despite these benefits, however, governments often approve policies, such as tariffs and quotas, that impede trade. Realizing the full benefits of trade requires developing international institutions that change the "rules of the game" so as to encourage increased global linkages.

### Concepts

- Choice
- Economic system
- Future consequences
- Incentives
- Opportunity cost
- Voluntary trade

### Objectives

*Students will:*

1. Explain why international trade has been expanding.
2. Identify the benefits of trade to consumers and producers.
3. Apply principles of economic reasoning to explain why international trade can have positive outcomes.

### Content Standard

- When individuals, regions, and nations specialize in what they can produce at the lowest cost and then trade with others, both production and consumption increase. (NCEE Content Standard 6)

### Lesson Description

Students examine an economic mystery regarding the importance of U.S. participation in the global economy. They participate in a demonstration regarding imported clothing. They use the **Guide to Economic Reasoning** to explain that, while exports and imports may be a relatively small part of the U.S. economy, international trade benefits the United States and its trade partners.

*Time Required: 45 minutes*

### Materials

- A transparency of Visuals 1 and 2
- Activity 1
- A $20 bill

### Procedure

1. Tell the class that globalization has become a topic of interest among many Americans. Some fear our global connections while others welcome them. But how connected are we? Does it matter? Display Visual 1. Ask:

    - What percent of GDP involves international transactions?

      *(About 25 percent.)*

    - What percent of the labor force is engaged in exports?

      *(Eight percent.)*

2. Display Visual 2. Ask the students to speculate about whether each statement is true or false.

    A. The global economy is a growing part of the U.S. economy. *(True)*

    B. Some American workers benefit from trade. *(True)*

    C. American consumers benefit from trade. *(True)*

    D. Prices in the United States are lower because of trade. *(True)*

    E. Trade barriers have been increasing around the world. *(False)*

# WHY GO GLOBAL?

3. Do a short demonstration regarding the widespread nature of international trade. Explain that you will give $20 to the "All American Kid" in the class. An "All American Kid" is one who is wearing only American-made clothing. Divide the class into pairs. Ask each person in the pair to search the clothing labels of the other — shoes, shirts, belts, pants, and so forth — to see where the clothing was made. The student who is wearing all American-made clothing gets the $20. It is highly unlikely that you have an "All American Kid" in your class.

4. Ask: Why don't we buy only American clothes?

    *(Apparently, we prefer to buy at least some clothing from other nations. The producers from other nations provide us with some clothing we like better, in quality and price, than what is offered by domestic producers.)*

5. Explain to the class that its behavior in the demonstration is similar to the behavior of many Americans and others living Canada, Mexico, Japan, and Europe. Refer the students to Activity 1 and ask them to read it. Then ask:

    A. Why are we going global?

    *(Decreasing communication and transportation costs.)*

    B. How do American workers and businesses benefit from international trade?

    *(The global economy offers a market for goods and services produced by American workers, farmers, and businesses.)*

    C. How do American consumers benefit from international trade?

    *(Consumers are able to obtain goods and services from around the world. Because of increased competition, consumers may obtain these goods and services at lower prices.)*

    D. How do our trade partners benefit from international trade?

    *(The benefits we see in the United States — in expanded markets for workers, increased competition, and lower prices — are the same benefits trade confers on our trade partners.)*

    E. Since international trade is a relatively small part of the American economy, why is there all the fuss about going global?

    *(It is relatively easy for people to notice how some Americans are harmed by increased trade. Plant closings, for example, have a visual impact. It is harder to recognize the advantages trade offers to the U.S. economy. It provides us with more choices at lower costs. It opens markets for American workers, farmers, and businesses. And, trade benefits our trade partners, which in turn helps to create stable and peaceful global relationships.)*

## CLOSURE

Review the key points of the lesson. Ask:

- How do American workers and businesses benefit from trade?

    *(The global economy offers a market for goods and services produced by American workers, farmers, and business.)*

- How do our trade partners benefit from trade?

    *(The benefits we see in the United States — in expanded markets for workers, increased competition, and lower prices — are the same benefits trade confers on our trade partners.)*

- Since international trade is a relatively small part of the American economy, why is there all the fuss about going global?

    *(Trade offers many advantages to the U.S. economy. It provides us with more choices at lower costs. It opens markets for American workers, farmers, and businesses. And, trade benefits our trade partners, which in turn helps to create stable and peaceful global relationships.)*

## MULTIPLE-CHOICE QUESTIONS

### (CORRECT ANSWERS SHOWN IN BOLD)

1. The portion of U.S. GDP related to international trade (total of imports and exports) has been:

    A. Stable.

    **B. Increasing.**

    C. Decreasing.

    D. Impossible to measure.

2. Which of the following is a benefit to nations that are open to trade?

    A. Lower prices

    B. More consumer choice

    C. More markets for business

    **D. All of the above**

## ESSAY QUESTION

The benefits of trade are well known. Economists have been explaining these benefits since the time of Adam Smith and the *The Wealth of Nations*. Yet there are nations that refuse to allow expanded trade. Explain why.

*(Open trade tends to benefit the society as a whole. For example, consumers, workers, and businesses all tend to benefit. But trade does involve costs to some. For example, some businesses benefit from less competition. In many developing*

# Unit 7 | Teacher's Guide

*nations, political leaders use the power of the state to keep out competitors. They enable friends, supporters, and family members to run businesses that charge higher prices than they could charge if open trade were permitted. These higher prices are a concentrated benefit to a few leaders, while the costs are spread out among many consumers.)*

# Why Go Global?

**Unit 7, Lesson 39**
Visual 1

## ARE WE REALLY GLOBAL?

The global economy is often in the news. We often hear stories about the United States and its relationships with its trade partners: Canada, Mexico, Japan, and the nations of the European Union. Yet, for much of our history, foreign trade (the value of exports plus imports) has been a relatively small part of our economy.

- In 2000, foreign trade accounted for about 25 percent of GDP.

- Only about 8 percent of our labor force is engaged in producing goods and service for export.

- *Since international trade is a relatively small part of the American economy, why is there all the fuss about going global?*

# Unit 7 | Teacher's Guide

**Unit 7, Lesson 39**
Visual 2

## True/False Clues

A. The global economy is a growing part of the U.S. economy.

   True or False?

B. Some American workers benefit from international trade.

   True or False?

C. American consumers benefit from international trade.

   True or False?

D. Prices in the United States are lower because of international trade.

   True or False?

E. Trade barriers have been increasing around the world.

   True or False?

# Unit 7 | Teacher's Guide

## Unit 7 Lesson 40

## Why Do People Trade Across National Borders?

**Economics**  Trade is the voluntary exchange of goods and services. The decision to trade is made because two or more parties involved in the exchange expect to gain from the trade. When one or both of the trading partners believe they can no longer gain from trading, the exchange will not take place. Trading partners may reside inside national borders. Increasingly, trading partners reside in different countries.

**Reasoning**  People judge the satisfaction they are likely to gain from an act of trade by economizing — by weighing the expected gains against the expected losses. Students should use this principle of economic reasoning to explain the choices made by participants in this lesson's trading simulation.

### CONCEPTS

- Benefits
- Costs
- Incentives
- Trade

### OBJECTIVES

*Students will:*

1. Participate in a trading session.
2. Describe the incentives that encourage them to trade.
3. List the anticipated costs and benefits of their trade.
4. Indicate their satisfaction before and after acquiring items in a voluntary trade.

### CONTENT STANDARD

- Voluntary exchange occurs only when all participating parties expect to gain. This is true for trade among individuals or organizations within a nation, and among individuals or organizations in different nations. (NCEE Content Standard 5)

### LESSON DESCRIPTION

This lesson involves students in a trading simulation that grows in complexity. Students use this experience to investigate the consequences of voluntary trade among individuals in increasingly larger groups.

*Time Required: 45 minutes*

### MATERIALS

- A number of small, easy-to-exchange items, such as miniature candy bars, small boxes of raisins, wheat germ, small school supplies, stickers, library passes, health and beauty items, used CDs, paperback books. Each item should be placed in a paper bag for distribution to the students.
- A transparency of Visuals 1, 2, and 3

### PROCEDURE

1. Tell the students that today they will be participating in a trading activity. The purpose of the activity is to investigate the motives for voluntary exchanges in the economy.
2. Ask: Why do people trade? Record a few student responses on the chalkboard. State that these responses are hypotheses. Now the class must gather some evidence to support or reject these hypotheses.
3. Assign one student the responsibility of helping you. His or her task will be to help distribute bags, keep a numerical record of satisfaction levels, and observe the trading behavior of other students.
4. Distribute the paper bags (which contain an item for trade: see materials section for directions) to the students — one bag per student. (Each student should receive a different item — a CD for Michelle, a box of paper clips for Tyrone, etc.) Explain that the item in each bag is a gift. It is for each student to keep.
5. When distributing the bags, try to create interesting contrasts — for example:
   - Some students with uninteresting items.
   - Some students with very popular items.
   - Some students with items that they do not want — candy for a diabetic student, gum for a student with braces, for example.

   *It is important to set up an atmosphere in which the motive for trade arises because people have a wide variety of items and some of them hold items that do not match their tastes or interests.*

6. Ask the students to open their bags and look at their items, without showing the items to anyone else. After looking into his or her bag, each student decides on a scale of 1-10 (with 10 as the highest rating) how much he or she likes the item. The students should write these numbers down and give the notations of their rankings to the student helper. The student helper should add all the numbers and record a total number for the entire class on a piece of paper. (For example, in Round 1 the total might be around 50.)

# Why Do People Trade Across National Borders?

7. Next, assign the students to groups of 3-6 people. Ask them to sit together and show one another the items in their bags. They may trade with one another if they wish to, but they cannot trade with people in other groups.

8. After five minutes, stop the trading activity and ask the students to rate the items in their possession again on a scale of 1-10. They should do this rating even if they have not traded an item. (Their assessment of their item may have changed after seeing other items.) Have the student helper collect the numerical ratings, add the numbers, and record a second total. (For example, in Round 2 the total usually rises to perhaps 85 or so.)

9. Ask the students to show their items to the entire class; they might even do a little commercial explaining how neat their items are. Then give the class another five minutes to trade. This time let the students trade with anyone in the class.

10. After five minutes, stop the trading activity and ask the students to return to their desks and (again) rate the items in their possession on a scale of 1-10. The student helper should collect these rankings and calculate a total for the entire class. (For example, in Round 3 the total usually increases to perhaps 120 or so.)

11. Write the results of the ranking on Visual 1 and display it to the class. Then discuss the results of the simulation. Ask:

    A. How many of you made trades?

    (Use a show of hands. It will be unusual if everyone trades.)

    B. Which items did you trade?

    (List some sample responses.)

    C. Did any of you trade more than once?

    (Several people probably traded more than once.)

    D. Why did you trade?

    (People tend to give up items they personally value less in order to obtain items they value more. They also tend to trade when it appears the cost of the trade is less than the benefits gained.)

    E. For those students who did not trade: Why did you not do so?

    (They will have many answers here — uninterested, shy, whatever. Usually they will indicate that the costs of trading were greater than any benefits they expected to receive, so they did not trade. Also, other people may not have wanted their items. It takes two people to make a trade occur.)

    F. What was the cost and what was the benefit of your trade?

    (The item traded away and the effort needed to negotiate were the costs; the benefit was the item received.)

    G. Were all of you happy with the results of your trading?

    (Probably not. Students who had little to trade may not have been pleased. Students who couldn't find what they wanted may have been dissatisfied. Students who traded and then realized they missed a better trade may have been unhappy. Finally, students who either underestimated the costs of a trade or overestimated its benefits — or both — may have been unhappy. Everyone can think of a better deal that should have taken place. Trading does not guarantee happiness. Economists merely observe that trade will continue if people think they will be better off after the trade than if they had not traded at all.)

    H. Ask the students to look at the class satisfaction summary on Visual 1. Why do the numbers grow larger?

    (As trade takes place, items move from people who value them less to people who value them more. This action causes the total satisfaction of the group to rise.)

    I. How does the trading simulation resemble the "real world"?

    (Voluntary trade takes place every time we buy groceries or movie tickets or gas for the car or pay rent for an apartment — the list goes on and on. Also, people obtain more items and items of greater variety when they trade with larger groups, as in international trade. The game is not real in that the students used barter. Most people now trade for most items using currency. Also, the students were given their items to trade. They did not have to incur any production costs.)

    J. Tell the students that when they were in groups, they resembled the countries participating in NAFTA (North American Free Trade Association). They were a group of regional trading partners. Display Visual 2 and discuss the bullet points.

    K. Indicate that when they traded with the entire class, the students resembled the countries participating in the World Trade Organization (WTO). They were engaging in international trade. Display Visual 3 discuss the bullet points.

# Unit 7 | Teacher's Guide

## Closure

Return to the statements the students provided earlier in the lesson about why people trade. Ask the students which hypotheses seem to be the most accurate as judged by the behavior observed in the trading activity.

*(Any statement suggesting that people expect to gain from trade will have been verified. Any statement suggesting other explanations will not be verified by the trading activity. Even if the statement is correct, the evidence may not support it.)*

## Multiple-Choice Questions

### (Correct Answers Shown in Bold)

1. Which of the following is an example of voluntary trade?
   A. A person is knocked down and rendered unconscious so a second person can take the first person's money.
   B. A person is kidnapped and returned to safety after the kidnappers have been paid $1million.
   C. A state legislature requires citizens to pay taxes to help cover the expenses of public schools.
   **D. A music teacher is paid to give private lessons to a violin student.**

2. Which of the following is *not* an example of voluntary trade?
   A. A Mexican farmer sells a truckload of watermelons to a grocery store in Texas.
   B. A Canadian winemaker sells a case of wine to an American tourist traveling in Canada.
   **C. An American importer bringing organic Italian olive oil into the country has to pay a 50 percent tariff on all the olive oil.**
   D. A customer decides to buy a car from an automobile dealer using a no interest loan to pay for the car.

3. Which of the following actions will encourage international trade and tend to increase the number of trades?
   A. A 50 percent tariff on all imported products
   **B. A loan from a Japanese bank to American wholesalers, enabling them to purchase computer games for sale in the United States**
   C. An U.S. law prohibiting trucks licensed in Mexico and Canada to travel on highways in the United States
   D. A parent requiring students to complete their homework before watching TV

## Essay Question

Read the following statement and write a response that demonstrates your understanding of gains and losses in international trade.

"International trade must be regulated and controlled to a greater degree. Companies in the United States are taking advantage of people in the rest of the world by selling them products they don't need. After all, poor people in China don't need our soft drinks, athletic shoes, Hollywood movies, hamburgers, and computer software! They should make their own food and clothing."

*(This statement ignores the basic idea behind trade. People don't base their trades on what someone else thinks they need. People choose to trade for goods and services because they find them more valuable than the resources they give up as part of the trade. These voluntary trades are made because people think they are better off after the trade. No one has forced people in China to buy soft drinks, shoes, movies, hamburgers, and computer software. Making your own food and clothing is very time- and resource-consuming. Often it is more efficient to purchase goods of this sort from someone else.)*

WHY DO PEOPLE TRADE ACROSS NATIONAL BORDERS?

**Unit 7, Lesson 40**
Visual 1

## CLASS RANKING OF TRADABLE ITEMS: A SUMMARY

|         | Total Points |
|---------|--------------|
| Round 1 |              |
| Round 2 |              |
| Round 3 |              |

**Unit 7, Lesson 40**
Visual 2

## NORTH AMERICAN FREE TRADE ASSOCIATION (NAFTA)

- Trading members: Canada, Mexico, USA
- Purposes:
    (1) Reduce trade barriers between countries in North America
    (2) Increase economic activity in North America
    (3) Improve the standard of living in member countries

**Unit 7, Lesson 40**
Visual 3

## WORLD TRADE ORGANIZATION (WTO)

- 142 countries are members. All the major economies in the world are included.

- Purposes:

    (1) Promote trade among countries around the world by reducing trade barriers

    (2) Establish common rules for trade

    (3) Increase international trade

    (4) Improve the world's standard of living

# Unit 7 | Teacher's Guide

## Unit 7 Lesson 41

## Why People Trade: Comparative Advantage

### INTRODUCTION

**Economics** *Comparative advantage* is a powerful idea that helps explain why individuals, companies, regions, and countries gain by specialization and trade, even when one is better than all its trading partners at producing all goods and services. The law of comparative advantage applied in international trade states that the total output of a group of nations is greatest when each nation specializes its production, exporting those goods and services it can produce at the lowest opportunity cost and importing goods and services it would produce at a greater opportunity cost.

**Reasoning** The comparative advantage principle is a subtle, difficult, and important extension of the opportunity cost principle. Link the idea closely to students' prior understanding of opportunity cost and encourage them to practice this reasoning. Most students must practice the idea repeatedly before they can use it well.

### CONCEPTS

- Comparative advantage
- Opportunity cost
- Specialization
- Trade

### CONTENT STANDARD

- When individuals, regions, and nations specialize in what they can produce at the lowest costs and then trade with others, both production and consumption increase. (NCEE Content Standard 6)

### OBJECTIVES:

Students will:

1. Review the concept of opportunity cost.
2. Define and apply the concept of comparative advantage.
3. Explain why nations and people often choose to specialize in the production of certain goods and services and trade to obtain other goods and services.

### LESSON DESCRIPTION

The students decide why people buy foreign goods, and they practice measuring the comparative advantage of different producers.

*Time Required: 90 minutes*

### MATERIALS

- A transparency of Visual 1
- Activities 1, 2, and 3

Note: To complete Activity 2, students will need to contact people in advance.

### PROCEDURE

1. Tell the class that the purpose of today's lesson is to introduce the idea of comparative advantage. Display Visual 1 and briefly discuss the concepts. Refer the students to Activity 1 and ask them to read it. Then ask:

    A. Why do people trade?

    *(Both parties expect to gain from the trade.)*

    B. Why does the United States import bananas?

    *(U.S. consumers want to eat bananas. U.S. farmers could grow bananas, but it would be very expensive. They gain more by growing wheat and trading for bananas.)*

    C. What is comparative advantage?

    *(The ability to produce a good or service at a lower opportunity cost than some other producer.)*

2. Refer the students to Activity 2. Ask the students to complete it as a homework assignment, comparing their behavior to that of the adults they interview by reference to the major points about trade in Activity 1. What incentives influence each group's behavior?

3. When the students have completed Activity 2, ask:

    A. What was the main criterion for their choice of shoes?

    *(Generally, it will be price.)*

    B. Why is price important in their decisions?

    *(A lower price frees more personal money to buy additional goods and services.)*

    C. Ask the students what types of foreign-produced products the merchants they interviewed had available for sale.

    *(Answers will vary.)*

    D. What did the people interviewed indicate were the main criteria for purchasing foreign goods?

    *(This response may emphasize both quality and price. Most people use both criteria when making a choice.)*

# Why People Trade: Comparative Advantage

4. Refer the students to Activity 3; ask them to read it and answer the questions about the Home-Building Mystery. Ask:

   A. Was Ms. Brickstrom correct? Could both builders benefit by specializing their production? Why?

   *(On the basis of comparative advantage, each builder can gain wealth by specializing and trading. Firman is able to produce more houses than Brickstrom, but he will gain by concentrating more on what he does best — making wood homes — and trading with Brickstrom for additional brick houses.)*

   B. Did anyone think that the two builders should not trade? If so, why?

   *(The arithmetic should illustrate the advantages of specialization and trade. However, there may be other important issues of dependency, quality differences, or personality clashes that might provide a reason for not trading.)*

*Answers to Activity 3*

**Annual Output before Specialization**

|  | Wood Houses | Brick Houses |
|---|---|---|
| Firman | 16 (4 months work) | 16 (8 months work) |
| Brickstrom | 6 (6 months work) | 6 (6 months work) |
| Total output | 22 houses | 22 houses |

**Annual Output after Specialization**

|  | Wood Houses | Brick Houses |
|---|---|---|
| Firman | 24 (6 months work) | 12 (6 months work) |
| Brickstrom | 0 (0 months work) | 12 (12 months work) |
| Total output | 24 houses | 24 houses |

**Annual Output after Specialization and Trade**

|  | Wood Houses | Brick Houses |
|---|---|---|
| Firman | 17 (6 months work) | 17 (6 months work) |
| Brickstrom | 7 (0 months work) | 7 (12 months work) |
| Total output | 24 houses | 24 houses |

## Closure

Have the students write a definition for three terms: *specialization, opportunity cost,* and *comparative advantage.* Display the definitions on Visual 1 and review the correct responses.

## Multiple-Choice Questions

**(Correct answers shown in bold)**

1. Which cost will be minimized if a person, company, or a country decides to specialize in production?

   A. Accounting cost

   **B. Opportunity cost**

   C. Sunk cost

   D. Average cost

2. An adult gives you the following advice: "Do what you want to do, youngster, just be sure to concentrate on your comparative advantage!" Which of the following answers best interprets what the adult means?

   A. Spend your time working on your highest opportunity cost projects.

   **B. Spend your time working on your lowest opportunity cost projects.**

   C. Spend your time looking up the definition of comparative advantage.

   D. Spend your time looking in the mirror admiring your comparative advantage.

3. Comparative advantage cannot be understood well unless a person also understands which of the following concepts?

   A. Money

   **B. Opportunity cost**

   C. Unemployment

   D. Inflation

## Essay Question

Consider the following example: A successful lawyer decides to fire the firm's only word-processing specialist. The lawyer has just completed a word-processing course and has learned to complete legal briefs in one-half the time it takes the word-processing specialist to complete them.

The lawyer typically charges $400 per hour for legal work, and she has plenty of legal work to do. The word-processing specialist makes $20 per hour. Explain, using the ideas of opportunity cost and comparative advantage, whether the lawyer is or is not making a choice that will increase the income of the firm.

*(The lawyer will reduce the income of the firm. When the lawyer is typing legal briefs, she cannot do her lawyer's work — work that pays much more income. Every hour the lawyer is typing, the firm is losing $400 per hour while saving $20 per hour. The lawyer's opportunity cost of typing is too high. The lawyer's comparative advantage is completing legal work.)*

# Unit 7 | Teacher's Guide

**Unit 7, Lesson 41**
Visual 1

## INTERNATIONAL TRADE CONCEPTS

**Opportunity Cost:** The highest-valued alternative that must be sacrificed (forgone) as a result of choosing among alternatives.

**Absolute Advantage:** The ability to produce more units of a good or service than some other producer, using the same quantity of resources.

**Comparative Advantage:** The ability to produce a good or service at a lower opportunity cost than the cost of some other producer. This principle suggests that individuals, firms, and nations can gain by specializing in the production of goods they can produce cheaply (low opportunity cost) and exchange those goods for more desired goods, which are more costly to produce (higher opportunity cost).

**Specialization:** A method of assigning different tasks to different workers.

# Unit 7 | Teacher's Guide

## Unit 7 Lesson 42

## Foreign Currencies and Foreign Exchange

### INTRODUCTION

**Economics**  Money has several functions. It serves as a medium of exchange, a store of value, and a measure of value. In world trade, money also functions as a medium of exchange used to carry out payments on international transactions. The value of a currency, when used in international exchanges, is frequently set in foreign exchange markets where the forces of supply and demand establish the price at which different currencies are exchanged. Foreign exchange rates set in such a market are called floating exchange rates. When currency values are not set by foreign exchange markets, they are set at fixed rates or between fixed limits by governments.

**Reasoning**  Decisions to buy or sell foreign currency are influenced by the same economic principles that affect all economic choices. In this lesson, students will apply their reasoning skills to explain changes in the exchange rate between two currencies.

### CONCEPTS

- Demand
- Exchange rate
- Foreign exchange markets
- Supply

### OBJECTIVES

*The students will:*

1. Explain why citizens or businesses in one country might require the currency of another country.
2. Explain how foreign exchange values are influenced by supply and demand.
3. Explain how an increase (or decrease) in the availability of a currency may cause a decline (or rise) in that currency's foreign exchange value.

### CONTENT STANDARD

- Voluntary exchange occurs only when all participating parties expect to gain. This is true for trade among individuals or organizations within a nation, and among individuals or organizations in different nations. (NCEE Content Standard 5)

### LESSON DESCRIPTION

Students participate in a simulated foreign exchange market. The exercise provides an opportunity for students to use supply and demand analysis to explain how flexible exchange rates are established in currency markets.

*Time Required: 45 minutes*

### MATERIALS:

- A transparency of Visual 1
- Mints, similar small candies, or other equally divisible goods such as unshelled almonds or peanuts. (A one-pound bag should be enough for three classes of 35 students.)
- Handout Material 1 and 2 (see pp. 278, 279)
- Activity 1

### PROCEDURE

1. Prepare for this lesson by making enough duplicates of Handout Material 1 (Japanese yen) to provide about 12 bills with varying denominations of yen for each student. Cut the currency out of the page so you can distribute the bills separately. Make a few extra yen to be sure you will not run out. You should make about 25 U.S. dollars out of Handout Material 2. The teacher keeps the dollars.

2. Announce that today the class will look at money and the process by which it is exchanged and valued by people in two or more countries. Have the students read Activity 1. (Don't have them answer the questions now; they will answer the questions later, in the Closure activity.)

3. Announce that you are setting up a foreign currency market so that the class can play The Foreign Currency and Exchange Game. Tell them you will sell one candy mint for one U.S. dollar.

4. Tell the students they will act as citizens of Japan. Distribute four or five Japanese yen notes, of various denominations, to each student. Give them the different amounts in random fashion.

5. Announce that the only way they can buy U.S. candy is with one of the U.S. dollars you hold. Also announce that you can sell only five pieces of candy during one session of the currency market. Students will therefore be required to trade their yen for your U.S. dollars before they can buy any of the five candies.

6. Appoint a student to serve as the banker. Pay the banker one piece of candy for the work done during each round. Give the banker the remaining yen and five dollars. Set up the bank at the front of the room.

# Foreign Currencies and Foreign Exchange

7. Appoint another student as tally keeper. You will also pay this student one piece of candy per round. Use Visual 1 to record the number of transactions. (Do not add the columns for Rounds 2 and 3 to the tally table until you are ready to begin those rounds. This procedure prevents the students from anticipating how many rounds there will be in the activity.) The tally keeper will make a mark in the appropriate space for each price at which you sell an American dollar in each round.

8. **Round 1.** Announce that the bidding for U.S. dollars will begin. The only acceptable payment is with Japanese yen. To simplify the chart, the minimum price will be 50 yen. Let students bid. Decide at what prices you will sell the U.S. dollars. At first, you will get low bids. Accept a few. Then the bids should start to increase. As each bid is accepted, the bidder should go to the bank and exchange the yen for U.S. dollars. The tally keeper should make a mark on the chart at the appropriate price, in yen, as each bid is accepted. Continue until the banker announces that you have sold the five U.S. dollars available for this round. Stop the bidding. Allow the owners of U.S. dollars to exchange the dollars for the candy.

9. **Round 2.** Increase the supply of Japanese yen by distributing another four or five yen to each student. Announce the beginning of Round 2. Have available another set of five U.S. dollars and five pieces of candy. The banker and the tally keeper will perform the same jobs as in the previous round. Repeat the bidding process. When the five U.S. dollars are sold, stop the bidding and allow the owners of the dollars to get their candy.

10. **Round 3.** Increase the supply of Japanese yen by distributing more yen to each student. Announce the beginning of Round 3. Have available another set of five U.S. dollars and five pieces of candy. The banker and the tally keeper will perform the same jobs as in the previous round. Repeat the bidding process. When the five American dollars are sold, stop the bidding and allow the owners of the dollars to get their candy.

11. Ask the students to focus on Visual 1.

    A. How many total yen were paid for the five U.S. dollars in Round 1? In Round 2? In Round 3? In other words, what was the price of a U.S. dollar in terms of yen in each round?

    B. How wide were the price variations of yen per dollar in each round?

    C. Did the successive rounds establish a price pattern?

    D. What determined the exchange rate of yen and dollars?

    *(You should steer students toward a supply and demand explanation if it does not occur naturally.)*

    E. How does the pattern of exchange rates illustrate the interaction of supply and demand.

    *(The exchange rate for dollars in terms of yen rose when the increased supply of yen resulted in a higher yen price for each U.S. dollar.)*

    F. In general, how is the foreign exchange value of a currency set in terms of other currencies?

    *(By the interaction of supply and demand.)*

    G. What factors might cause the exchange rate between two countries to change?

    *(Changes in the supply of or the demand for the currencies.)*

## Closure

Refer again to Activity 1. Ask the students to answer the questions:

- What are the three functions of money?

  *(Medium of exchange, store of value, measure of value.)*

- What determines the value of any currency?

  *(Supply and demand.)*

- What do we call a decrease in value of a currency? An increase?

  *(In a decrease, the currency depreciates; in an increase, it appreciates.)*

- What do we call the places or means of communication by which currencies are traded and the value of one country's currency is established in terms of other currencies?

  *(Foreign exchange markets.)*

- Assume the United States produces new products that citizens of other countries buy in large quantities. All other things being equal, what will happen to the value of the U.S. dollar in terms of foreign currencies?

  *(It would increase.)*

- Assume the number of U.S. citizens traveling to foreign countries greatly increases. All other things being equal, what will happen to the value of the U.S. dollar in terms of foreign currencies?

  *(It would decrease.)*

# Unit 7 | Teacher's Guide

## Multiple-Choice Questions

(Correct answers shown in bold)

1. Which of the following actions will increase the supply of U.S. dollars on the foreign exchange market?

    A. U.S. citizens buy fewer imported products.

    **B. U.S. citizens increase their purchases of imported products.**

    C. U.S. citizens reduce the number of trips taken to other countries.

    D. German businesses increase their purchases of U.S.-manufactured robots for use in German factories.

2. Recently a TV commentator reported that the U.S. dollar declined in value against the European currency (the euro). Which of the following statements is consistent with that report?

    **A. One hundred U.S. dollars buy fewer euros today than those dollars could purchase on the previous day.**

    B. One hundred U.S. dollars buy more euros today than those dollars could purchase on the previous day.

    C. A Gallup poll found that more people worldwide preferred euros to U.S. dollars.

    D. The U.S. dollar is backed by fewer gold reserves today than it was on the previous day.

3. Which currencies serve as a store of value, a medium of exchange, and a measure of value?

    A. The U.S. dollar

    B. The New Zealand dollar

    C. The Japanese yen

    **D. All three currencies serve all three functions.**

## Essay Question

Imagine a situation in which there is an increase of thousands of U.S. citizens (tourists, business representatives, and government officials) who choose to visit Japan. All of these visitors, arriving in the Tokyo airport, buy thousands of Japanese yen to use during their stay in Japan. Assuming that no other changes are taking place with the yen, explain what effect these visitors' actions will have on the supply of and demand for the U.S. dollar in the U.S.-Japan foreign exchange market, on the supply of and demand for the yen, and on the price of each currency.

*(The supply of U.S. dollars increased when U.S. citizens paid dollars to buy yen. The demand for the U.S. dollar did not change. The demand for the U.S. dollar in this example would change only if Japanese citizens were attempting to buy U.S. dollars in greater numbers than before. The demand for yen increased when the U.S. citizens attempted to purchase yen with U.S. dollars. The supply of yen did not change. The exchange value of the yen [the price in U.S. dollars] would rise. The U.S. dollar would decline in value relative to the yen.)*

# Foreign Currencies and Foreign Exchange

## Unit 7, Lesson 42

### Handout Material 1

Yen (Approximately one page per student)

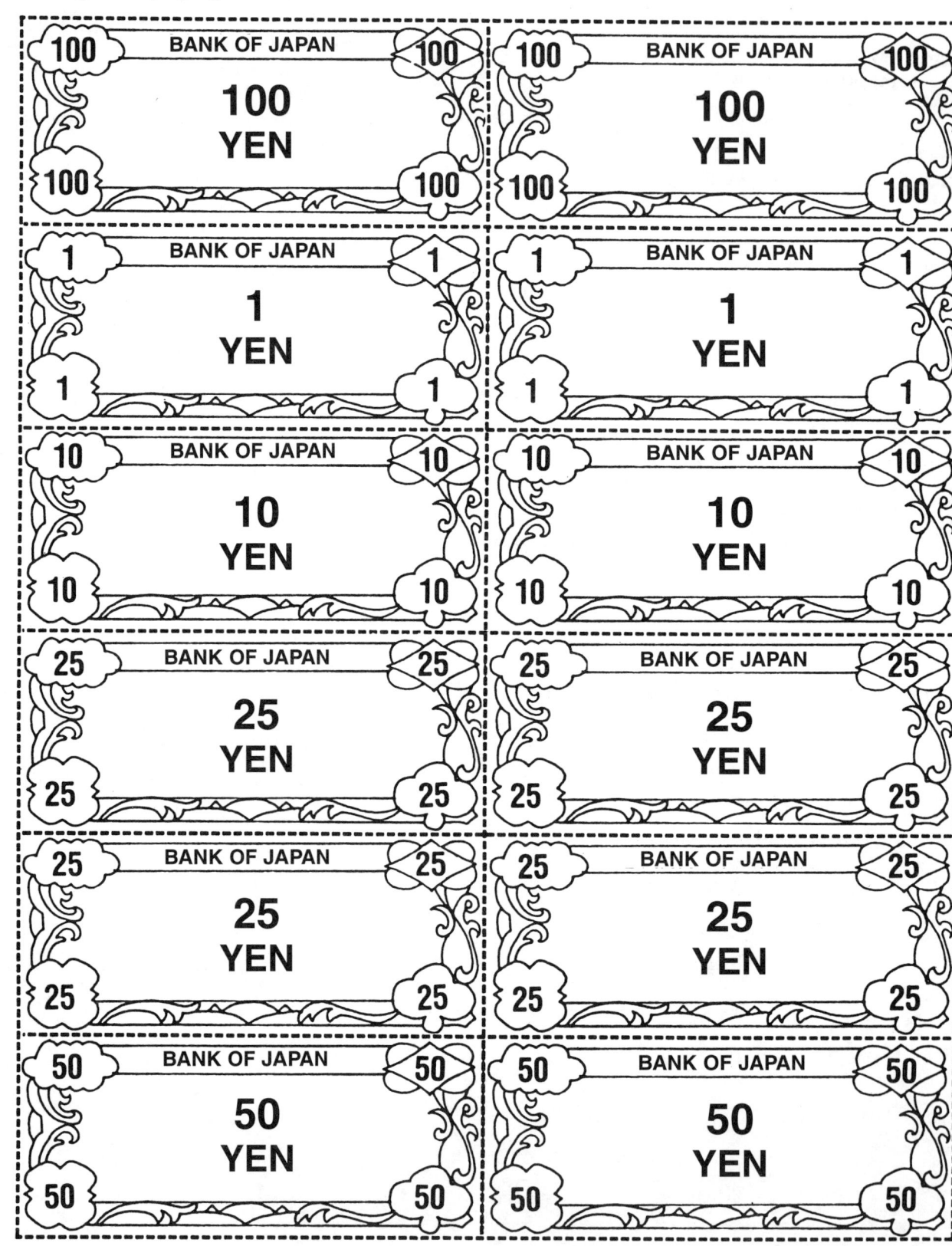

# Unit 7 | Teacher's Guide

## Unit 7, Lesson 42

**Handout Material 2**

U.S. Dollars (You will need to provide 25 U.S. dollars per student)

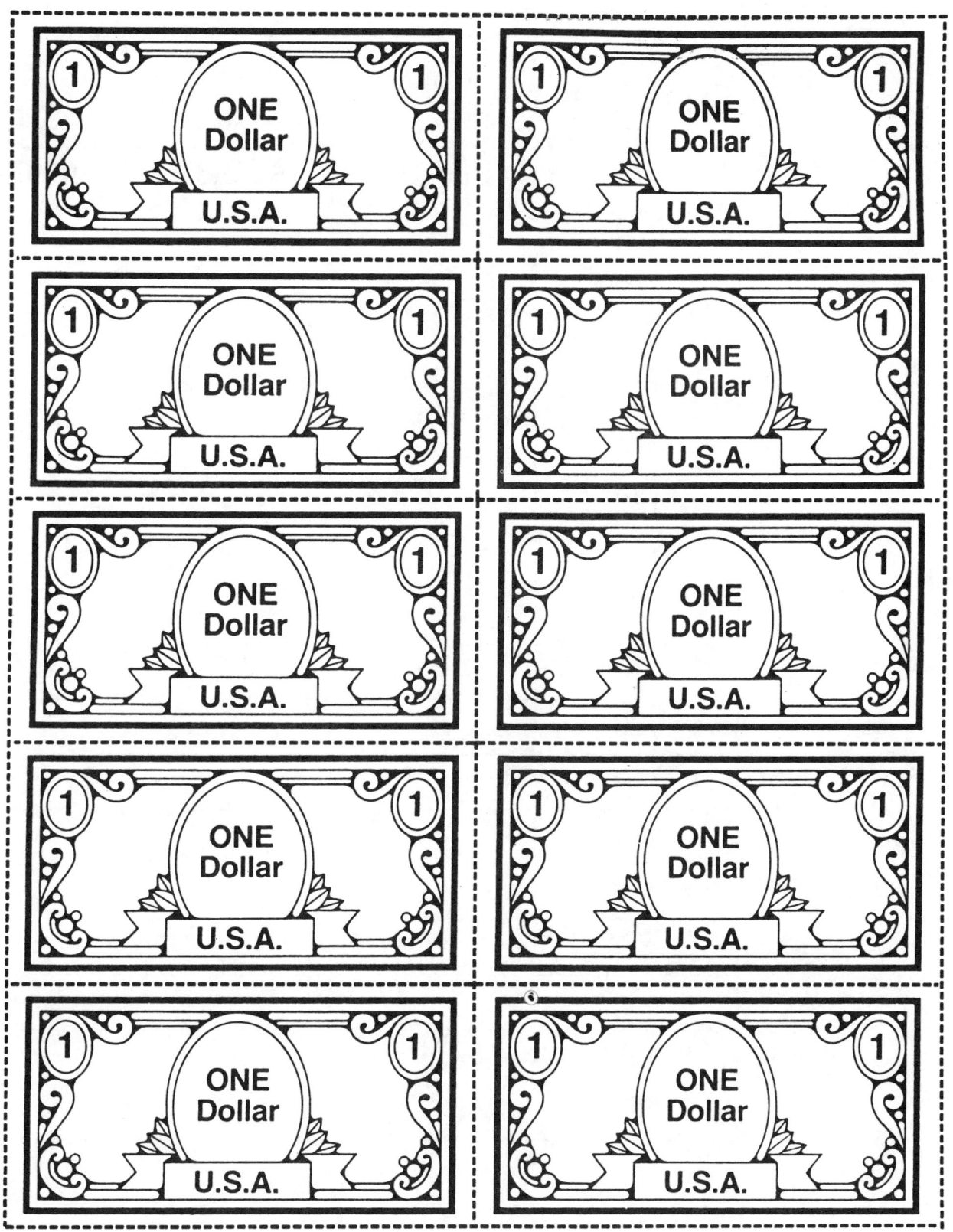

**Unit 7, Lesson 42**
Visual 1

# TALLY TABLE

| Price (in Yen) | Round 1 | Round 2 | Round 3 |
|---|---|---|---|
| 220 | | | |
| 210 | | | |
| 190 | | | |
| 180 | | | |
| 170 | | | |
| 160 | | | |
| 150 | | | |
| 140 | | | |
| 130 | | | |
| 120 | | | |
| 110 | | | |
| 100 | | | |
| 90 | | | |
| 80 | | | |
| 70 | | | |
| 60 | | | |
| 50 | | | |

# Unit 7 | Teacher's Guide

## Unit 7 Lesson 43

## Why Are Some Nations Wealthy?

### INTRODUCTION

**Economics** The contentious debate on globalization often centers on why some nations are rich and others remain in poverty. A nation's wealth affects the standard of living of its citizens. The key to economic prosperity is long-term economic growth. What explains the differences among nations in long-term economic growth? Economists have identified the keys to economic growth; they include technological innovation, investment in physical and human capital, low inflation, political stability, and a decentralized market economy.

**Reasoning** The anti-globalization movement is a major threat to world prosperity. According to Steven Landsburg, "the particular responses endorsed by the anti-globalization crowd — kick back, relax, keep your environment clean and don't worry so much about where your next meal is coming from — are responses that have never worked well for poor people in the U.S. or anywhere else" *(The Wall Street Journal,* July 23, 2001).

The way to achieve economic growth is to create incentives to save, invest, and innovate. Every year the Heritage Foundation and *The Wall Street Journal* publish the "Index of Economic Freedom." Every year the findings are similar. Countries with the most economic freedom (low taxes, less government regulation, sound monetary policy, protection of property rights, decentralized markets) also have the highest rates of economic growth.

### CONCEPTS

- Economic growth
- Human capital
- Natural resources
- Physical capital
- Productivity
- Property rights
- Saving and investment policy
- Trade

### OBJECTIVES

*Students will:*

1. Predict factors associated with national long-term economic growth and prosperity.

2. Explore the relationship between economic growth and the factors commonly associated with market economies, including property rights, institutions promoting saving and investing in human capital and physical capital, and free trade.

### CONTENT STANDARD

- Investment in factories, machinery, new technology, and the health, education, and training of people can raise future standards of living. (NCEE Content Standard 15)

### LESSON DESCRIPTION

Students work in groups to examine data from several nations regarding size, natural resources, and population. Using these data, they try to identify the nations and predict whether each nation is rich or poor. Students rank the nations from richest to poorest. After the mystery nations are revealed, students discuss economists' findings about the factors that contribute most to long-term economic growth.

*Time Required: 45 minutes*

### MATERIALS

- A transparency of Visuals 1, 2, 3, and 4
- Activity 1

### PROCEDURE

1. Explain that in this lesson the students will predict which nations of the world are wealthy and which are not, using data on different nations' size, natural resources, and population.

2. Divide the class into groups of three.

3. Refer the groups to Activity 1; ask the students to identify the nations and then rank them from richest to poorest.

4. Have each group report its findings to the class. Discuss why they ranked the countries as they did. (Most will focus on the amount of natural resources the nations possess.)

5. Use Visual 1 to reveal the mystery nations and go over the answers for Activity 1.

*Answers to Activity 1*

| Richest / Poorest | Country Letter | Country Name |
|---|---|---|
| Richest | 1. E | Singapore |
|  | 2. B | Japan |
|  | 3. A | Argentina |
|  | 4. D | Russia |
| Poorest | 5. C | Nigeria |

# Why Are Some Nations Wealthy?

6. Have the students answer the following questions, but do not comment on their answers until everyone has had a chance to answer.

    - How can some nations with few natural resources, such as Japan and Singapore, be relatively wealthy?

    - How can other nations with vast amounts of natural resources, such as Nigeria and Russia, be relatively poor?

7. Explain that some economists call this problem "the natural resources paradox." Natural resources have certainly contributed to the economic success of some nations, including the United States, South Africa, and the oil-rich nations of the Middle East. But there are many examples of nations such as Japan and Singapore that have achieved great economic success with relatively few natural resources. And some nations with vast stocks of natural resources, such as Nigeria and Russia, remain relatively poor. Ask the students to list other factors that might promote or discourage long-term economic growth and high standards of living.

8. Display Visual 2 and discuss the major points:

    - High investment levels in physical and human capital. Investments in both physical capital (factories and machines) and human capital (the health, education, and training of workers) promote long-term economic growth.

    - Both are also related to the widespread use of new technologies, which often require new machinery and training of workers. Over the past two centuries, technological innovations have been the single most important determinant of economic growth, followed closely by investments in physical and human capital.

    - Wealthier nations are usually in a better position to fund additional investments in human and physical capital, but less developed nations often present other opportunities for new investments. For example, lower levels of income mean that labor costs are lower in those nations, and it is often possible to transfer new technologies and production methods from wealthier nations to the poorer nations.

    - Greater economic freedom.

9. Display Visual 3. Explain that countries with the highest levels of economic freedom have higher rates of long-term economic growth. Note on Visual 3 the freest nations economically in 2002. Note that these nations are rich or have high levels of economic growth.

10. Display Visual 4. Explain that these are the most repressed nations. Note that these nations are not only poor but are incubators of terrorism.

11. Display Visual 2 again and discuss the remaining bullet points:

    - Strong incentives to save, invest, and increase productivity. Successful economies have institutions that encourage saving and investment. Saving means not spending all of the nation's income for the current consumption of goods and services. Resources that are consumed today can't be used for investment, and vice versa. Successful investments lead to higher future levels of production, income, and consumption.

    - Competitive markets. Competitive markets generate innovation and lower prices.

    - Low inflation. A stable currency (low levels of inflation) enhances incentives by maintaining the value of financial assets, which encourages saving and investment. Preventing inflation also keeps people's efforts directed at work, saving, and investing, rather than searching for ways to protect their assets from the effects of inflation.

    - Political stability. Political stability means a change in government won't cause confiscation of its citizens' property. There is an incentive for long-term investment.

    - Free trade. The high-income nations of the world are heavily involved in world trade — and, in fact, the United States is both the wealthiest nation in the world and the world's largest trader. Canada, Germany, the United Kingdom, Japan, France, Singapore, and Hong Kong are also heavily engaged in international trade. Trading leads nations to specialize in the production and export of the goods and services they can produce at the lowest opportunity cost. Trading those exports for other products that can be produced at a lower cost in other nations reduces the total cost of production and allows higher levels of consumption worldwide. Free trade also results in increased competition, which keeps prices lower for consumers and helps insure that businesses are responsive to consumer demand. Levels of trade have increased dramatically over the past 25 years. As much as one-third of U.S. economic growth during the 1990s was attributed to the international trade sector of the economy. Nevertheless, international trade is controversial because it adversely affects businesses that must compete with foreign producers.

# Unit 7 | Teacher's Guide

## CLOSURE

Ask the following questions.

- How important are natural resources to a nation's wealth?

    *(Natural resources have certainly contributed to the economic success of some nations. But there are many examples of nations and regions, such as Japan and Hong Kong, that have achieved great economic success with very few natural resources.)*

- What are the major factors that encourage long-term economic growth?

    *(Successful economies encourage greater productivity through investments in physical capital, human capital, and technology; control inflation and maintain political stability; experience moderate but not rapid population growth; encourage international trade; and provide strong financial incentives and protect property rights, which encourage people to work, save, and invest in themselves and in business opportunities. Over the past century, the nations with the greatest economic growth were those that adopted the key characteristics of a market economy.)*

- How does per capita GDP relate to the quality of life? Why is this important?

    *(The higher the per capita GDP, the higher the quality of life. Nations with a high per capita GDP have high literacy rates, low infant mortality rates, and long life expectancies. Successful economies provide their citizens with a higher quality of life.)*

## MULTIPLE-CHOICE QUESTIONS

### (CORRECT ANSWERS SHOWN IN BOLD)

1. Which of the following factors contributes least to economic growth?

    A. Greater economic freedom

    **B. Large amounts of natural resources**

    C. Low rates of inflation

    D. High investment in physical and human capital

2. Greater economic freedom is associated with:

    A. Lower life expectancy.

    B. Terrorism.

    C. Political repression.

    **D. Greater economic growth.**

3. What do we mean by "investment in human capital"?

    **A. Higher spending on education and training**

    B. Higher spending on population control measures

    C. Government spending on exploration of natural resources

    D. All of the above

## ESSAY QUESTIONS

1. President Bush claims that "when we negotiate for open markets, we are providing new hope for the world's poor." Does freer trade help or hurt the world's poor?

    *(By allowing nations, organizations, and individuals to specialize in what they do best, trade makes more goods and services available to everyone, raising living standards to all. Freer trade also increases competition, spreads knowledge and skills, and provides for the transfer of technology. These factors increase living standards.)*

2. What factors most increase the wealth of a nation?

    *(Students should emphasize the factors listed on Visual 2.)*

3. What do we mean by "economic freedom," and how does it relate to economic growth?

    *(Economic freedom means that people can make economic decisions without restrictions from government. Economic freedom involves low taxes, less government regulation, protection of property rights, freedom of enterprise, and a commitment to free trade. Greater economic freedom correlates strongly with greater economic growth.)*

WHY ARE SOME NATIONS WEALTHY?

**Unit 7, Lesson 43**
Visual 1

## MYSTERY NATIONS REVEALED*

### COUNTRY A

| | |
|---|---|
| Name of country: | Argentina |
| Population: | 37,384,816 |
| Per capita GDP: | $12,900 |
| Life expectancy: | 75.26 years |
| Literacy rate: | 96.2% |
| Infant mortality rate: | 17.75/1000 |

### COUNTRY B

| | |
|---|---|
| Name of country: | Japan |
| Population: | 126,771,662 |
| Per capita GDP: | $24,900 |
| Life expectancy: | 80.8 years |
| Literacy rate: | 99% |
| Infant mortality rate: | 3.88/1000 |

### COUNTRY C

| | |
|---|---|
| Name of country: | Nigeria |
| Population: | 126,635,626 |
| Per capita GDP: | $950 |
| Life expectancy: | 51.07 years |
| Literacy rate: | 57.1% |
| Infant mortality rate: | 73.34/1000 |

### COUNTRY D

| | |
|---|---|
| Name of country: | Russia |
| Population: | 145,470,197 |
| Per capita GDP: | $7700 |
| Life expectancy: | 67.34 years |
| Literacy rate: | 98% |
| Infant mortality rate: | 20.05/1000 |

### COUNTRY E

| | |
|---|---|
| Name of country: | Singapore |
| Population: | 4,300,419 |
| Per capita GDP: | $26,500 |
| Life expectancy: | 83.35 years |
| Literacy rate: | 93.5% |
| Infant mortality rate: | 3.62/1000 |

*All data from *CIA World Factbook 2001*, www.odci.gov.

**Unit 7, Lesson 43**
Visual 2

## FACTORS CONTRIBUTING TO LONG-TERM ECONOMIC GROWTH

- High investment levels in physical and human capital

- Greater economic freedom, including lower taxes, fewer government regulations, sound monetary policy, protection of property rights, and decentralized decision-making in most sectors of the economy

- Strong incentives to save, invest, and increase productivity (including property rights)

- Competitive markets

- Low inflation

- Political stability

- Free trade

**Unit 7, Lesson 43**
Visual 3

## COUNTRIES WITH THE HIGHEST LEVELS OF ECONOMIC FREEDOM, 2002

1. Hong Kong
2. Singapore
3. New Zealand
4. Estonia
   Ireland
   Luxembourg
   Netherlands
   United States
9. Australia
   Chile
   United Kingdom
12. Denmark
    Switzerland
14. Finland

**Unit 7, Lesson 43**
Visual 4

## COUNTRIES WITH THE LOWEST LEVELS OF ECONOMIC FREEDOM, 2002

144. Yugoslavia
145. Burma
     Syria
147. Zimbabwe
148. Belarus
     Uzbekistan
150. Turkmenistan
151. Iran
     Laos
153. Cuba
     Libya
155. Iraq
     North Korea

# Unit 7 | Teacher's Guide

## Unit 7 Lesson 44

## World Environmental Issues: Is the Market at Fault?

### INTRODUCTION

**Economics** Markets tend to operate best when all the costs and benefits of an action are borne by the two parties involved in the trading activity. Markets also work best when property rights are clearly defined and enforced. Environmental problems usually occur when property rights are unclear and/or when costs are borne by third parties — people uninvolved in the trading activity. Environmental problems also occur when people treat scarce goods as if they were not scarce.

**Reasoning** Markets are often blamed for environmental abuse. This analysis is only half correct. Markets can contribute to environmental abuse by overusing a resource, but only when ownership rights do not exist, are unclear, or are not enforced. Clearly established property rights can help make the market more environmentally friendly because environmental problems are usually wasteful and inefficient. People with property rights who bear the costs and benefits of their actions tend to avoid wasteful, inefficient uses of their property.

### CONCEPTS

- Incentives
- Markets
- Private property ownership
- Scarcity
- Tragedy of the commons

### OBJECTIVES

*Students will:*

1. Compare and contrast environmental issues to find common characteristics among the problems.
2. Analyze the argument that markets create incentives to degrade the environment.
3. Identify and evaluate market-oriented environmental solutions.

### CONTENT STANDARDS

- Productive resources are limited. Therefore, people cannot have all the goods and services they want; as a result, they must choose some things and give up others. (NCEE Content Standard 1)
- People respond predictably to positive and negative incentives. (NCEE Content Standard 4)

### LESSON DESCRIPTION

Students study four short case studies. They identify similarities and differences across these five case studies. After noting this information, they assess several environmental policy solutions. They must decide which policies set up incentives that encourage good stewardship of the resources.

*Time Required: 50 minutes*

### MATERIALS

- A transparency of Visual 1
- Activities 1 and 2

### PROCEDURE

1. Explain to the students that they will be studying world environmental problems. Using economic reasoning, they must decide first whether a resource is scarce and second if people are treating the scarce resource as scarce. They must also decide whether market activity is contributing to the environmental problem.

2. Refer the students to Activity 1 and ask them to read it. Then ask:

   A. In which of the situations do people own the resource before it is harvested?

   *(Only in the case involving rice.)*

   B. Which of these resources are scarce? Do people treat these resources as scarce?

   *(All of them are scarce. They have more than one valuable use. Only rice is treated as scarce. Trees are treated as waste, and fish and elephants are treated as having only one valuable use.)*

   C. Which resources are growing more abundant?

   *(Rice.)*

   D. Which resources are growing less abundant?

   *(Fish, trees, elephants.)*

3. Display Visual 1. Enter the students' answers on the grid.

*Answers to Visual 1*

**What Do They Have in Common?**

| Characteristics | Fish | Rain Forest Trees | Elephants | Rice |
|---|---|---|---|---|
| Scarcity | Yes | Yes | Yes | Yes |
| Treated as Scarce | No | No | No | Yes |
| Markets | Yes | Yes | Yes | Yes |
| Ownership | No | No | No | Yes |
| Abundance Increasing | No | No | No | Yes |

CAPSTONE: EXEMPLARY LESSONS FOR HIGH SCHOOL ECONOMICS @ NATIONAL COUNCIL ON ECONOMIC EDUCATION, NEW YORK, NY

# World Environmental Issues: Is the Market at Fault?

4. Encourage the students to develop generalizations about markets. Ask: When are markets environmentally friendly toward the resource? When are markets environmentally unfriendly toward the resource?

   *(When nobody owns the resources in question, market incentives tend to encourage behavior that reduces or degrades the resource. This outcome is sometimes referred to as the tragedy of the commons. When ownership exists, market incentives tend to encourage an increase in the resource or at least protection of it.)*

5. Refer the students to Activity 2. Ask them to examine the alternative environmental policies and predict which policies would encourage more environmentally friendly behavior.

### Answers to Activity 2

*(Statements 1, 3, and 5 will encourage voluntary cooperation to protect the resource. Statements 2, 4, and 6 will not encourage voluntary cooperation to protect the resource.)*

## Closure

Ask the following question: "Why do valuable things owned by no one tend to disappear or be overused and abused?"

*(Everyone is rewarded for using or taking the resource. No one is rewarded for the work of conserving the resource.)*

## Multiple-Choice Questions

### (Correct answers shown in bold)

1. Which of the following is/are likely to suffer from the "tragedy of the commons"?
   - A. Public parks
   - B. River water
   - C. Wildlife
   - **D. All of the above**

2. Markets can lead to the destruction of wildlife, such as elephants, under what conditions?
   - A. When the demand for animal products like ivory is low
   - B. When the supply of animal products like ivory is abundant
   - C. When the market clearing price for ivory changes
   - **D. When ownership rights to the wildlife (elephants) do not exist**

3. Markets for fish tend to be environmentally friendly under what conditions?
   - A. When fishers have clear property rights to the fish
   - B. When the property rights of the fisher can be enforced
   - C. When the fishers are rewarded for protecting the fish
   - **D. All of the above**

## Essay Question

Use economic reasoning to explain the following statement:

"The rain forest cannot be saved from the tragedy of the commons until the trees become scarce to the poor farmers who now burn the rain forest to clear the land for farming."

*(Currently, the trees are not scarce to poor farmers because, so far as the farmers are concerned, the trees do not have two or more valuable uses [See Lesson 3 on scarcity]. If the trees could produce food or income for the farmers, they would not destroy the trees. They would have an incentive to care for the trees in the forest. Now, however, the trees only create a problem for the farmers. By contrast, crops produce food and income for their families. Farmers destroy the trees to create the crops. Therefore the trees are not scarce to the farmers.)*

## Unit 7 | Teacher's Guide

**Unit 7, Lesson 44**
Visual 1

# WHAT DO THEY HAVE IN COMMON?

| Characteristics | Fish | Rain Forest Trees | Elephants | Rice |
|---|---|---|---|---|
| Scarcity | | | | |
| Treated as Scarce | | | | |
| Markets | | | | |
| Ownership | | | | |
| Abundance Increasing | | | | |

# Unit 7 | Teacher's Guide

## Unit 7 Lesson 45

## International Trade: How Do We Measure Trades Across Political Borders?

### INTRODUCTION

**Economics** Several measurements are used to keep track of international trade. This lesson examines the balance of payments. The balance of payments account is a periodic report that summarizes all financial transactions between one country and all other countries for a specific time period. All transactions are grouped into three basic categories: current account, capital account, and official reserve account.

**Reasoning** Information within the balance of payments report is often taken as a measure of economic health. Using the report in this way is misguided. The report is only a summary of trading activities among individuals and businesses who happen to live in different countries. In other words, when an American tourist travels to Brazil and stays in a boat on the Amazon River, or when Bank of America lends money to a Japanese auto producer, these actions are recorded in the balance of payments report. Very few trades between the government of one country and the government of another country are recorded in this report. By analyzing the changes in these international activities, economists can better describe the current status of international transactions as part of the United States economy. This lesson teaches students to disregard distracting statements and clues about international trade and to focus on more meaningful conclusions.

### CONCEPTS

- Balance of payments
- Capital account
- Current account
- Deficit
- Surplus

### OBJECTIVES

*Students will:*

1. Name the principal components of the balance of payments account.
2. Construct a balance of payments account for a hypothetical economy.
3. Explain what is meant by a *deficit* or *surplus* in the country's balance of payments accounts.

### CONTENT STANDARDS

- Voluntary exchange occurs only when all participating parties expect to gain. This is true for trade among individuals or organizations within a nation, and among individuals or organizations in different nations. (NCEE Content Standard 5)
- When individuals, regions, and nations specialize in what they can produce at the lowest cost and then trade with others, both production and consumption increase. (NCEE Content Standard 6)

### LESSON DESCRIPTION

Many popular misconceptions evolve from reading balance of payments reports. Newspaper stories warn us of the perils of a deficit in the U.S. trade balance and a surplus in the Chinese trade balance. This lesson will introduce students to the balance of payments reports and help them draw accurate conclusions about the economy from these reports.

*Time Required: 90 minutes*

### MATERIALS

- Activities 1, 2, and 3

### PROCEDURE

1. Explain that the purpose of this lesson is to deepen students' understanding of international trade by examining government reports on international trade flows. Reassure them that this work will do them no permanent harm, help them avoid some common misunderstandings, and be accomplished in a straightforward way.

2. Refer the students to Activity 1. Have them read Part 1 of the conversation and the accompanying explanation. Ask:

   A. Do you understand what a credit is? Which way does the payment of money flow?

      *(The money flows to someone in the United States.)*

   B. Do you understand what a debit is? Which way does the payment of money flow?

      *(The money flows to someone living outside the United States.)*

   C. All trades must involve payment of money. What is not counted in these reports?

      *(Any trades made without money payment; also illegal trades.)*

   D. How would these reports change if the flow of money from illegal drug sales were reported?

# INTERNATIONAL TRADE: HOW DO WE MEASURE TRADES ACROSS POLITICAL BORDERS?

*(More debits from the flow of U.S. money to foreign drug supply sources. More credits from the flow of illegally obtained money reinvested in the United States to launder it and make it clean for other uses.)*

3. Turn next to Activity 2. Ask the students to complete the sample balance of payments accounts.

*Answers to Activity 2*

|  | United States | | Germany | |
|---|---|---|---|---|
|  | Debit | Credit | Debit | Credit |
| U.S. company sells $1 million of steel to German builder. |  | 1 m | 1 m |  |
| Bank of America pays $5 million in interest to German depositors. | 5 m |  |  | 5 m |
| U.S. citizens spend $3 million on Mercedes automobiles. | 3 m |  |  | 3 m |
| A U.S. firm receives a $2 million dividend on its German investments. |  | 2 m | 2 m |  |
| German tourists spend $3 million in the United States, while American tourists spend $5 million in Germany. | 5 m | 3 m | 3 m | 5 m |
| A German firm pays $1 million to a U.S. shipping line to transport a load of cars. |  | 1 m | 1 m |  |
| U.S. exchange students spend $8 million for tuition at a German university. | 8 m |  |  | 8 m |
| The German government buys a $10 million missile for the U.S. Army to improve German defenses. |  | 10 m | 10 m |  |
| Total | $21 m | $17 m | $17 m | $21 m |

4. Ask the students to read Part 2 of Activity 1 and the accompanying explanation. Ask:

    A. What does the current account measure?

    *(Buying and selling of imports and exports; cash flow from travel and foreign aid.)*

    B. What does the capital account measure?

    *(Borrowing and lending between countries.)*

    C. Is borrowing entered as a debit or a credit?

    *(Borrowing money from other countries brings money in and is thus entered as a credit.)*

5. Refer the students to Activity 3. Ask them to examine a real balance of payments report for the United States and answer the questions.

*Answers to Activity 3*

A. A deficit: the total of imports of goods and services exceeds the total of exports of goods and services.

B. A net borrower: the balance of capital account is positive, showing the United States as a net exporter of IOUs.

C. Yes. Unless mistakes are made, voluntary exchanges are beneficial to both parties. The U.S. importers voluntarily purchased their goods and services abroad and the borrowers voluntarily exchanged IOUs for foreign currency.

D. The $117,676 billion deficit on current account is offset by the $94,670 billion surplus on capital account, plus the $23,006 billion statistical discrepancy. Put differently: the $117,676 billion deficit is balanced by the sum of + $94,670 billion and + $23,006 billion equals +$117,676 billion.

6. Ask the students to read the remaining part of Activity 1. Have them point out the misunderstandings expressed by Herr Plus and Ms. Deficit.

*(The key misunderstanding is to not notice that all exchanges benefit both parties and therefore the exchanges must balance. They cannot have deficits and surpluses as a total trade action.)*

## Closure

Ask the students to explain how the following two transactions would be recorded in the balance of payments accounts.

1. The Unites States gives a foreign-aid grant to Egypt.

    *(This transaction would be an outflow of payments from the United States and be recorded as a debit to the current account portion of the balance of payments account.)*

2. A rich Egyptian citizen decides to provide a loan to a Las Vegas casino to build a pyramid in Las Vegas to attract customers to the casino.

    *(This transaction would be an inflow of payments to the United States and be recorded as a credit to the capital account portion of the balance of payments.)*

# Unit 7 | Teacher's Guide

MULTIPLE-CHOICE QUESTIONS (CORRECT ANSWERS SHOWN IN BOLD)

1. In which part of the balance of payments account does the United States usually have a deficit?

   **A. The current account**

   B. The capital account

   C. Both the capital account and the current account

   D. Neither the capital account or the current account

2. In which part of the balance of payments account does the United States usually have a surplus?

   A. The current account

   **B. The capital account**

   C. Both the capital account and the current account

   D. Neither the capital account or the current account

3. If a car dealer imports $10 million worth of automobiles produced in Japan, in which balance of payment account is this transaction recorded?

   **A. The current account**

   B. The capital account

   C. Both the capital account and the current account

   D. Neither the capital account or the current account

ESSAY QUESTION

Explain what it means to have a deficit in the nation's trade balance (the current account).

*(Both the dollar value of imports and exports are recorded in the current account. If the United States has a current account deficit, that only means that the total number of dollars spent on imports was greater than the total amount of dollars received by the sale of U.S. export items.)*

# Glossary* | Teacher's Guide

**Absolute advantage**  The ability to produce more units of a good or service than some other producer, using the same quantity of resources. See also **Comparative advantage.**

**Adaptive expectations**  Expectations about inflation or other economic events.

**Aggregate demand**  A schedule (or graph) that shows the value of output (real GDP) that would be demanded at different price levels.

**Aggregate supply**  A schedule (or graph) that shows the value of output (real GDP) that would be produced at different price levels. In the long run, the schedule shows a constant level of real GDP at all price levels, determined by the economy's productive capacity at full employment. In the short run, the aggregate supply schedule may show different levels of real GDP as the price level changes.

**Alternative**  One of many courses of action that might be taken in a given situation.

**Assumptions**  Beliefs or statements presupposed to be true.

**Balance of payments**  The record of all transactions (in goods, services, physical and financial assets) between individuals, firms, and governments of one country with those in all other countries in a given year, expressed in monetary terms.

**Balance of trade**  The part of a nation's balance of payments accounts that deals only with its imports and exports of goods (also called merchandise or "visibles"). When "invisibles," or services, are added to the balance of trade, the result is a nation's balance on the current account section of its balance of payments.

**Barriers to entry**  Factors that restrict entry into an industry and give cost advantages to existing firms. Examples would include the large size of existing firms, control over an essential resource or information, and legal rights such as patents and licenses.

**Barter**  Trading a good or service directly for another good or service, without using money or credit.

**Benefit**  The advantage(s) of a particular course of action as measured by good feeling, dollars, or number of items.

**Bond**  A contractual obligation to repay a specified amount of money in a specified amount of time, including a set rate of interest on the amount that is borrowed.

**Budget**  An element of financial planning where all income is listed and compared to all expenditures. Often expenditure decisions need to be made to hold spending less than or equal to income.

**Budget deficit**  Refers to national budgets; occurs when government spending is greater than government income from taxes and tariffs in a given year. A yearly deficit adds to the public debt.

**Budget surplus**  Refers to national budgets; occurs when government income is greater than government spending in a given year.

**Business cycles**  Fluctuations in the overall rate of national economic activity with alternating periods of expansion and contraction; these vary in duration and degrees of severity; usually measured by real gross domestic product (GDP).

**Capital account**  Part of a nation's balance of payments accounts; records capital outflows — i.e., expenditures made by the nation's residents to purchase physical capital and financial assets from the residents of foreign nations; also records capital inflows — i.e., expenditures by residents of foreign nations to purchase physical capital and financial assets from residents of the nation in question.

**Capital**  Resources and goods made and used to produce other goods and services. Examples include buildings, machinery, tools, and equipment.

**Choice**  Course of action taken when faced with a set of alternatives.

**Collusion**  An agreement between firms to fix prices or engage in other activities to restrict competition in an industry.

**Command economy**  An economy in which most economic issues of production and distribution are resolved through central planning and control.

**Comparative advantage**  The ability to produce a good or service at a lower opportunity cost than some other producer. This is the economic basis for specialization and trade. See also **Absolute advantage**.

**Competition**  Attempts by two or more individuals or organizations to acquire the same goods, services, or productive and financial resources. Consumers compete with other consumers for goods and services. Producers compete with other producers for sales to consumers. See also **Market structure**.

**Complements**  Goods and/or services that are often consumed together; e.g., left and right socks, or tennis rackets and tennis lessons.

*Support for the development of this glossary was provided to the National Council on Economic Education by the United States Agency for International Development through the Eurasia Foundation.

# Glossary*

**Compound interest** Interest that is earned not only on the principal but also on the interest already earned.

**Consumer price index (CPI)** A price index that measures the cost of a fixed basket of consumer goods and services and compares the cost of this basket in one time period with its cost in some base period. Changes in the CPI are used to measure inflation. See also **Implicit price deflator**.

**Concentration ratio** The percentage of total industry sales by the largest firms (generally four or eight) in an industry. The concentration ratio provides a measure of domination in an industry by a few firms and serves as a measure of whether an industry is an oligopoly.

**Consumers** People who use goods and services to satisfy their economic wants.

**Consumer surplus** The difference between the price a consumer would be willing to pay for a good or service and what that consumer actually has to pay.

**Consumption** Spending by households on goods and services.

**Contractionary fiscal policy** A decrease in government spending and/or an increase in taxes designed to decrease aggregate demand in the economy and control inflation.

**Costs** The disadvantages of a particular course of action as measured by bad feeling, dollars, or numbers of items.

**Credit** The opportunity to borrow money or to receive goods or services in return for a promise to pay later.

**Crowding out** Increased interest rates and decreased private investment caused by government borrowing.

**Current account** Part of a nation's balance of payments accounts; records exports and imports of goods and services, net investment income, and transfer payments with other countries.

**Cyclical unemployment** Unemployment caused by fluctuations in the overall rate of economic activity. See also **Business cycles**.

**Debt** Money owed to someone else. Also see **Debt for individual** and **National debt**.

**Debt for individual** Money a person owes to someone else, usually a financial institution.

**Deficit** See **Budget deficit**.

**Deflation** A sustained decrease in the average price level of all the goods and services produced in the economy.

**Demand** A schedule (or graph) showing how many units of a good or service buyers are willing and able to buy at all possible prices during a period of time.

**Determinants of demand** Factors other than the price that change (shift) the demand schedule, causing consumers to buy more or less at every price. Factors include income, number of consumers, preferences, and prices of related goods.

**Determinants of supply** Factors other than price that change (shift) the supply schedule, causing producers to supply more or less at every price. Factors include number of firms, production costs, and new technology.

**Diminishing marginal utility** A widely observed relationship in which the additional satisfaction (marginal utility) associated with consuming additional units of the same product in a given amount of time eventually declines.

**Distribution** The allocation or dividing up of the goods and services a society produces.

**Division of labor** An arrangement in which workers perform only one or a few steps in a larger production process (as when working on an assembly line).

**Economics** The study of how people, firms, and societies choose to use scarce resources.

**Economic functions of government** In a market economy, government agencies establish and maintain a legal system to regulate both commercial and social behavior, promote competition, respond to market failures by providing public goods and adjusting for externalities, redistribute income, and establish macroeconomic stabilization policies. To perform these functions, governments must shift resources from private uses by taxing and/or borrowing.

**Economic growth** An increase in real output as measured by real GDP or per capita real GDP.

**Economic incentives** Factors that motivate and influence the behavior of individuals and organizations, including firms and government agencies. Prices, profits, and losses are important economic incentives in a market economy.

**Economic profit** A firm's total revenue minus all explicit and implicit costs of production, including opportunity costs.

**Economic system** The institutional framework of formal and informal rules that a society uses to determine what to produce, how to produce, and how to distribute goods and services.

**Economic wants** Desires that can be satisfied by consuming a good or service.

# Glossary* | Teacher's Guide

**Economizing behavior**  Considering the costs and benefits of various alternatives and choosing the one with the greatest net benefits.

**Elasticity**  See **Price elasticity of demand, Price elasticity of supply.**

**Employment rate**  The percentage of the total population aged 16 or over that is employed. See also **Unemployment rate**.

**Entrepreneurship**  A characteristic of people who assume the risk of organizing productive resources to produce goods and services; a resource.

**Equilibrium price**  The price at which the quantity demanded by buyers equals the quantity supplied by sellers; also called the market-clearing price.

**Equilibrium quantity**  The quantity demanded and quantity supplied at the equilibrium or market-clearing price.

**Exchange**  Trading a good or service for another good or service, or for money.

**Exchange rate**  The price of one nation's currency in terms of another nation's currency.

**Expansionary fiscal policy**  An increase in government spending and/or a decrease in taxes designed to increase aggregate demand in the economy, thus increasing real output and decreasing unemployment.

**Exports**  Goods and services produced in one nation and sold to consumers in other nations.

**Externalities**  Economic side effects or third-party effects, in which some of the benefits or costs associated with the production or consumption of a product affect someone other than the direct producer or consumer of the product. See also **Market failures**.

**Federal Reserve**  The central bank of the United States. Its main function is controlling the money supply through monetary policy.

**Financial planning**  Setting short-, medium-, and long-range goals; then collecting and analyzing income and expenditure information to determine how to meet one's goals.

**Firms**  Economic units that demand productive resources from households and supply goods and services to households and government agencies.

**Fiscal policy**  Changes in the expenditures or tax revenues of the federal government, undertaken to promote full employment, price stability, and reasonable rates of economic growth.

**Fixed costs**  Costs of production that do not change as a firm's output level changes. See also **Variable costs**.

**Foreign exchange market**  Market where demand for and supply of foreign currencies determines exchange rates.

**Fractional reserve banking system**  Under such a system, banks are required to hold only a specified fraction of each depositor's money. The rest can be lent out, thus "creating money."

**Free rider**  One who enjoys the benefits of a good or service without paying for it.

**Future consequences**  Costs and/or benefits of a choice that will be paid or gained at a later time.

**Goods**  Tangible objects that satisfy economic wants.

**Government failure**  Policy and budget choices by government officials that result in inefficiency.

**Government spending**  Spending by all levels of government on goods and services; includes categories like military, schools, and roads.

**Gross domestic product (GDP)**  The market value of all final goods and services produced in a country in a calendar year. See also **Gross national product (GNP)**.

**Gross national product (GNP)**  An alternative to **Gross domestic product (GDP)** as a measure of the value of final goods and services produced in one year. **GNP** measures the value of output produced by resources owned by a nation's residents, regardless of where the resources are located. **GDP** measures the value of output produced by the resources located in a nation, regardless of who owns the resources.

**Heterogeneous products**  Products (goods or services) that are differentiated by real or imagined differences in quality or other features, such as color, taste, styling, warranties, or complementary services provided to those who buy the products. See also **Homogeneous products**.

**Homogeneous products**  Products (goods or services) that are identical, with no differentiating features. See also **Heterogeneous products**.

**Households**  Individuals and family units that buy goods and services (as consumers) and sell or rent productive resources (as resource owners).

**Human capital**  The health, education, experience, training, and skills of people.

**Hyperinflation**  A very rapid rise in the overall price level.

**Imperfect competition**  Any market structure in which firms are not price takers, but instead must seek the price and output levels that maximize their profits. See also **Perfect competition**.

# Glossary*

**Implicit price deflator** A price index that compares the prices of all the goods and services produced in the current-year gross domestic product (GDP) to the price levels that prevailed for those same goods and services in an earlier year or years. The implicit price deflator is used to adjust values of nominal or current-price GDP to obtain values for the real GDP. See also **Consumer price index**.

**Imports** Purchases of foreign goods and services; the opposite of **Exports**.

**Incentive** Any reward or benefit, such as money or good feeling, that motivates choices and behaviors.

**Income** Payments earned by households for selling or renting their productive resources. For example, workers receive wage or salary payments in exchange for their labor.

**Income inequality** The unequal distribution of an economy's total income among people or families.

**Inflation** A rise in the general or average price level of all the goods and services produced in an economy.

**Interdependence** A situation in which decisions made by one person affect decisions made by other people, or events in one part of the world or sector of the economy affect other parts of the world or other sectors of the economy.

**Interest** Payments for the use of real or financial capital over some period of time; paid by those who use the resources to those who own them, as in mortgage payments paid by a borrower to a lender.

**Investment** Purchase of capital goods (including machinery, technology, or new buildings) used to make consumer goods and services.

**Invisible hand** A figure of speech representing the idea that firms and individuals making decisions in their own self-interest will at the same time create economic order and promote society's interests; coined by Adam Smith.

**Keynesian theory** The macroeconomic theory holding that business cycles are caused by changes in aggregate demand and that such cycles can and should be influenced by fiscal and monetary policy undertaken to promote economic stability.

**Labor** The quantity and quality of human effort available to produce goods and services.

**Labor force** The people in a nation who are aged 16 or over and are employed or actively looking for work.

**Land (or Natural resources)** "Gifts of nature" that can be used to produce goods and services; for example, oceans, air, mineral deposits, virgin forests, and actual fields of land. When investments are made to improve fields of land or other natural resources, those resources become, in part, capital resources.

**Law of diminishing marginal returns** Describes a phenomenon observed in all short-run production processes, when at least one input (usually capital) is fixed. As more and more units of a variable input (usually labor) are added to the fixed input, the additional (marginal) output associated with each increase in units of the variable input will eventually decline. In other words, successive increases in a variable factor of production added to fixed factors of production will result in smaller increases in output.

**Loanable funds market** Market in which the supply and demand for money, in the form of bank deposits and loans, determine the interest rate.

**Macroeconomic equilibrium** The equilibrium level of output and the price level where aggregate demand equals aggregate supply.

**Macroeconomics** The study of economics concerned with the economy as a whole, involving aggregate demand, aggregate supply, and monetary and fiscal policy.

**Marginal analysis** A decision-making tool for comparing the additional or marginal benefits of a course of action to the additional or marginal costs.

**Marginal benefit** The additional gain from consuming or producing one more unit; can be measured in dollars or satisfaction.

**Marginal cost** The change in a producer's total cost when output is increased by one unit; can be measured in dollars or negative feeling.

**Marginal revenue** The change in a producer's total revenues when one additional unit of output is sold.

**Market economy** An economy that relies on a system of interdependent market prices to allocate goods, services, and productive resources and to coordinate the diverse plans of consumers and producers, all of them following their own self — interests.

**Market failures** The systematic overproduction or underproduction of some goods and services that would occur in an unregulated market system when problems such as public goods, externalities, or imperfect competition are present.

**Markets** Places, institutions, or technological arrangements where or by means of which goods or services are exchanged.

# Glossary* | Teacher's Guide

**Market structure**  The degree of competition in a market, ranging from many buyers and sellers to few or even single buyers or sellers. See also **Competition**.

**Microeconomics**  The study of economics concerned with individual units of the economy such as consumers and businesses and firms, including individual markets and specific prices for goods, services, and resources.

**Monetarist theory**  A macroeconomic theory holding that the main cause of changes in the business cycle are changes in money supply.

**Monetary policy**  Changes in the supply of money and the availability of credit initiated by a nation's central bank to promote price stability, full employment, and reasonable rates of economic growth.

**Money**  Anything that is generally accepted as final payment for goods and services; serves as a medium of exchange, a store of value, and a unit of account; allows people to compare the relative economic value of different goods and services.

**Money supply**  Narrowly defined by economists as currency in the hands of the public plus checking-type deposits; also called M1.

**Monopoly**  A market structure in which a single seller produces or sells all the units of a good or service in a particular market, and where the barriers to new firms entering the market are very high.

**Monopolistic competition**  A market structure in which slightly differentiated products are sold by a large number of relatively small producers, and where the barriers to new firms entering the market are low.

**Multiplier effect**  The idea that a small increase in spending by consumers, businesses, or government can cause large changes in economic production. The multiplier also works in reverse when spending decreases.

**National debt**  The total amount owed by the national government to those from whom it has borrowed to finance the accumulated difference between annual budget deficits and annual budget surpluses; also called public debt.

**Natural resources**  See **Land**.

**Net exports**  Exports minus imports.

**New classical theory**  A macroeconomic theory holding that government policies will have a limited effect on the business cycle since individuals and firms will take government policies into account when making decisions.

**Non-exclusion**  A property of certain goods and services such that (once the goods or services are provided) they cannot be denied to or withheld from people who have not paid for the goods or services; examples include street lights or national defense.

**Non-price competition**  Competition by firms trying to attract customers by methods other than reducing prices; examples include advertising and promotional gifts.

**Normal rate of profit**  Profits just high enough to compensate producers for the explicit and implicit costs (including opportunity costs) they incur in producing a particular good or service, without leading to any net entry or exit by producers in that market. Also called normal profits. Normal profits are an economic cost of production; they mark a point at which any lower level of profit would lead a producer to pursue some other use of his or her resources.

**Oligopoly**  A market structure in which a few, relatively large firms account for all or most of the production or sales of a good or service in a particular market, and where barriers to new firms entering the market are very high. Some oligopolies produce homogeneous products; others produce heterogeneous products.

**Opportunity cost**  The second-best alternative (or the value of that alternative) that must be given up when scarce resources are used for one purpose instead of another.

**Perfect competition**  A market structure in which a large number of relatively small firms produce and sell identical products and where and there are no significant barriers to entry into or exit from the industry. Firms in perfect competition are price takers and in the long run will earn only normal profits. See also **Imperfect competition**.

**Personal distribution of income**  A classification of the income received by individuals or families; shows the number of people in various income categories, ranging from those receiving the highest level of income to those receiving the lowest.

**Poverty**  The state of being poor, variously defined. Sometimes defined relatively — by reference, for example, to the average household income in a nation or region. Sometimes defined absolutely — by reference, for example, to the income needed to provide for adequate food, housing, and clothing in a nation or region.

**Price**  The amount of money that people pay when they buy a good or service; the amount they receive when they sell a good or service.

# Glossary*

**Price ceiling**  A legally established maximum price for a good or service. See also **Shortage.**

**Price elasticity of demand**  The responsiveness of the quantity demanded of a good or service to changes in its price. The price elasticity of demand is the percentage change in quantity demanded divided by the percentage change in price.

**Price elasticity of supply**  The responsiveness of the quantity demanded of a good or service to changes in its price. The price elasticity of supply is the percentage change in quantity supplied divided by the percentage change in price.

**Price floor**  A legally established minimum price for a good or service. See also **Surplus.**

**Price level**  The weighted average of the prices of all goods and services in an economy; used to calculate inflation. See also Consumer price index.

**Private good**  A good that provides benefits only to the purchaser.

**Producers**  People and firms that use resources to make goods and services.

**Producer surplus**  The difference between what a supplier is paid for a good or service and what it costs to supply the good or service. Added to **Consumer surplus**, it provides a measure of the total economic benefit of a sale.

**Production possibilities frontier**  A table or graph that shows the full employment capacity of an economy in the form of possible combinations of two goods, or two bundles of goods, that could be produced with a given amount of productive resources and level of technology.

**Productivity**  A ratio of output (goods and services) per unit of input (factors of production) per unit of time.

**Profit**  Income received for entrepreneurial skills and risk taking, calculated by subtracting all of a firm's explicit and implicit costs from its total revenues.

**Property rights**  Legal protection for the boundaries and possession of property. Assigning of property rights to individuals, collectives, or governments will depend on the economic system.

**Public-Choice analysis**  The study of decision making as it affects the organization and operation of government and other collective organizations. Involves the application of economic principles to political science topics.

**Public goods**  Goods for which use by one person does not reduce the quantity of the good available for others to use, and for which consumption can not be limited to those who pay for the good. Lighthouses, streetlights, and national defense are examples of public goods.

**Purchasing power**  The amount of goods and services that a monetary unit of income can buy.

**Quantity demanded**  The amount of a good or service a consumer will buy at a given price in a given period of time.

**Quantity supplied**  The amount of a good or service a producer will sell at a given price in a given period of time.

**Quotas**  In international trade, limits on the quantity of a product that may be imported or exported, established by government laws or regulations; in command economies, more typically a production target assigned by government planning agencies to the producers of a good or service.

**Rational expectations**  Expectations about the future rate of inflation or other economic events that people form using all available information, including predictions about the effect of present and future policy actions by the government.

**Rational expectations theory**  A branch of New Classical theory which holds that firms and individuals have rational expectations about the economy and government policies and thus may pursue their own interests in such a way as to render those policies ineffective.

**Rational ignorance**  A decision not to obtain information about political issues or candidates because the costs of doing so outweigh the benefits.

**Real gross domestic product (GDP)**  GDP measured in dollars of constant purchasing power. The measure is obtained by adjusting nominal GDP (GDP measured in current prices) by an appropriate price index — usually the implicit price deflator. Often used as a measure of economic activity.

**Real interest rates**  The nominal (posted) interest rate minus the rate of inflation.

**Recession**  A decline in the rate of national economic activity, usually measured by a decline in real GDP for at least two consecutive quarters (i.e., six months).

**Resources**  The three (or four) basic kinds of resources used to produce goods and services: land or natural resources, human resources (including labor and entrepreneurship), and capital.

**Salaries**  Payments for labor resources; unlike wages, not explicitly based on the number of hours worked. See also **Wages**.

# Glossary* | Teacher's Guide

**Savings**   Disposable income (income after taxes) minus consumption spending.

**Scarcity**   The condition that exists when human wants exceed the capacity of available resources to satisfy those wants; also a situation in a resource has more than one valuable use. The problem of scarcity faces all individuals and organizations, including firms and government agencies.

**Secondary effects**   Effects indirectly related to a course of action whose influence will only be seen or felt later in time.

**Secured debt**   Credit with collateral (a house or a car, e.g.) for the lender.

**Services**   Activities performed by people, firms, or government agencies to satisfy economic wants.

**Shared consumption**   A property of a good or service such that it can be used by many without diminishing another's ability to consume the same good; examples include street lights or radio broadcasts.

**Shortage**   The situation that results when the quantity demanded for a product exceeds the quantity supplied. Generally happens because the price of the product is below the market equilibrium price. See also **Price ceilings**.

**Special Interest Group**   An organization of people with a particular legislative concern. They work together to gather information, lobby politicians, and publicize their concern.

**Specialization**   A situation in which people produce a narrower range of goods and services than they consume. Specialization increases productivity; it also requires trade and it increases interdependence.

**Substitute**   A good or service that may be used in place of another good or service; examples include tap water for bottled water (or vice versa) and movies for concerts (or vice versa).

**Supply**   A schedule (or graph) showing how many units of a good or service producers are willing and able to sell at all possible prices during a period of time.

**Supply-side fiscal policy**   Policy intended to increase an economy's productive capacity by shifting aggregate supply; e.g., a tax cut giving businesses an incentive to invest and expand.

**Surplus**   The situation that results when the quantity supplied of a product exceeds the quantity demanded. Generally happens because the price of the product is above the market equilibrium price. See also **Price floors**.

**Tariff**   A tax on an imported good or service.

**Taxes**   Compulsory payments to governments by households and businesses.

**Total cost**   All costs associated with producing a good or service; the sum of fixed costs plus variable costs.

**Total revenue**   All money received from selling a good or service; the price times the quantity sold of each item.

**Trade**   Voluntary exchange of goods and services for money or other goods and services.

**Traditional economy**   An economy in which customs and habits from the past are used to resolve most economic issues of production and distribution.

**Tragedy of the commons**   Overuse or misuse of a commonly-owned resource, such as public grazing land or fishing waters.

**Transaction costs**   Costs associated with buying or selling goods and services that are not included in the money prices of those goods and services. Examples include obtaining information on prices and product quality, searching for sellers, and bargaining costs.

**Transfer payments**   Payments for which no goods or services are provided in return. Examples of government transfer payments include social security payments and unemployment insurance payments.

**Unemployment**   Unemployment exists when people who want to work in jobs they are qualified to do at current wage rates are not able to find jobs, or are waiting to begin a new job, or are actively looking for work but do not have the skills required to fill the jobs that are currently available.

**Unemployment rate**   The percentage of the labor force that is unemployed. See also **Employment rate**.

**Unsecured debt**   Debt without collateral; credit card debt, for example.

**Utility**   An abstract measure of the satisfaction consumers derive from consuming goods, services, and leisure activities.

**Variable costs**   Costs that change as a firm's level of output changes. See also **Fixed costs**.

**Voluntary trade**   See **Trade**.

**Wages**   Payments for labor services that are directly tied to time worked, or to the number of units of output produced. See also Salaries.